A History of Bancroft's School
1737–1987

Francis Bancroft
Citizen and Draper
1667–1728

A HISTORY OF
BANCROFT'S SCHOOL
1737–1987

by

K. R. Wing

OLD BANCROFTIANS ASSOCIATION
Bancroft's School
Woodford Wells
Essex
1987

First published 1987 by
The Old Bancroftians Association
Bancroft's School,
Woodford Wells,
Essex, IG8 0RF
Copyright © K. R. Wing 1987

ISBN 0 9511884 0 2

Printed in Great Britain by
Villiers Publications Ltd,
26a Shepherd's Hill,
London N6 5AH

Contents

List of Plates

vii

To: J.W.M.C., P.M.P. & J.B.T.
Good friends, loyal and true

Acknowledgements

This Book is the work of many appearing under the name of one. A large number of people have given their time freely and I am also grateful for the encouragement given me by numerous people. The Book is published by the Old Bancroftians Association and of the numerous O.B.s whom I must thank, the members of the History sub-committee must be to the fore. My successor as Chairman, B. R. Gates, successfully chaired our interesting and lively discussions on the Book's format; K. J. Campbell, the O.B.A. Archivist helped in sorting through the Association's numerous records; B. M. F. Youd and A. M. Le Grove gave sound fiscal advice;.and J. Buck, D. H. Giles, M. T. Rossiter, P. D. Warner, F. Winmill, J. J. Wisdom and Messrs R. L. Bowley and J. G. Bromfield each contributed to the creation of the Book. I am especially grateful to Giles, Warner and Wisdom for assisting to bring my rough drafts into cogent English. The following O.B.s also saw the manuscript in whole or,in part and I appreciate the constructive comments which they each made: W. M. Caldow, E. B. Graham, A. M. Le Grove, P. M. J. Mantle, G. S. H. Smeed and N. C. Suckling. Dr P. C. D. Southern, and Messrs I. M. Richardson and D. C. R. Francombe also gave helpful advice and encouragement, and the last I must thank for his generous hospitality. A special thank you is due to Alan Palmer whose professionl expertise was much appreciated. May I thank the sixty or so O.B.s who kindly sent in their reminiscences, these proved invaluable in writing the 20th century chapters and have been deposited with the O.B.A. Archivist.

Much of the research was done at Drapers' Hall and I must express my thanks to the Company for their great encouragement, especially to the Clerk, Mr R. G. C. Strick, and the Clerk to the Governors of Bancroft's School, Mr G. C. Watts. They read the whole manuscript and made some very helpful suggestions, pointing out various factual errors. Mr R. Lynch advised me on the Bancroft's Trust properties and Mr E. J. Standen, the Beadle, provided refreshment during my days at the Hall. Most especially may I thank Mr R. T. Brown, the Company's Archivist, for his friendly help and sense of humour. Several members of the Court have shown an interest in the project, and I am especially grateful for the assistance given by Messrs E. Playne, W. R. Winterton, W. B. G. Simmonds, and F. L. Monro.

Most photographs and illustrations are the property either of the Drapers' Company or the Old Bancroftians Association, and I acknowledge their respective copyrights. May I also thank Kenneth Bray for arranging the photographing at Drapers' Hall. The copyright of the photographs rests with the names appearing next to the individual descriptions on pages vi–viii.

I am very grateful to my Mother and to Mrs M. Campbell for translating my appalling handwriting into a typed draft; to the other ladies who typed individual chapters for the first draft; to Mrs Ford for preparing an index, and to Mr Sankey of Villiers Publications Limited for his help and patience. Mrs L. Wilsher, B. R. Gates' secretary has also been most helpful.

Finally may I thank my various friends for patiently stifling their yawns during the last few years when I have bored them with the details of my research; to Mr J. B. Thole for reading the draft and correcting my syntax; Mr J. W. M. Chadwick for legal advice, and P. M. Pelling for endorsing my opinion of certain mutual acquaintances.

To each and all, my thanks.

K. R. Wing
January 1987

Author's Foreword

I have always enjoyed looking through old papers and, on coming down from the University, was delighted to discover the Muniment Room of Drapers' Hall. Not only was I welcomed there but was positively encouraged to sift through the Bancroft papers, especially by the archivist, Mr Robert Brown. I discovered a great deal about Francis Bancroft and his family, which I am currently putting into a separate book, but little about the School. I was therefore reluctant to become too involved with the Old Bancroftian sub-committee which hoped to bring up to date *Bancroft's School 1737–1937*, mainly because I thought that the Mile End era had never been properly covered and that the Symns and Playne period had not been fully researched at the time. The 1937 book never claimed to be 'history' in the proper meaning of the word, the editors denying themselves that title, so it seemed to me that the whole book had to be rewritten. When this was agreed I became chairman of the history sub-committee.

The idea was to divide the research into three parts: Mile End, Woodford up to the death of Wells, and the recent period. In the event I found myself researching all the official records, namely minutes and account books, with other helpers collating and forwarding the reminiscences of O.B.s. In the absence of anyone more capable being both willing and able to write the book, the lot fell to me – at least I could read my notes. The many thanks that I owe to numerous people will be found elsewhere, but here is the place to apologise to those who have been omitted from the text but who, perhaps, might have been mentioned. The chapters on the last fifty years contain numerous references to the names of those who have achieved success at School or beyond; the decision to include or exclude had to be made at random, and to those robbed of immortality herein, I apologise. I am, perhaps, more conscious of this fault with the two wartime chapters: truly, for many brave and gallant Bancroftians there is no memorial save for the tablets in the School and elsewhere and the fading memories of old comrades. In all humility I ask their pardon.

Of the book itself, the chapters up to 1906 rely almost exclusively on records at Drapers' Hall. One day, perhaps, it will be re-written in a more fitting style, but our knowledge of that period is complete. The chapters which follow, up to the retirement of Mr Adams, or perhaps until 1977, rely on the memories of Old Bancroftians as much as on formal evidence. I trust the living will agree with my broad conclusions, for a history must concern itself with reaching such conclusions. Perhaps with the benefit of longer hindsight these will have changed by 2037 and be ready for re-writing. For the Richardson era, especially the last eight years, I cannot bring to bear my limited grasp of the science of history, but must merely report what has happened, so the true finishing date of this book as 'history' is 1977: such are the perils in writing of a continuous, vibrant and prosperous institution.

Finally, I must of course declare an interest; I am an Old Bancroftian inordinately fond of his old school. I am aware of its weaknesses but truly believe that its manifest strengths greatly outweigh them, a conclusion which I trust readers of this book will also reach. All opinions and views expressed in this book are those of the author.

K. R. W.

Glossary

'All-in'   Summons to school meals. It was cried as one
                long drawn out word by a monitor. Now
                redundant except at occasional O.B. dinners.

Assy   Hard-surfaced areas around the school, possibly
                derived from asphalt.

Black Hole   Place of confinement at Tottenham.

The Bryn   Boarding house kept by the Hall family, firstly in
                Whitehall Road, then Monkhams Drive. Closed
                down in 1920.

Bunkers   First floor dormitory for senior boys, wooden
                partitions gave some privacy.

Busters   Slabs of bread and butter, principal content of
                boarders' tea until 1930.

C.R.   Committee Room, from room where Bancroft's
                Committee, i.e. the Governors met, then used by
                the monitors, finally restricted to boarder moni-
                tors and prefects. Ceased to exist in 1973.

Friends   Name given by Drapers' Company to parents
                and guardians of boys.

Impositions   Punishment sheets, collected from housemaster
                who duly recorded the details in a register.

Monitors   Appointed at Mile End to help keep discipline,
                these were most senior and responsible boys.
                When the House system developed, monitors had
                power over all pupils, assisted by prefects whose
                power was (officially) restricted to boys in their
                own houses. The office of prefect has ceased to
                exist.

Monkhams   Playing fields between Monkhams Avenue and
                Drive, in use 1906–30 when sold for development.

Odds & Evens   When houses were introduced day boys were
                divided into East and West Houses, and boarders
                were sub-divided into two groups, depending on
                whether their boarder number was odd or even to
                create four teams. This practice fell into abeyance
                after the 2nd World War, and the creation of

	North House in 1964 finally enabled a four-House competition to begin.
Riggs' Retreat	An area of Epping Forest off Whitehall Road used for games until the 1950s.
Sides	A form of imposition – see illustration.
Sickers	Sick rooms in the boarder block.
Swappers	Changing rooms, alongside the old swimming pool.
Usher	Originally an untrained junior master, it remained in use to describe young masters at least until the move to Woodford.
Vis Day	Visitation Day, now a Friday in July when the Master and Wardens visit the School, equivalent of speech day.
West Grove	Playing Fields beyond Woodford Station.

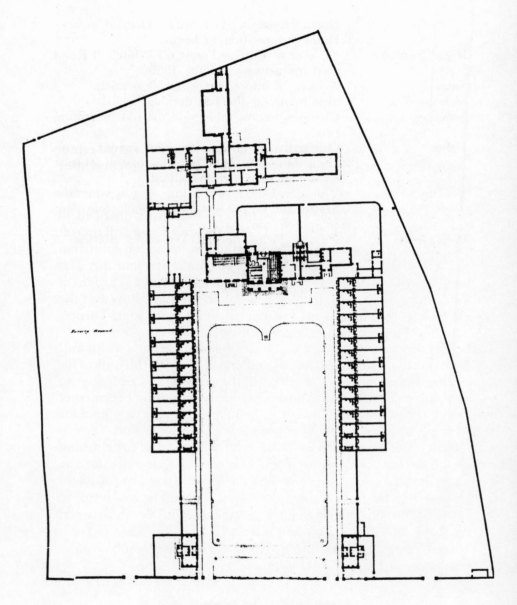

Plan of Bancroft's Hospital, 1855

CHAPTER I

Fundatoris Nostri

'HAVING heard that Mr Bancroft had died and left a great estate to the Company it was ordered that his Will be brought and after supper at the Star and Angel was opened and read.'

The Estates Committee of the Drapers' Company chanced to have met on the 19th March, 1728,* the day Francis Bancroft died at his temporary lodgings in Islington, to which suburban village he had been taken a fortnight earlier for its clean air. The members of the Committee included the Master and Wardens of the Company who were named as Bancroft's Executors and the Will was presumably read to them by their Clerk, John Turner, who had prepared it for Bancroft a week before.

The document ran to six large sheets of scrivener's script and gave specific legacies to friends and relations, with the bulk of his estate, estimated at £28,000, to the Drapers' Company to establish and maintain Almshouses for twenty-four Freemen of the Company of good health and conversation and a school for one hundred poor boys aged between seven and fifteen. Instructions were given for the school syllabus and for clothing the boys and almsmen; an allowance of coals was made for the latter and the two masters whose salaries were fixed at £30 each. Instructions for the funeral were also stated: the cost was not to exceed £200, it was to take place a week after his death between the hours of 8 and 9 pm and his lead-lined coffin was to have a hinged lid and be placed in the vault of his grand tomb already erected in St Helen's Bishopsgate.

---

*In 1728 Great Britain still adhered to the Julian Calendar; apart from making her eleven days behind the Gregorian Calendar which was in use throughout the rest of Western Europe it meant that the year end occurred on March 24th. Hence, by contemporary reckoning, Bancroft died on 19th March, 1727 and was buried on 29th March, 1728. Except where a date is quoted in a document the author has taken the year to begin on January 1st, a change which occurred in 1753.

1

Whatever the small group of diners thought of this last testament it probably came as no surprise that the Company was the principal beneficiary. Bancroft had never been an active member of the Company and had declined the livery when called to it in 1709 but it was the main legatee of his 1720 Will and he made known his intention to do something for the Company in his Will.

Bancroft had been an important City official for thirty years, his livelihood dependent on knowing everyone in the business community; one can assume him to have been acquainted with his Draper contemporaries, who would further have known him to be a wealthy bachelor at odds with his family and desirous of immortality through a munificent obituary act. In 1723, he had bought an eight foot square plot in St Helen's Church, obtained a Faculty from the Bishop of London recognising his perpetual freehold and built on it a large tomb designed by George Dance the Younger. Bancroft had no connection with that church but it was, significantly, the burial place of Sir Thomas Gresham and Sir Andrew Judd, who both founded educational trusts, and of numerous other City worthies, and Bancroft perhaps wanted to be included amongst their number. Those who have enjoyed the benefits of his largesse in the last quarter millenium must thank him for devising his estate as he did; they must also thank the heavens that he had been a Freeman of the Drapers' Company since 1690.

The Master and Wardens and Brethren and Sisters of the Guild or Fraternity of the Blessed Mary the Virgin of the Mystery of Drapers of the City of London had emerged in the eleventh century as a group of woollen cloth merchants initially to maintain standards of quality and measure and latterly as a mutual support group. Their power grew with the expansion of the City, a fact recognised by the granting of a Royal Charter in 1364. In the Middle Ages the Drapers' Company controlled all drapers in the City and its environs and began to accumulate communal property and wealth and also a Hall, firstly in St Swithins Lane and since the Reformation in Throgmorton Street. As third Senior of the twelve Great Livery Companies it played a prominent part in City life, those companies enjoying the privilege of providing the Lord Mayor and other great officials from amongst their number: membership was much sought after.

2

As London developed as a great mercantile centre and cloth ceased to be England's staple export, the affected companies – Drapers', Mercers', Haberdashers', Merchant Taylors' – began to admit freemen not involved with their particular trades and by the seventeenth century it was purely coincidental if a Draper followed that trade or 'mystery'. In that century the Great Companies lost the last of their monopolies but, in that spirit of adaptability which is the glory of the English race, the Drapers' Company and its kind emerged as societies whose members enjoyed certain privileges as Freemen of the City and in return administered the various trusts which the companies had been accumulating since the Reformation. In the early eighteenth century the Company administered almshouses in Greenwich, Wokingham, Tower Hill, Shoreditch and Southwark and schools in Stratford-atte-Bow, Kirkham in Lancashire and Greenwich. It paid a lecturer at St Michael's, Cornhill, £50 a year for weekly sermons; sent £5 a year to a poor scholar at Oxford or Cambridge, the gift of one Theophilus Russell; and gave to the orphans of Christian, Godly, English men and women Mr Pennoyer's gift of £45 to set them up in apprenticeships.

The Company also administered a large estate in Ulster, a legacy of James the First's plantations, and within the City helped to run the tacklehouse porters on the river front and guaranteed a significant quota of the City's needed corn supply. Having seen to the needs of others through these and other trusts the Company also distributed pensions and alms to its own members who had fallen on hard times or had been so unfortunate as to find themselves locked in the Marshalsea Prison by their creditors. To this impressive portfolio of diverse interests was added the Bancroft Trust, it becoming the largest Drapers' trust at that time.

As the Company figures at every stage of Bancroft's School's development, its eighteenth century structure, which remains unchanged to this day, must be explained. The Company admits men and women to its Freedom by one of three ways: paternity, being born the legitimate child of a Freeman; by apprenticeship to a Freeman; or by redemption, or payment of a fine. From the Freemen are chosen the Liverymen who in Bancroft's time had to show a personal fortune of £1,000. They enjoy certain privileges in the Company and the City and form a pool of eligible and capable men from which are drawn members of the

3

Court of Assistants. This Court is the general committee of the Company and effectively runs it. At its head is the Master elected annually from amongst its number; he, with the four wardens, forms the Court of Wardens. Its duties include the administration of almshouses and it was primarily responsible for administering Bancroft's Hospital in its early years.

The Drapers' Company still administers the Bancroft Trust and also enjoys a considerable income in its own right from which it makes great charitable donations. The School has received great benefit, not only financial, from this connection over the years and it is not insincere to say that the present school would not be in its present healthy state but for the Company's wise guidance and careful husbandry over two hundred and fifty years. We can but be grateful for Francis Bancroft being a Draper; the reason why he chose that Company rather than any other lies in his immediate ancestry.

The name Bancroft is thought to mean an enclosed field (croft) on the bank of a river and there are early references to the name in the counties of Cheshire and Lancashire. An early reference also occurs in East Anglia when in 1361 John de Bancroft, an innkeeper, was admitted a Freeman of the Borough of King's Lynn and occasional references occur throughout the later Middle Ages. It would seem that Francis Bancroft's family lived near Woodbridge in Suffolk at the time of the Reformation and moved to Wingfield in the north of that county in the following years. His great grandparents Samuel and Lucy brought up their four sons there and their baptismal entries are found in Wingfield's parish register. Of the four, John remained in Wingfield, dying there in 1650, and was Francis Bancroft's grandfather. From his Will and such records as ship money returns, we know him to have been a prosperous yeoman farmer who added to his land holdings during his lifetime. He married a Bridget Collinge of the neighbouring village of Hoxne who bore him six children. One can but imagine the lifestyle of this East Anglian family of farmers removed from the political world of London by a week's hard riding, and concerned more with their crops and hunting than with the religious debates of pre Civil War England. There might have been Bancrofts farming at Wingfield today but for the fact that John had a very ambitious and successful elder brother.

Thomas Bancroft is one of those early seventeenth century

4

characters whose name appears on the periphery of history but of whom very little is known. He was never a Freeman of the City of London, the obvious first step to acquiring a fortune at the time, and it is not known when he went to London. It seems likely that he was taken up by the influential Knyvett family whose kinsman owned Wingfield Castle and that he moved in Court, rather than City, circles. He married well, a girl called Margaret Hide, whose father combined the life of the squire of Wallingford, Berkshire with that of a City merchant, and whose brother Andrew, a rich silk merchant, was a Freeman of the Drapers' Company. Thomas was one of the two Burgesses for the pocket borough of Castle Rising near King's Lynn in the Parliaments of 1623, 1624, 1625 and 1629 and enjoyed a no doubt lucrative position in the Government for he is referred to as 'Mr Bancroft of the Exchequer'. This wealth enabled him to buy from the Earl of Surrey, probably his political master, the Manor of Santon in Norfolk some twenty miles west of his birth place. He is commemorated there in the church which he rebuilt for his own use in 1634 and which was re-consecrated by Bishop Harsnett on his journey north following his translation from Norwich to York – an irrelevant aside except that the worthy prelate later endowed a grammar school in the small Essex village of Chigwell.

Thomas had three daughters, two of whom made socially successful marriages, but there was no son to continue his name. He had maintained contact with his family; his brother Samuel inherited his Castle Rising house when he died in 1636 and, more importantly for our story, his young nephew John travelled to London at his behest and with his active support. John was apprenticed to Andrew Hide in 1631, Thomas standing surety for £200, and lived with Hide in the Langbourne Ward of the City. On finishing his eight year apprenticeship he was admitted a Freeman of the Drapers' Company on the 15th January, 1640 and twenty months later he became an official of the Lord Mayor's household.

John was to hold office for fifty years, a period which began with the Long Parliament and ended shortly after the Glorious Revolution of 1689. The City was heavily involved in all the intervening events of Civil War, Commonwealth, Restoration, Exclusion Bill and the flight of James the Second. We know nothing of his politics which he doubtless kept to himself,

Family tree showing Francis Bancroft's relationship to Thomas Bancroft, MP

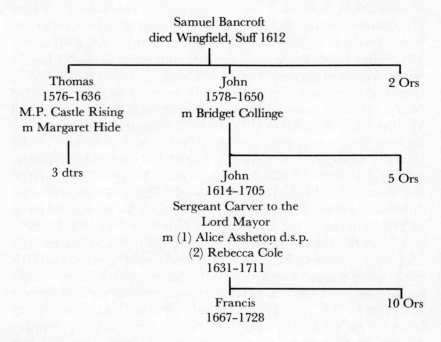

```
                    Samuel Bancroft
                 died Wingfield, Suff 1612
                            |
    ┌───────────────────────┼───────────────────────┐
  Thomas                   John                    2 Ors
 1576–1636               1578–1650
M.P. Castle Rising      m Bridget Collinge
m Margaret Hide                 |
     |              ┌───────────┴───────────────────┐
  3 dtrs                       John                5 Ors
                             1614–1705
                       Sergeant Carver to the
                             Lord Mayor
                      m (1) Alice Assheton d.s.p.
                          (2) Rebecca Cole
                             1631–1711
                                 |
                     ┌───────────┴───────────────────┐
                            Francis               10 Ors
                           1667–1728
```

Family tree showing relationship of Bancroft and Hide & Assheton families

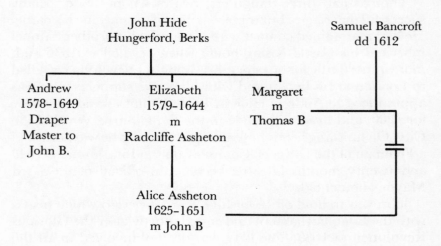

```
            John Hide                          Samuel Bancroft
         Hungerford, Berks                        dd 1612
                |                                    |
    ┌───────────┼───────────────┐                    |
  Andrew     Elizabeth        Margaret               |
 1578–1649   1579–1644          m                    |
 Draper         m           Thomas B ────────────────┤
 Master to  Radcliffe Assheton                       ╪
 John B.        |                                    |
            Alice Assheton                           |
            1625–1651 ────────────────────────────────
            m John B
```

6

trimming his sails to meet views of particular Mayors like a secular Vicar of Bray. He married in 1645 the common niece of his master and his aunt-in-law, Alice Ashton or Assheton, whose father Radcliff was a member of a prominent Lancashire family.

They lived just north of the City Wall in Postern, the name for the western end of Fore St in the Parish of St Giles Cripplegate in which district he and his family were to live until Francis' death eighty years later. The marriage does not appear to have been fruitful, his wife dying in 1650. In 1654 he re-married, again to a well-connected young lady called Rebecca Cole. The Coles lived in Carshalton in Surrey and styled themselves as Gentlemen. Rebecca's father Henry was one of several children and sired nine children by his wife Rebecca, and their descendants will figure in the story of Francis and his Will. Henry's wife had been a member of the influential Garland family, her half-brother Augustine being one of the Regicides, notorious even amongst that group of gentlemen for having spat in Charles the First's face when the King was being led from his trial in Westminster Hall to martyrdom and an incorruptible crown. Augustine was to disappear after the Restoration but in 1654, as MP for Queenborough in Kent, he was an important man to know and John's new wife brought Garland property in Birchin Lane as a dowry. As John had few relatives in London he joined his wife's close-knit family and doubtless this network of cousins and connections was beneficial to his City career.

The marriage of John and Rebecca lasted over fifty years, an event even rarer in the seventeenth century than today, and they had ten children, five of whom survived the rigours of childhood in the London of the Great Plague. The eldest son, John, was a Barber Surgeon and married the daughter of a prominent Lincolnshire squire, Edward King, who settled a generous dowry on his daughter Diana, the groom's father doing well by his son with property in Fetter Lane. The young couple lived in fashionable Covent Garden where John moved in literary circles, writing three plays which enjoyed success in their day. The author of *Henry II with the Death of Rosamond, Edward III and the fall of Mortimer* and *The Tragedy of Sertorius* finds honourable mention in contemporary lives of the poets. Of their five children all but Martha predeceased their father who died in 1696. Her disastrous marriage to William Turner was to cause problems for Francis in later years.

7

Two of John and Rebecca's daughters, Elizabeth and Martha, survived to adulthood, though the latter remained at home, no doubt tending her ageing parents until her death aged 30 in 1701. Margaret married George Bond, a Leather-seller, and their only daughter Elizabeth married Thomas Catmore whose son Thomas was to be Francis' principal personal legatee. The youngest of the family, Benjamin, separated by twenty years from his brother John, was apprenticed to an Apothecary but died aged twenty-one before taking up his profession. His notebook, in which various receipts are written, has survived, for his brother Francis kept it to use the remaining sheets as an account book. Francis was born on 26th October, 1667 in the suburb of Spitalfields and was christened in the ancient church of St Dunstan, Stepney, in which large parish Spitalfields then stood.

The Bancrofts' house in Postern had, presumably, burned down in the Great Fire of the previous year, their home being in the only part of London where the fire spread beyond the old city wall. The year before, in 1665, the family had fled the Great Plague and stayed at Chigwell where a son Samuel was born and christened. As the eldest son John would have been eleven years old, it is not impossible that he may have spent some time at the Latin school in the village – regrettably, that seat of learning does not have complete records for the seventeenth century.

It has been stated that the Bancrofts were poor when Francis was young. It is clear from surviving family papers that such was not the case as both his parents owned property in London and Middlesex and were generous to their children and grandchildren on marriage. There is no doubt that for all Londoners the aftermath of the fire was a difficult time as they rebuilt their homes and furnished them without the benefit of insurance payments. The Bancrofts returned north of the wall at some stage, to a house at the Moorgate end of Fore Street.

All Bancroftians know the stories about their benefactor – that he was a mean, unscrupulous City shark, the unacceptable face of early eighteenth century capitalism; the bizarre circumstances of his last days and the making of his Will; the funeral and its riot and the embezzlement of the estate by Bancroft's landlord. Here is not the place to give a detailed account of his career nor to write a vindication of his life but it is important to see the man in the light of his times.

The City of 1690 had changed immeasurably from the one known to Francis Bancroft's father when he first joined the Lord Mayor's household fifty years before, and it was to undergo further change during Francis' period of office. The medieval City had been a great centre of trade and commerce and the power of its merchants had been expressed through the influence of the great livery companies. As the City changed and a new type of commerce emerged in the form of Government supported trading companies – the East India Company, the Merchant Venturers – so the livery companies admitted the new type of merchant to their privileges and ensured both their own survival and a voice in the government of the City for these entrepreneurs.

The power of the new class of merchants became apparent during the Civil War when the hitherto loyal City supported their Parliamentary compatriots and became the paymaster of the Roundhead army. That that force would eventually dismiss its masters and seize the City was not foreseen at the time and the body mercantile was to learn the price of power by such a jolt to its system that it was evermore reluctant to indulge in naked unilateral power-mongering.

The Civil War over and the monarchy restored, the City grew in prestige, defeating the Dutch for trading supremacy and taking advantage of the chaos rendered in Europe by the Thirty Years War to spread its influence into the Baltic at the expense of the declining Hanseatic League merchants. The Royal Exchange had been built in the time of Queen Elizabeth as a place for merchants to meet, and by the late sixteen hundreds a new class of individual had developed in the City, the broker or middle man who, for a percentage of the price, would introduce buyers to sellers and sellers to buyers in property, bonds, stocks, insurance or any other commodity in demand. Lloyd's Coffee House was already a recognised place for insuring ships and cargo and the Bank of England opened its doors in 1691. The City was emerging as a modern centre of commerce with new institutions still recognisable today and with its old companies adapting to the new world.

The only institution slow to change was the lynchpin of the system, the City Government itself. In medieval times the Lord Mayor lived in a style equal to that of a great lord with a court of officials such as the Chamberlain to assist him to run the City and a series of lesser gentlemen, such as Cupbearer and Sergeant

Carver, to maintain his dignity. There was nothing demeaning in these offices and they were filled by freemen of the City who considered it an honour to serve the Lord Mayor in this fashion. As the lifestyle of great persons changed and the ceremony was largely removed from the serving of dishes at dinner (in favour of hot food) so the officers became bureaucrats and tax gatherers in the City. They received nominal salaries for services which would occupy them for but a few hours a week and would supplement their income from a fixed share of dues and fines collected in the course of their labours. Assuming that the flow of trade remained steady and that the officers were not complete rogues, this system of tax farming worked well, as the collector and the City both knew what income they would enjoy, the collector how much time would be expended in his duties and the City its overall annual income. The official then had time to pursue some other career, usually as an agent for a third party or as a broker, often using the contacts he made in his official capacity.

The system had always been open to abuse and to the eyes of a later age, accustomed to senior public servants receiving a KCB for administering the common weal, the idea of a man gaining a fortune from office – and Francis was the third generation of his family to do so – is indefensible, and by 1690 it could not even be claimed that the system continued to work efficiently. The City was still collecting revenues in the same manner and on the same goods as it had done for hundreds of years, taxing coal, wool, wine and food arriving and leaving its wharves, and at a time of slight inflation the City's revenue was dropping in real terms, as it failed to tax the new markets in stocks and bonds, and by the end of the century the City was almost bankrupt. For the officers also it meant a reduction in real incomes, but with the City corporation pressing for an increase in revenue, it caused them more work for less return.

The officers may be divided into two classes: the holders of a specific office, such as Sword Bearer or Yeoman of the Waterside, each with its specific duty and source of income; and the 'Young Men' of the household who were more akin to general messengers, presumably taking a share of the spoils when serving a senior official. Francis Bancroft began in 1690 as a Young Man to Mr Common Hunt and moved through a series of offices before becoming Sergeant of the Chamber in 1697. This he soon resigned, for a consideration, and became a Young Man again. Dismissing any Faustian motive in this move, we can assume he found it more beneficial to have a capital sum – the office of Sword Bearer changed hands for £1,500 in 1695 – than to enjoy the revenue of office, and that he preferred the extra freedom enjoyed by a Young Man to further his career.

We know very little of the detail of his career; the records of the Corporation contain numerous references to him, including a complaint against him and others for summoning people without good cause, presumably in the hope of receiving a 'gift' for dropping the summons, but it is probable that the duties of office occupied but a small part of his time. For the most he acted as a broker or agent, collecting his quarterage which he invested, mostly in Government bonds. He looked after his family's affairs and continued to live in the family home, presumably at little cost to himself. His aunts made him their executor – would they have so acted if he were completely without scruples? – and he protected the interest of his niece, Martha, whose husband William Turner deserted her while keeping her substantial dowry; and his sister-in-law, Diana Bancroft, made him trustee for her grandchildren. He maintained the family home for their benefit after the death of his father in 1706 and mother in 1709 until Martha died in 1722 when he moved to bachelor lodgings at the Red Lion in Coleman Street, then the main road north from Mansion House to Moorgate and close to his parents' former address 'next to the Greengate in Fore Street'.

He retired in 1720, the year of the South Sea Bubble which

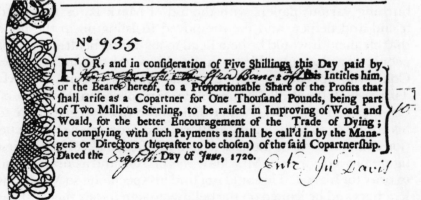

No 935

FOR, and in confideration of Five Shillings this Day paid by *Fr* *Broughil* *the* *New Bancs of* *this* Intitles him, or the Bearer hereof, to a Proportionable Share of the Profits that fhall arife as a Copartner for One Thoufand Pounds, being part of Two Millions Sterling, to be raifed in Improving of Woad and Woald, for the better Encouragement of the Trade of Dying; he complying with fuch Payments as fhall be call'd in by the Managers or Directors (hereafter to be chofen) of the faid Copartnerfhip. Dated the *Eighth* Day of *June*, 1720.

Entr Jno Davis

One of Francis Bancroft's Share certificates

11

brought to an end the years of reckless gambling in stocks. In a letter to an old friend who had bought land in Lancashire to which he had retired, he wrote of surviving the great crisis of the year though not without some loss. He also spoke of his loneliness, for he was fast becoming an old and eccentric bachelor. His retirement years were spent in good husbandry of his capital, in visiting his properties in Essex and Suffolk, which he had been acquiring since his father's death, and in preparing for his own death. His Will of 1720 left his farm property to the Turner children and gave details and instructions for a tomb to be built in St Helen's, Bishopsgate. The rest of his property went to the Drapers' Company to found the school and almshouses though there was less detail than in the 1728 document. The tomb was finished by 1726 at a cost of some £600. He left the lodgings of Mrs Marsh and her daughter Mrs Shaw and returned to Fore Street to Mr Hadley's at the Sign of the Angel and Still with a considerable increase in rent, from £1.15s.0d. to £7.12s.6d. a quarter: presumably that included board. He remained close to the two ladies, however, leaving each a legacy and annuity and granting them permission to be buried in his tomb.

His rooms were furnished with his own belongings including a dozen pictures and prints and one hundred books, a sizeable library for an early eighteenth century layman. Here he lived his last lonely years, arguing with his surviving relations and becoming a cantankerous old man. He summoned the Clerk of the Drapers' Company, John Turner, to his rooms when he was dying and gave instructions for the famous Will. He set about burning various papers with the aid of Mark Bates, a trusted friend and helper, and then removed to Islington in the hope that cleaner air would be beneficial to his failing health. Various people travelled out to him including his young cousin Nathaniel Cole, who appears to have acted as Francis's agent, and Mr Turner with the Will. The final scene is recorded in the Drapers' Company's records by Turner. Bancroft refused to give more to his family or to Hadley, his landlord, and ordered the computation of his estate to be increased from £25,000 to £28,000 (the first figure proved correct). Mrs Shaw was present and a curate found to pray for his soul. He could not find his spectacles so Mrs Shaw lent hers and he leaned on the bellows to sign the six sheets. That was on the 18th March and the following day he died.

Francis Bancroft: Esq: D. to G. Dance

for Mason's Work done in a Tomb Erected
in S:t Hellen's Church

1726
Decem.r 15.th

for 369 f.t 6 in.s of Cubical Portland Stone at 2.s p.r foot ————	36:17:00
for 730 f.t of Superficial Workmanship at 10.s p.r foot	55:07:00
for 4 Vas.s & flames at 30.s p.r Vas & flame ————	6:00:00
for 56 f.t 3 in.s of purbeck paving at 7.s ½ p.r foot ————	1:13:01 ¾
for Carving the Coat of Arms & flames—	5:05:00
for cutting 330 letters at 1.d p.r letter—	1:07:06
for cutting 93 holes for the iron work at 2.d p.r hole ————	0:15:06
for letting in 96 Cramps, plugs & hooks at 2.d each ————	0:16:00

£ 108:01:01 ¾

Rec.d the full Contents of this bill
& all demands   p.r Geo: Dance

Jn Cont

Bill for Bancroft's Tomb

13

YOU are desir'd to Accompany the Corps of **Francis Bancroft**, Esq; from Draper's-Hall in Throgmorton-Street, to the Parish-Church of St. Hellen's in Bishopsgate-Street, on Friday the 29th of March, 1728. at Seven of the Clock in the Evening, and bring this Ticket with you.

N.B. The Corps to be mov'd soon after Eight a-Clock.

Perform'd by the Company of Upholders in Leadenhall-Street.

An invitation to Bancroft's funeral

CHAPTER II

A Death and a Birth

THE WILL* now dictated the actions of its executors, or rather of their clerk, John Turner. The rooms in Fore Street were sealed after the removal of the tombkey and the windows screwed down, as nothing was to be removed for a month. The body was embalmed and placed in a lead-lined coffin and brought to Drapers' Hall for the funeral on the 29th March.

The 'guests' – Bancroft's estranged family, his City friends and the Court of the Drapers' Company – were summoned by invitation, a ghoulish document typical of the esoteric temperament of the time. The cortege, consisting of twelve carriages and lit by footmen carrying torches, was accompanied by sixty boys from the poor house on its short journey from Drapers' Hall, all hung in mourning, in Throgmorton Street, and into Bishopsgate, beneath the campanile of St Helen's which stood on the street, and into Gt St Helen's Place. With members of the Court acting as pall-bearers the coffin was taken into the church and placed in the tomb. For some reason it was not placed in the vault for some one hundred and fifty years, when it was finally buried in circumstances that do no credit to St Helen's and show the Drapers' Company forgetting their duty for the only time in their long trusteeship.

The events of the funeral form an important part of Bancroft's lore: according to Strype's 1735 edition of Stow's *Environs of London*, 'The persons who attended his funeral obsequies with great difficulty prevented his corpse from being jostled off the bearers' shoulders in the church by the enraged populace who seizing the bells, rang them for joy at his unlamented death, a deportment heretofore unheard of among the London Rabble.' One must work on the assumption that something untoward happened though no contemporary record refers to such a riot. The church records, the parish minutes, the Drapers' Company's

___

* See appendix

15

meticulous narrative of everything to do with the funeral and executors' work all fail to mention any such incident and the surviving newspapers do not make any reference to a disturbance. Most significant is the reference in the 'Death Bed Charity' pamphlet to the 'ostentatious funeral' but without mentioning the near riot. It hardly seems possible that the pamphleteer would have lost such a wonderful opportunity to press home his point; the pamphlet was published in 1728. St Helen's church is a fifteenth century re-building of an even earlier church and its ground level is much below the street level and consequently is entered down a broad flight of steps inside the church. In 1728 it was a small impecunious parish – probably the only reason why Bancroft could buy a freehold plot within the church – and the burial was lit only by a handful of torches. It would be easy for the bearers to tumble and come near to losing their step, to the amusement of the crowd that doubtless gathered to watch the free spectacle, and the mob of Hogarthian London were no respecters of funereal sobriety. In the confusion, the darkness, the scary atmosphere of an old church it is easy to imagine how such an event grew by 1735 into a riot. The other old canard concerning the annual viewing by the boys of the body will be dismissed below.

When the month following Francis Bancroft's death had passed, the executors opened his rooms in Fore Street and began to assess his estate. It consisted of an extensive portfolio of properties, with farmland in Essex and Suffolk, houses in the City, Westminster and at Chiswick and Prittlewell, and two inns with other tenements in High Holborn. There were also the notes of people to whom Bancroft had lent money, including a mortgage on a house in Hanover Square. By far the largest part of the estate however was in government and charter company bonds and bank notes (meaning money owed him by a bank). In those days such bonds and bank notes were registered at their respective houses and Mark Bates, Bancroft's assistant, had a list of the numbers. It soon became clear that £500 in bank notes and £900 of South Sea Company stock were missing along with a diamond ring and silver tankard. The Company informed the Bank and the South Sea Company and advertised the numbers and began an enquiry as to how they disappeared. At the same time Bancroft's relations began to demand more than their small bequests. The relations to whom small legacies had been left were: firstly, William and Martha Turner, the son and daughter of his brother John's daughter Martha; his sister Elizabeth's grandson Thomas Catmore – his principal heir; the grandchildren of his mother's brother John, one Nathaniel Cole and his sister Ann Wallis; and another cousin Mr Eade whose mother was a Garland.

Francis Bancroft had made a good deal of money in his lifetime but he had also inherited from his father and from his mother and her childless sisters who, it might be argued, had left money to an astute bachelor to invest wisely before passing it on to the next generation. If litigation ensued the case could drag on for years, so when the relations' intentions became clear, the Company sued first.

William Turner, the heir-at-law of Francis Bancroft, argued for a larger legacy which he would have received under the 1720 heads of instructions, instead of which he received £10 and a diamond ring – which was missing. Turner claimed that a house in Barbican that Bancroft was purchasing at the time of his death and for which a large deposit had been paid, was his by right as it was not specifically mentioned in the Will and furthermore, that the estate should pay the balance of the purchase money. The Company refuted this and eventually challenged Turner in the Court of Chancery to prove any claim on the estate – a clever move, putting the control of the litigation in their hands. Turner who with his sister had received money from Bancroft during his lifetime declined to press his case, settling for £100. Following this the Coles' case was dismissed by the Prerogative Court; the Wallises were given £100 in addition to the £5 annuities to each of their five children – they were to prove a nuisance to the Company for some time afterwards – and Nathaniel Cole was given £242 for past services to his cousin as well as his £100 legacy – he went on to be attorney to the East India Company and clerk to the Stationers' Company and his firm of attorneys survived until 1971. Thomas Catmore received his great uncle's linen, his library of 110 books, his pictures and most of his plate. He had to wait until 1734, his twenty-first year, to receive his £500 legacy.

The Company also recovered the £1,500 of missing notes and bonds. It was quite clear that they had been taken by Hadley, Bancroft's landlord, to whom he had entrusted a duplicate set of keys in case of fire during his absence. It is not sure when he took them but a lurid story emerges from the Company's enquiries

17

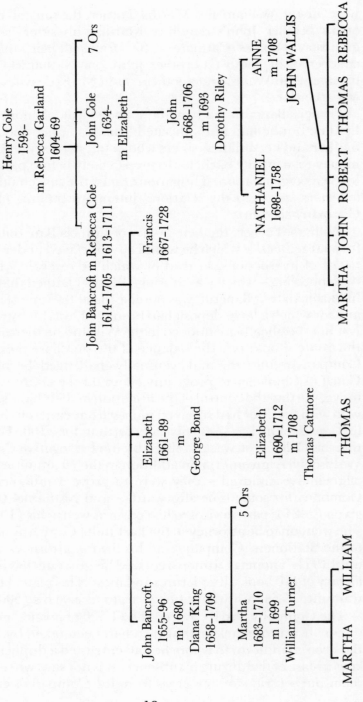

Family tree showing principal legatees of Francis Bancroft's Will

Henry Cole
1593–
m Rebecca Garland
1604–69

John Cole
1634–
m Elizabeth —

7 Ors

John
1668–1706
m 1693
Dorothy Riley

ANNE
m 1708

NATHANIEL
1698–1758

JOHN WALLIS

MARTHA   JOHN   ROBERT   THOMAS   REBECCA

John Bancroft m Rebecca Cole
1614–1705   1613–1711

Francis
1667–1728

Elizabeth
1661–89
m
George Bond

Elizabeth
1690–1712
m 1708
Thomas Catmore

THOMAS

John Bancroft,
1655–96
m 1680
Diana King
1658–1709

5 Ors

Martha
1683–1710
m 1699
William Turner

MARTHA   WILLIAM

with which Bancroft's distaff relatives readily assisted. While Bancroft lay dying, Cole went to Fore Street to collect papers for his cousin and while at the desk Hadley suggested that they remove some notes. Cole refused. Then, when Ann Wallis called to ask after her ailing relative, Hadley followed her to her cousins, the Eades, where he suggested that they should burn the Heads of Instructions and 'forget' to summon the Clerk of the Drapers' Company to Islington.

Later, after the death, when visiting the Wallises, he was wearing the stolen diamond ring and was openly accused by Ann Wallis of displaying the stolen money. All this was very damning evidence and the Court of Assistants instructed their Clerk to take whatever action against Hadley he thought necessary. We do not know what was said but the money reappeared – it was probably worthless to the thief as the numbers had been circulated – and Hadley received £120 for past services and back rent due from Bancroft and nothing was said of the various notes of Hadley's which Bancroft had held at his death. The other notes were called in, the interest in the Hanover Square and Barbican properties disposed of, the various legacies paid and Bancroft's debts met. £50 in annuities fell due and were paid from the income of the estate rather than by a capital purchase. When Catmore came of age in 1734 and was paid his £500, the executors passed to the Company cash, notes and bonds valued at almost £24,000 and land worth £400 a year.

The Company had accepted the Trust in principle within two months of Bancroft's death and they were now ready to put the great scheme into operation. The site had to be within the Bills of Mortality parishes of London, that is those suburban parishes which with those of the City and of Westminster provided statistics of births and deaths for the Government's growing statistics office. The Court of Wardens who were to oversee the Bancroft foundation thought it prudent to place it near existing almshouses and several trips were made in 1733 to assess suitable sites, followed by a good supper. The entry in the Company accounts '28th November paid Dinner, Coaches and viewing Newington Butts for Almshouses = £4 10s 8d' is repeated in varied form on a number of occasions. Eventually the Newington Butts site, as well as sites in Hoxton and Kingsland Road, were rejected in favour of a plot of nearly five acres on the Mile End Road, in the Hamlet of Mile End Old Town.

19

The land was purchased from Elizabeth Bodham and Nathaniel Owen for £580 plus various legal costs. The four-sided plot had three well-defined borders: the main road to the south, a well-defined ditch to the west and the wall of the Old Portuguese Jews' cemetery to the east. Only on the long north boundary, sloping northeastwards from the western ditch, was it ill-defined, so here the Company placed four boundary stones bearing their arms. The task of designing and building the Hospital was put out to tender and awarded to Edward Porter, a Freeman of the Company, whose estimate of £4,586 10s 4d was neither the cheapest nor dearest but who, as a member of the Company, could be relied upon to honour his contract of employment, a document rich in the legal verbosity of those days. The simple plan, for the execution of which John Osborne received £20, is shown in relation to the whole site on page 00.

With the buildings well under way the Company set about writing rules for the regulation of the Foundation and filling the two houses, twenty-four almshouses and large schoolroom with masters, almsmen and 100 day scholars respectively. By 1738 as the last coat of paint dried and the gravel paths were laid, Bancroft's began its life in earnest.

No part of the building survives *in situ* so a description of this stately edifice is relevant. It was built square on the grand geometrical scale and the buildings were specifically designed for the benefit of the three degrees of inmates, namely the Masters, Almsmen and Boys. All came together in the Chapel with its portico in the centre of the Main Block (its pediment surmounted by the clock now at Woodford) facing the road. The entrance or porchway was flanked by buildings, that on the left the school house, that on the right, in the East, the Masters' lodgings. These were each on two main floors with basement and attic, two rooms per floor. The schoolroom measured 40' 2" by 18' 6" and held the whole school. The Chapel was divided into pews for masters, almsmen and boys and the altar was similar to the one at the Woodford school, that being based on the grand original.

The twenty-four brother almsmen, fellows called from the labour of a long life to the refreshment of retirement, lived in the houses, twelve each on the west and east sides of the square. The boys attended to their labours in the schoolroom for seven years before being entered apprentice in the City or locally. The south side had gates and railings, with small lodges which were replaced in the early nineteenth century by larger buildings. The red bricks with their white stone facings made a fine site, its three constituent parts creating a harmonious whole in which the study of the liberal arts and sciences in their most basic form could be made and where masters, almsmen and boys could pursue their vocations, that pleasure and profit could be the result.

Calculation for Stationary per Ann

	£ S d	£ S d
10 Boys in Arithmetic ea. 2 Copy. Books	0..2..8	1..6..0
D.º 8 Copy Books each	0..3..2	1..11..8
Pens & Ink for D.º	0..3..0	1..10..0
10 Boys in Writing each 10 Copy Books	0..3..9	1..17..6
Pens &c for D.º	0..3..0	1..10..0
5 Bibles for the whole per Ann		0..15..0
6 Testaments for the whole per Ann		0..7..0
8. Spell.g Books D.º		0..5..4
Navigation. Stationary per Ann about		0..10..0
		9..12..6
Slates about 6 per Ann. 3 large 3 Small		3..9
Total		9..16..3

Bill for stationery

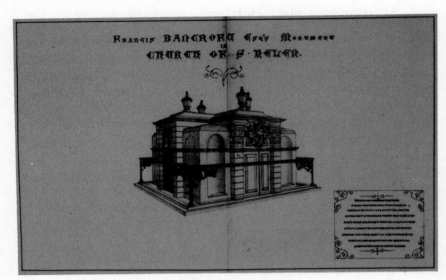

Bancroft's Tomb

Architect's Drawing of Bancroft's Hospital

To the Church Wardens and Overseers of y'r Poor of
the Hamlet of Mile End Old Town in the Parish of
S'r Dunstan Stepney in the county of Middlesex.

Middlesex
to wit   We the Church Wardens and Overseers of the Poor
of the Parish of S'r Mary White Chapel in the County of Middlesex
do hereby Certify that We Own and Acknowledge Benjamin
Lacey, Draper and Citizen of London to be an Inhabitant
Legally Setled in our said Parish of S'r Mary White Chapel in the County
of Middlesex aforesaid And We do Promise for Our selves and Successors to
Receive Him in our said Parish Whenever He shall become Chargeable
In Witness Whereof We the Church Wardens and Overseers of
the Poor aforesaid have hereunto respectively Set our Hands and Seals
Dated the 19 Day of Sep'r 1739.

Witness   Sam Gower   Church Wardens
Rob't Askew   Jn'o Shower
Arthur Noy

John Matthews
Wood Kintish   Overseers
John Abraham

We whose Names are hereunto Subscribed two of His Majesty's Justices
of the Peace for the County of Middlesex
aforesaid do Allow of the above Written Certificate. And We do also Certify that
Robert Askew one of the Witnesses who attended the Execution
of the said Certificate hath made Oath before us We did See the Church
Wardens and Overseers whose Names and Seals are to the said Certificate
Subscribed and Set Severally Sign and Seal the said Certificate and that the
Names of the said Robert Askew and Arthur Noy whose Names
are above Subscribed as Witnesses to the Execution of the said Certificate are of
their Own Proper hand writing Dated the 19 Day of Sep'r 1739
Rich Ricards

Robert Dennett

Alsman Lacey's sureties

23

CHAPTER III

The Eighteenth Century

BANCROFT'S cannot claim to be unique: it is, however, a most singular foundation. As a school it appears well after the grammar schools of Edward VI and the first Elizabeth yet a full century and more before the great Victorian schools, be they those for the 'fathers of gentlemen' or to educate the nation's new political masters. Furthermore its curriculum was quite different from either of the type of school which sandwiches it. The old grammar schools dated largely from the post-Reformation period when the predecessors of Bancroft and his ilk endowed schools to teach the rediscovered humanities of Greek and Latin. They taught the catechism of the Church as established by God and Act of Parliament, but such teaching was really an aside to the Classics and did not dominate the syllabus as in the old monastic schools.

The England of Bacon, Raleigh and Sidney was above such dogmatic pedantry and needed rulers at all levels versed in the works of Homer and Virgil, and for this reason grammar – that is Latin and Greek grammar – schools were founded throughout the realm, typically with an endowment to support one or two masters and between six and twenty boys. Their scholars went on to Oxford, Cambridge or the London Bar and they either returned to their estates, be they thirty thousand acres supporting a great house, or a glorified farm with its cosy manor house, or entered the recognised professions, namely the Church, with its close kinsman teaching, the Law, or the as yet small Civil Service. Within three generations England would be ruled from the Court, Parliament, the Bench and the Pulpit by enlightened Platonic philosopher kings.

It is not known where Bancroft went to school, if he did so, for at the time of his birth the grammar school dream had died. For John Bancroft, an important City official, the education given at Mercers', Merchant Taylors', St Pauls' or Charterhouse or any other of the City's small grammar schools was an irrelevance. It is more than likely that Francis and his brothers were tutored at home, his playwright brother and his own library and extant papers contradicting any imputation of illiteracy.

The grammar schools whose fixed incomes had diminished with inflation were failing to educate young men for the City and the emerging professions, and England was entering an educational Dark Age when schoolmastership became a lucrative additional stipend for the local rector, the universities the finishing schools for the aristocracy and the study of the arts the fad of a handful of dilettanti. Edward Gibbon, whose grandfather was a Bancroft-type City figure and may well have known our founder, talked of his Oxford days as the fourteen most wasted months of his life, with an ill-used, perpetually-locked college library and a Senior Common Room dominated by Port and Prejudice. The whole system was decayed. It is important to appreciate the educational world into which Bancroft's was thrust in 1738.

We can but surmise the reasons for Francis Bancroft bequeathing his money to charity but it seems a natural conclusion that after years in the City, having seen its growth and development, he appreciated the need for apprentices able to read, write and cast accounts and so he gave to the City from which he had made so much money an institution that produced each year fifteen literate, numerate boys to work its wheels of commerce. That assumed intention must be understood if Bancroft's Hospital's one hundred and fifty years in the environs of London are to be appreciated. It must also be remembered that the joint foundation was to provide for twenty-four almsmen over whom the two masters had charge and that this requirement not only took a large slice of the charity's income but produced problems more than commensurate with its cost.

The first two masters selected were Thomas Downes, Gentleman, of St Albans and John Entick. They were equal in every respect but Entick was by far the more dominating character. As Downes was to die within four years of his appointment it is probable that he was already elderly. Entick, on the other hand, was about thirty and was to become the most celebrated of Bancroft's distinguished line of masters, enjoying an entry in the Dictionary of National Biography. Born about 1703, he was a curate in St Stephen's, Coleman Street at the time of his appointment as master, this being Francis Bancroft's parish. Possible he and Bancroft knew each other, which may have

25

helped secure his appointment. He had a school of some description in his parish before his appointment and had already in 1728 published the *Speculum Lectuam* intended to make Latin more amenable to the average schoolboy – or vice versa. Whilst teaching at Bancroft's he had charge of the petty cash and persuaded the Company to give him an allowance for preaching in Chapel on a Sunday. He also acted as agent for the Company in some local property of theirs at Bett Street which helped supplement his income.

He had taken a wife, Jane, during his curacy and she had borne him a son, John, who was baptised at St Stephen's, Coleman Street on the 4th May 1731. His wife had presumably died by the time of his enforced resignation in 1753 as she is not mentioned in the curious tale which was related to the Court by the various parties. Downes had been replaced in 1740 by Joseph Fisher as co-master. By 1755 Fisher was complaining of his wife's infidelity with Entick, her defence – most flippant by the standards of the time – being that her husband had forsaken her owing to his predilection for whores whom he frequently took to their – Mr and Mrs Fisher's – nuptial bed. The Company, fearing a scandal, dismissed Entick, paying him £97. 14s. 11d. 'if he left immediately'. Entick continued living in the parish of St Dunstan's, Stepney and joined Mr Shebbeare and Jonathan Scott in producing *The Monitor*, a High Tory broadsheet attacking the Whig Government, his salary being £200 a year. The attacks were unfavourably received by the King's Ministers and in 1762, following a particularly scurrilous broadside, his house was raided under a general warrant and his papers seized. He sued the authorities and, following a legal decision known as Entick's Case which severely limited the use of the general warrant, he was awarded £300 compensation in 1765; the case created a significant part of those laws which keep all Englishmen free. He went on to write a number of books, including an edition of Stow's *Environs of London*, and died in Stepney in 1773. A portrait by Burgess survives and his dictionaries remained standard works until the nineteenth century.

The two masters each had to find persons to stand surety to the value of £100 and took office on Lady Day, 1737. The 24 almsmen were selected by the Court of Assistants and were all freemen of the Company. During this period it was accepted by the Drapers' Company that men of humble substance would apply for the freedom of the Company in order to enjoy such charitable munificence as the Company's charities and trusts bestowed. Except in rare circumstances liverymen seldom applied for Company charity and, as the number of poor freemen declined in the nineteenth century, the Company found it increasingly difficult to fulfil some of their trusts owing to a lack of poor Drapers. Bancroft's merely gave preference to Drapers and in later years more and more of the almsmen were 'outsiders'. In 1738 however there was no such problem. We tend today to think of almshouses as homes for the elderly but Bancroft's Hospital was not exclusively filled with ancient Drapers. Several of them were employed and others were married, though a wife or dependants had to leave the house on the death of the almsman.

On appointment they took an oath to obey the Master and Wardens and the Hospital bye-laws and had to find two friends to stand surety. They also obtained a certificate from their parish wardens agreeing to be liable in the event of their expulsion from the almshouses. This was necessary under the Poor Laws as otherwise the Company or the ratepayers of the Mile End Old Town would have been liable for their maintenance. The almsmen, with their wives, were obliged to attend Chapel twice a day and the Hospital gates were closed from nine o'clock in Winter and ten o'clock in Summer until eight o'clock or seven o'clock the next morning, during which time a check was made on them, absence invoking a shilling fine for the first offence and expulsion for persistent breach of gate hours. The rules, a copy of which was given to each almsman, and which were publicly displayed, established other rules necessary for the orderly running of a civilized society.*

They were forbidden to take apprentices, or marry, or use their houses for business purposes, nor could they keep animals or chickens. In compensation for keeping these rules they were accommodated free, given half a chaldron of coal each year, £2 a quarter and a new gown every three years. From their number, one was appointed porter and another chapel clerk, each with an extra £8 a year. The almsmen were an important feature of the foundation for 150 years, their numbers increasing to 28 and then to 30 in 1812 when two lodge houses were built. As this

---

* See appendix for full list

History modestly hopes to record the development of every facet of the foundation and as the almsmen occupied a good deal of the time allotted to the Bancroft Trust by the Drapers' Company, mention will be made of them in the narrative of this work.

The boys began attendance in the Spring of 1738, in their uniforms of blue coats, caps, stockings, shoes and linen, rather like those still worn (on certain occasions) by the 'Blue Coat' scholars of Christ's Hospital. The selection process was quite simple. Each year the Masters and four Wardens had the right to nominate boys to a vacancy. The boys had to be able to read and write, come from respectable homes, be aged seven to ten on entry and live within travelling distance of the school, as there were no boarders before 1802.

In 1738 Mile End was one of the Tower Hamlets, an ancient description of the small settlements east of the City along or near the Colchester Road. Ribbon development meant that spacious villas or the occasional row of houses stretched from Aldgate Bar to the School site and beyond but north lay open country, mostly market gardens.

The boys attended the School every day of the week, as Chapel was compulsory on Sundays. The working day began with Chapel at eight o'clock from Michaelmas to Lady Day followed by lessons until eleven. These resumed at one until four when the day ended with another Chapel Service. For the Spring and Summer the day began at seven and lasted till five. These long hours were relieved on Thursday and Saturday by a half holiday. 'Breaking Up' consisted of three weeks at Christmas and a fortnight each at Easter and Whitsun.

The Instructions for the syllabus, emanating from the Will, are simply set out in the book of rules:

'That (The Masters) shall carefully Teach the children to Read, Write and cast accounts: and Instruct them as well in the Principles of the Christian Religion according to the Doctrine of the Church of England as in Loyalty to the King.'

There is nothing to suggest that this regime changed to any great degree for a hundred years. The Instructions for their behaviour could, with certain minor modifications, he applied to pupils of today.*

---

* See appendix for full list

The two masters, we assume, taught at the same time in different parts of the school room, as there must have been a variance in academic attainment according to age. Before long, monitors were appointed, partly to keep discipline and partly to aid the masters. These boys were given 6d. rather than the 1d. allowed to all boys on Visitation Day and the boy who made the oration, presumably the Head Boy, received half-a-crown. Until 1886 the school observed the two religious services prescribed by Bancroft in his Will. In October a service was held either in St Michael's, Cornhill (the Company Church) or elsewhere and in March near to the anniversary of Francis Bancroft's death a service was held in St Helen's, Bishopsgate. At both these services the boys were catechised and afterwards a supper was provided costing no more than £5.

It is part of Bancroft folklore that at the service in St Helen's the boys in accordance with his Will filed past Francis Bancroft's mummified corpse, clearly seen through the glass top of his coffin. There is little substance for this story. The Will makes no such instruction and the coffin was of solid oak, lined with lead and encased in an oak box.

The story may have arisen, from a custom of the Drapers' Company, as trustees of Francis Bancroft's estate, of inspecting the condition of his tomb from time to time. By 1748 a new oak case was needed for the coffin and the maintenance of the tomb was the first charge on the trust's London and Middlesex property. Certainly on one occasion – 1865 – this inspection was on the same day as the annual service, a convenient circumstance for the Master and Wardens. The tomb was opened – the Drapers' Company still have the key – and the state of the coffin examined. It is possible that one of the school masters was permitted to join in the inspection, or even that a boy surreptitiously looked through the open doors and then saw the coffin, but there is no record of the ceremony which tradition maintains occurred each year.

The eighteenth century, as has been said, was one of stagnation in the development of education. At Bancroft's Hospital the boys attended each day, learning to read, write and count and were then apprenticed out at fourteen or fifteen to anyone who would take them, the foundation paying £4. William Child was apprenticed to William Simpson in June 1743 and from that date regular appearances of similar payments appear in the Company's accounts. Numerous other sorts of payments were also made and their interest lies in showing the management of the Hospital and the Trust by the Drapers' Company, the alterations in dress, for example, showing the extent to which they interested themselves in the School.

The original clothing bill for one hundred boys was:

	£	s	d
100 Blue Jersey suits	50	0	0
200 Shirts at 2/3d	22	10	0
200 Prs Stockings at 10d	8	6	8
200 Bands at 3d	2	10	0
100 Prs Shoes at 2/9d	31	15	0
100 Caps & Strings at 9d	3	15	0
100 prs gloves at 7d	2	18	4
100 prs buckles at 3d	1	5	0
	£123	0	0

Inflation and a slight change in detail increased this to £155 by the end of the century. The boys received a new set of shoes half way through the year, an allowance increased to three pairs in 1761. In the early years the boys' parents or 'friends' had to give bonds for the cost of the uniform, that is, find a guarantor for £1 5s 0d in case their children absconded with the clothing. This changed in 1769 to a straightforward note.

The Company showed concern in 1750 at the standard of cloth and ordered samples to Drapers' Hall, and they occasionally changed the purveyor of the various articles, more to improve standards than to save money. In 1783 the school cap whose descendant survived until the 1970s was temporarily replaced by a hat. All the clothing when no longer fit for use by the scholars was given to the poor. The accounts also show the purchase of such school necessities as spelling books, inkwells, Prayer Books and a regular supply of stationery. They also show the rising costs of repairs and the wise husbandry of the Trust's endowment.

The first repainting of the buildings occurred in 1743 and the cost and extent of repairs increased by the year. In 1749 the following bills were paid:

		£	s	d
Richard Sparks	Carpenter	32	7	8
John Bundy	Bricklayer	25	19	10
Jane Holloway	Plaisterer		13	4
Peter Chuflou	Glazier	1	11	11
David Machen	Plumber	3	12	10½
John Slock	Painter	1	0	8
Thomas Cope	Paviour	5	9	0
		70	15	3½

and these bills continued. In 1746 a new lead roof had been placed for £110 and in 1766 the portico had to be replaced, costing £404 11s 2d.

We tend to think of Georgian builders as men who made their structures to last but it would seem that Mr Porter was an early example of a jerry builder. The plumbing arrangements of the school and the masters' and almsmen's dwellings were primitive by our standards, each dwelling having its own small cesspool with a main cesspool in the grounds which had to be emptied regularly, for which service in 1754 Mary Harper was paid £6 or 4/-d a ton for 'emptying and carrying away 30 tons of soil from the boys' necessary'. Similar bills are found for performing these tasks at the almshouses. Even with the advent of sewage pipes in the following century the sanitary arrangements at Mile End were never good and caused much concern when the school admitted boarders. The original water supply came from wells dug into the Hospital grounds but in 1763 the Hospital received water from the Stratford and West Ham Waterworks Company whose reservoir was east of the school, at a cost of £6 a year, an arrangement that was to last until the school's demolition.

Other changes were made to what the minutes of the Drapers' Company ominously call 'The Institution': the ditch in front of the school was bricked over and proper gates made for a carriage to drive up to the Chapel portico. It was also proposed in 1769 that a gallery be added to the Hospital Chapel and a licence be obtained to hold regular services, an idea abandoned by the Company for fear that the Bishop of London would claim some jurisdiction over the school and the appointment of Masters. For similar reasons an earlier request by local residents to attend the chapel on Sundays – the Parish Church was St Dunstan's, Stepney – had been declined. All these matters concerned the Court of Assistants in those years and any decision had formally to be voted upon and agreed by the Court. Their principal work during this period, however, was the deployment and development of the trust fund.

Francis Bancroft left the Drapers' Company six silver plates; he also offered them a great fortune to be held in trust to finance and administer his Hospital. It was from this trust that the school was financed wholly until 1889 and it continued to educate all, and provide bed and board for about seventy of the hundred foundation scholars from that date until after the second world war. The Trust still exists and the Company as trustee pays the income each year to the Governors who use it to finance scholarships in accordance with the spirit of the original foundation. The Company have, since 1975, covenanted from their own funds money to maintain extra scholarships at the school.

As will become apparent throughout this History, Bancroft's' debt to the Company is beyond calculation. They have given buildings to the foundation in 1800, 1883, 1910, 1937, 1964, 1969, and 1987. On other occasions they have given interest-free loans and even, like a good parent, paid off debts as well as endowing leavers' scholarships, the latter mainly from defunct trusts. The Company has seldom, however, allowed the School to became an annual recipient of its income, drawing a distinction between ordinary expenditure and capital improvements, the exceptions being when the school's future was in doubt in the 1870s and during the first world war when the trust income was not able to fulfil all its obligations.

Bancroft's estate in 1728 amounted, after specific legacies, to about £23,000 in bonds and a certain amount of property, consisting of three farms in Essex and Suffolk and various houses in London, Westminster, Middlesex and Essex. The farmland consisted of 260 acres at Clopton Hall near Dunmow, where the trustee also became lord of the manor; Saltcoats Farm, an 80-acre copy-holding at Woodham Ferrers; and Benton End Farm at Hadleigh in Suffolk with 242 acres. Copy-hold meant that certain dues were paid to the lord of the manor, especially on inheritance. The Drapers' Company therefore appointed three trustees to hold the land at Hadleigh – and the Chiswick Houses – and paid the dues when the last of the trustees died. In recompense, the dues received from the Manor of Clopton enhanced the income from that property.

The house property consisted of three messuages in Chiswick inherited by Francis Bancroft from his father; houses at Prittlewell, Essex; two houses in King Street, Westminster; two inns and a house in High Holborn; and a house in Godliman Street, alias St Pauls Chain, in the City.

The income for 1732 was as follows:

	£	s	d
John Stokes Clopton Hall	100	0	0
Manorial dues	4	8	11
John Tumpion Hadleigh	155	0	0
Thomas Cornel W. Ferrers	25	0	0
Edward Earlmer Chiswick	10	0	0
Peter Rowland Westminster	10	10	0
John Brown H. Holborn	24	0	0
Elizabeth Budgeon H. Holborn	13	0	0
Joseph Ellis H. Holborn	19	0	0
Wallis Hutchins St Pauls Chain	26	0	0
Rowland English Prittlewell	Peppercorn		
	£386	18	11

The Prittlewell houses were being developed. Added to this were the bonds consisting of South Sea stock of £2,596 5s 4d and annuities of £21,293 13s 2d. Income since Bancroft's death had added £1,454 0s 0d to these investments and the executors also transferred £1,524 0s 0d in 1734, the two sums paying a substantial amount of the cost of building the Hospital.

The Company was wary of holding a large proportion of the trust's funds in stocks and bonds – the South Sea Bubble was but a few years before – and during the eighteenth century they expanded the property portfolio. In 1737 the houses at Holborn were merged into one block by the purchase of the Angel Inn for £1,200 and in 1740 and '43 rent charges – dues liable on freehold properties – were purchased in Yorkshire for £9,200 and in Lincolnshire for £2,800, the incomes of £339 and £100 respectively being above the 3% offered on bonds at that time.

The Westminster houses were compulsorily purchased for £320 in 1745 to allow the construction of the approach road to the new Westminster Bridge, but that loss was more than recompensed by the purchase for £250 of Nos. 10 and 11 Poultry in 1747 and a quit rent, (an annual charge) on a property the following year in All Saints, Honey Lane. In 1751, Bancroft's became a minority co-owner with the Rainey Trust of 55–56 Gracechurch Street and 1–18 Talbot Court, the Bancroft share costing £160, and in the same year a property in Basinghall Avenue was purchased for £260.

The London property rents and the substantial farm rents were easily collected, but Chiswick, and especially Prittlewell, had to be collected through agents, whose shilling in the pound brought so little that the properties were often neglected. Similar problems were also had at times in collecting the rent charges and it was necessary every few years to hold a court baron at Clopton. Despite these problems the Trust remained a landowner until the 1920s.

Throughout the eighteenth century the annual income of the Trust exceeded the expenditure by about £300 and the entry, 'Purchased £300 3% South Sea stock' occurs regularly. Although the expenditure increased, it failed to keep pace with the income growth caused by the reinvestment and by a rise in property values. In 1773 the Trust lent Lord Selbourne £19,400 on a mortgage of his Irish estates giving an income of £900 a year, and by 1786 the income was:

Rents	£1,134	
Bonds	£270	value £10,500
Mortgage	£970	value £19,400
	———	
	£2,374	

By 1799 the value of the bonds had increased to £26,000 and the rent roll to £1,900 per annum. This excess of income over expenditure was a grave embarrassment to the Company who as trustee felt duty bound to use up the entire income each year. From 1783 onwards, various ideas were mooted and eventually a boarding school was decided upon. The Trust was allowed to accumulate more capital to generate the income assessed for this purpose and the boarding house opened in 1802. An easier way to use the cash would have been an expansion of the almshouses. This was to happen when four almshouses were added in the early nineteenth century and two more when the lodge gates were built, though the problems caused by Bancroft's almsmen and their licentious behaviour led to the Company's belief that it had sufficient almsmen already.

In 1737, within a year of his appointment, William White was expelled for drunkenness and the minutes of the Court of Wardens for the next hundred and fifty years contain regular repetitions of this type of entry. The almshouses had their uses, especially as a place for retired Company servants; John Clark, bargemaster, being admitted in 1747, but the behaviour of the almsmen made this of little recompense. In 1770, following a series of scandals including the expulsion of the aptly named Mr Maidman who showed too keen an interest in the young girls of the neighbourhood, the Court carried out a full investigation of the almshouses. A complaint was found against most of the inmates, either of drunkenness or of immoral living, and they were asked to produce their marriage certificates. Several were reprimanded for breach of the rules.

In 1791 a further enquiry was held following an argument between almsman Palmer and the gatekeeper. From this it was discovered that Palmer was twenty-eight years old and earned 18/-d a week as spectacle-maker, a calling which obliged him to miss the daily chapel service and breach the gate hours. He was expelled and the compulsory attendance of chapel enforced. As the income of the Trust increased the allowance and pensions of the almsmen were increased: the coal allowance increased from six to twelve sacks in 1749, with an extra half chaldron in 1787, and the pension was increased by instalments to £18 a year in 1784 though a request for candles in 1788 was declined.

When the almsmen died they were buried in a small graveyard adjoining the Hospital, but they often left wives whom the Company had to place elsewhere. This led to a suggestion in 1783 that the Trust be extended to almswomen; it was also suggested that girls might be educated by the Charity but this suggestion was defeated by the Master's casting vote at the Court of Assistants. The almsmen remained at Mile End until the Hospital was demolished, a constant thorn in the side of the Company, for twenty-eight men were more vociferous than a hundred boys, and no further attempt was made to extend the size of the foundation.

The office of joint master lasted from 1737 until 1802, during which time eight masters occupied the houses to the east of the porticoed chapel. Until 1784 one of them was in Holy Orders.

Entick had been a curate at St Stephen's, Coleman Street, until he was appointed first joint master with Mr Downes in 1737. On the latter's death Joseph Fisher came to the foundation and it was his wife's friendliness with Entick which ensured that master's expulsion. In what appears to have been a confused election at Drapers' Hall Entick was replaced by the Rev Nehemiah Ring, BA, of Merton College, Oxford. His namesake uncle was Master Warden of the Company that year, succeeding as Master shortly thereafter, and was Church Warden of St John's, Hackney. Ring, the schoolmaster, with his wife and children lived at the school until his death in 1768. He preached in the chapel and several times it was suggested that he be paid £40 extra a year for this service but the Trustees were reluctant to break the Will. Instead the Company appointed him to Rainey's Lectureship at St Michael's, Cornhill, which increased his income. On his death the Company gave 20 guineas to his widow.

On Fisher's death in 1759, Phineas Barratt was appointed and he was joined by Rev Arthur Dawes in 1768. Barratt's reign lasted forty-three years, a period unsurpassed by any other Bancroft's Master. The salary increased to £60 in 1770 and £76 in 1784 and they were allowed to expand their gardens in 1775. Barratt was clearly well regarded by the Company as they made him a gift of £50 from their own funds in 1778. Dawes also must have been in good favour for in 1784 he was appointed to the Company's living at St Michael's, Cornhill, where he lived until his death in 1793. Instead of a cleric the Company appointed in 1784 George Franklin to Dawes' mastership. A Liveryman of the Company, he was retired on a Company pension of £105 in 1800 to make way for George Peché who became the boarding school's first Head Master. Franklin died at Bethnal Green in 1803, the same year as Barratt.

Little is known of the above masters except for Entick and he alone survives in portrait form. There are no anecdotes concerning them; they simply carried out the duties of their office in which a majority of them died. They were, however, the first in a long line of masters, head masters and assistant masters who have moulded Bancroft's and given something of their personalities to create the school and for that reason their memories should be as revered as those of more recent and better known names.

Slating done for the Worshipful Company of Drapers

April past due   By H & S. Sharpe   £ s d   £ s d

At Bancrofts Hospital Mile end

22	6	. dupl Countess slating on boards with copper nails - - - - - - -	⅔	44.2.8
		Items in Wates.16 in Day Works from May 18th to Nov. 25th 1826 collected from Books and vouchers of Clerk of Works -		
		Slater 24 a days - - - - - -	5/.	6.10.8
		Labour 11 day - - - - -	3/6	1.18.6
		Boy 1 day - - - - - - -		. 2.6
	6	. dupl welsh rag slating - - - 8		. 3 -
	144	. —— westmorland do	7/	4.4 -
		60 doubles slates - - - - 7/6		. 4.2
		962 Ladies slates - - - - 4/.		6.14.8
		70 Countess do - - - - 7/		. 16.9½
		ett 8 & 3 nails - £ct copper do -		. 17 -
		cartage - - - - - - -		. 7 -

         £ 66.0.8½

Rich. Davis

Ex.d U.J Booth   Jn.o Parsons

J.B.Smith ——

Bill for repairs, c1785

Worthy Sirs

From my very infirm state of Health, —
I find it impossible for me to Discharge the Duty, of
the Office of one of the Masters of Mr Bancroft Hospital
either with Justice to the Boys committed to my Care —
and Instruction — or Satisfaction to my Self; I have
for 15 Years past endeavoured to perform the Duty of my
Office, flattering my Self to your Satisfaction; ———
I therefore humbly beg your Permission to resign the
said Mastership; that an Able Person may be —
chosen in my Room; ——— Permit me Worthy Gentl.
to state that at the Advanced Age of 67 — infirm and
helpless as I am. I have not had an Opportunity of —
making any Saving for future Provision; & having
the Honour of being related to the Worshipful Comp.y
of Drapers — a Livery Man thereof for 30 Years; — I throw
my Self upon the Court, humbly submitting my Case
to Your Worships Consideration and Humanity; trusting
from the well known Liberality and Goodness of the Court
on all occasions; flatter my Self they will so consider —
as that the Remainder of my Life will be Happy &
Comfortable; I am with all due Respect, Worthy Sirs,
Your obliged and obedt. hble Ser.
Geo. Franklin.

Mr Bancroft Hosp.l
16 Decr 1799.

George Franklin's retirement letter

38

CHAPTER IV

Boarding School

THE DECISION to extend the provisions of the Trust to board as
well as clothe and educate the boys was not taken lightly; figures
were studied, projections taken, comparisons made with other
schools and legal advice sought, so that fifteen years elapsed
between the proposal and fruition of the plan.

As mentioned above, the Trust income regularly exceeded the
present expenditure. The question then arose as to whether this
surplus was sufficient to board a hundred boys and the answer in
1790 appeared to be that it was not. The Court of Wardens
enquired of the financing of Christ's Hospital, to which great
school the Company, then as now, enjoyed the right of
nominating a scholar under the Will of John Buck. They
discovered the cost of maintaining a boy was £17 a year, though
they decided that it would cost more per head to keep one
hundred boys at Bancroft's, as opposed to the larger number of
boys at Christ's. Even relying on the figure of £1,700 a year, the
position was not very promising. The expenditure on day boys
broke down as follows:

Apparel	£300	9	10
Masters	£152	0	0
Coals	£20	0	0
Stationery	£27	3	0
Apprenticeships	£32	0	0
	£531	12	10

To this could be added the annual surplus of £720, giving £1,250,
producing a shortfall of £450 a year. There was no obvious way
of reducing this proposed expenditure of £1,700 and they needed
a minimum staff consisting of the two masters and a chaplain
plus a steward, a matron, a cook, nurse and washer woman. The
Court therefore dropped the plan for the time being.

In 1796 the state of account was again laid before a special
committee appointed by the Court, from which it was clear that

39

the income was now sufficient to maintain a boarding establishment, though not capable of funding the new buildings. The Committee suggested that the Company should give from its corporate funds the cost of building and furnishing the new building. The Court were not indisposed to the suggestion but first submitted the plan to learned counsel. They received an opinion from the Attorney General Sir John Scott. That great jurist who, as Earl of Eldon, was Lord Chancellor from 1801 to 1827 with only one short break, has been described as a Tory of the bluest hue. During the long premiership of Lord Liverpool he personified the will of that administration to oppose constitutional change. It is perhaps not strange therefore that he opposed the proposed alteration to Bancroft's without the benefit of a Chancery hearing.

After careful consideration the Company took the view that as the Will allowed them to make such improvements as they saw fit to the school they were entitled to spend their own money in doing so. They therefore declined the Attorney General's advice and avoided a lengthy and costly legal action, at the same time voting £3,500 for building and furnishing two dormitories, a classroom, dining hall, sick rooms and domestic offices.

In November 1797 they formed themselves into a committee of the whole Court to consider the building work and furnishing in some detail. The Company's surveyor, Gorham, prepared plans for the new buildings on the land behind the range that comprised the school room, chapel and masters' houses: the two masters were compensated for the loss of the land with £16 each. Several builders applied for the contract and it was given to Joseph Stewart who stood surety for the estimated £2,000 cost. The work started in 1799 and it was thought that by 1801 as the buildings approached completion the income of the Trust would at last reach a level sufficient to meet all regular expenditure. The Company was pleased with the new buildings and gave Stewart a hundred guineas to show their appreciation of his efforts. They now had to consider the new rules for the Institution.

The two masters, Franklin and Barrett, were growing old and Franklin, a liveryman of the Company since 1770, was given, in 1800, a pension by the Drapers' Company of a hundred guineas a year. In his place they appointed George Peché who became Head Master on Barrett's death in 1803. The entire new building was furnished for £600 and plans were made for the re-opening.

The pupils had to be selected and a new method was chosen which acknowledged the Court's grant of money. Every year the Master and four wardens would each have the right to nominate a boy to a vacancy, the other places being filled by nominations from individual members of the Court of Assistants chosen by rote. This system, which lasted until 1883, had the pleasant effect of providing a wide cross-section of boys for the school, as anyone was permitted to approach a member of the Court and the member might use his nomination in favour of an impecunious nephew, his clerk's son, his gardener's grandson or simply for the boy of someone fortunate enough to know whom to approach to beg a place for his son.

The rules forbade the sons of rich parents and the standard of literacy demanded excluded the offspring of the ignorant poor but Bancroftians came from all the classes in between and this social mixture has always been one of Bancroft's great assets.

As selection procedure began the Committee announced that, contrary to what they had previously believed, the income would only support fifty boarders at that stage. After due consideration it was decided to continue the appointment of the boys at a rate of fifteen a year, hoping the income to be sufficiently large within seven years to take the full cost of the establishment. The alternative of boarding out the boys for a short time was dismissed as most unsatisfactory, the Company agreeing to underwrite any initial deficit. The Committee then devised and printed the new regulations.*

The two masters were no longer to be equal but one was to be Head Master on £120 a year plus 48 sacks of coal and his house free of rates and taxes, with his subordinate on £90 a year enjoying the same perquisites. They were to share the duties of teaching under the Head Master's supervision, the undermaster deputising in his absence. One master was always to be on the premises and be present at all meals; the Head Master alone was able to beat the boys; and was also to keep accounts and oversee the administration of the kitchens.

The syllabus which the masters taught remained the same as before according to the Will: the boys were to learn to read, write

---

* See appendix

and cast accounts and know their duty to God and the King. The chaplaincy was not a full time appointment but the incumbent had to hold divine service on Sundays and the principal feast days, for which he received thirty guineas a year. The important office of housekeeper was to be filled by an unmarried woman with no dependent children. She was to supervise the other staff – cook, house maid and scullery maid – as well as the boys outside school hours, to ensure that they washed properly. She also had to order all the food and keep domestic accounts and see that the boys received sufficient food.

To ensure that the staff did not short change the boys, all leftover food was sold to an outside contractor rather than become a perk for the servants. All four servants lived in and had coals and laundry paid for: the housekeeper received £40 a year, cook £15 and the maids £12 each.

The regime under which the boys lived at the Hospital was naturally very strict, but their conditions appear to have been reasonable when compared to those existing at other boarding schools of the time. They arrived with a certificate from their parish acknowledging their right of residence there (these were similar forms to those produced by the almsmen and for the same reason, namely to protect the poor law guardians of Mile End Old Town from liability for them on their leaving the Hospital), another form from their 'Friends' giving the Master and wardens powers *in loco parentis*, and a third certificate from the doctor stating they were fit and clean and had been inoculated for smallpox.

The uniform had altered slightly, the coat being shorter than before, and an experiment was tried of making the boys breeches of leather, no doubt to make them last longer. There were three linen shirts, changed on Thursdays and Sundays, and four pairs of stockings changed once a week. Hair was cut once a month 'as close as scissors can be got to the head' and the sheets of the beds were changed once a fortnight, all boys but the four monitors sleeping two to a bed. There were two dormitories of equal size.

The boys rose at six in summer and seven in winter and after performing their ablutions and having breakfast of bread, cheese and cocoa (or milk on alternate days), began school an hour later with prayers. At eleven the boys did their chores and then had free time until luncheon which consisted of ½lb. meat each and vegetables.

Afternoon school was from two till five, except on Wednesdays and Saturdays when they had a half-holiday and the day ended with Chapel. They supped at six on bread and cheese, performed other chores then washed with soap and sand and retired at eight in Winter and nine in Summer. There was a covered playground where the boys could go during this time but they were forbidden the dormitories except for sleeping and making their beds and they were also forbidden to enter the long front court, no doubt to limit their contact with the almsmen as much as to keep that area tidy.

Holidays were from Christmas Eve to January 7th and the third Thursday in August until the Monday fortnight following, Easter and Whitsun being spent at school. There were also Red Letter days when a special meal was served as follows:

Founder's Day (March 18th)	Roast beef & dumplings
St. George's Day	Roast beef & plum pudding
Last Sunday in April	Roast beef & plum pudding
Easter Sunday	Roast beef & Yorkshire pudding
Whit Sunday & King's Birthday	Shoulder of veal & gooseberry Pies
Drapers' Company Election Day	Shoulder of veal & fruit pies
November 5th	Roast beef & dumplings
Lord Mayor's Day	Roast Pork, apple pies
Christmas Day	Roast beef & dumplings

School was kept running every day of the year for those boys whose 'Friends' could not take them away during the vacation. Alternatively boys wishing to spend a night outside school during term had to apply to the Master, Wardens or Clerk of the Company for permission and if received they were given a special badge and their names entered in a book. Sick boys were sent to the London Hospital to which the Drapers' Company had long subscribed and to which the Bancroft trust now donated £20 a year. The Medical Officer appeared at the school daily for the benefit of the boys and almsmen.

The Draper's Company were aware that an added responsibility was placed on their shoulders by this new venture and they appointed a committee of five of their number, of whom at least one was always a Warden, to oversee the school. They visited the school about once a fortnight, their agenda including the ordering of food. Furthermore, the Clerk of the Company attended once a month to see that the accounts were kept in order.

By 1802 it was realised that the income of the trust would not keep pace with inflation and the Committee of the whole Court suggested that at least £300 a year be reinvested and that the opening of the school be delayed until £9,000 was saved from income to give an extra £300 a year, for they estimated that the charity's cost in the first year would be £3,293 6s 3d as set against an income of £3,203 5s 11d. Regrettably the forecast of inflation was to prove only too accurate, because of the great war being financed and fought by England against the tyranny of Napoleon.

Inflation was increasing in England for the first time since Stuart times. It adversely affected the trust finances in two ways; the income decreased in real terms and the capital value of the 3% stock dropped to acknowledge the 5% interest rate, thus in 1802 the trust bought £400 worth of 3% stock for £227. Accordingly, had they attempted to sell the large amount of stock held by the Trust, it would have been at a price below what it cost seventy years earlier. Under these and other circumstances the real income of the trust failed to keep pace with the cost of living, and this was to cause great debate at Drapers' Hall in the middle of the century.

Peché became the first Head Master, John Woolley Lessingham the under master, the Rev Thomas Thirlwall the chaplain and Mary Chamberlain housekeeper. The school opened on August 1st, 1802 with a service by the chaplain which was printed by order of the Court. Thus began the one hundred and seventy-nine year period of Bancroft's as a boarding school.

For the next fifty years, while England underwent the most far-reaching and radical changes in its social, economic and political structure, Bancroft's remained almost static. The same is true of most boarding schools during the period who also enjoyed the other feature of early nineteenth century Bancroft's – outbreaks of insurrection by the boys. The great educational reformers – Vaughan at Harrow, Arnold at Rugby and other evangelical clergymen – were a feature of the immediate post-Reform Bill period. Like other schools throughout the country

Bancroft's remained immune to change before then. Indeed, in a decision in the Court of Chancery, the same Lord Eldon who had advised the Drapers' Company not to create a boarding foundation without a court agreement, delivered a judgement against Leeds Grammar School forcing it to teach only the original syllabus of Greek and Latin, and making the Governors abandon 'Modern' subjects such as mathematics. In view of such a decision it is hardly surprising that the Company were reluctant to alter the syllabus before being forced to by Royal Commissions and Acts of Parliament in the middle of the century.

Bancroft's had three Head Masters between 1803 and 1855, George Peché until 1836, Henry Mackenzie for four years and Richard Thomas from 1840–1855. Peché took Holy Orders in 1812 when the Company found difficulty in finding a clergyman to hold a service once a week for a stipend of only 30 guineas and decided against raising it to 50 guineas. Thirlwall had resigned in 1808 and his successor, William Lowfield Fancourt, served for just three years, complaining of the difficulty of the journey from the City. Peché therefore returned to Oxford and took Holy Orders at Pembroke College.

The office of under master changed twice in the early years: Mr Laundy replaced Lessingham in 1807, retiring in 1819, to be replaced by Charles Dinham. Dinham, who figures in Bancroft's famous riot of 1838, died in office in 1851 and his successor Cornelius Laycock survived until 1886 when the school moved from Mile End, a joint period of sixty-seven years. The income of the two masters grew steadily throughout this period, the Company giving a gift of £50 each year to Peché and £25 to Dinham from their own funds as those of the trust could not always afford it. Peché also had the Rainey Lectureship. Peché appears to have been a kindly man, popular and respected at the school and at Drapers' Hall. Boys were expelled during his reign and there were minor disturbances but in general the school was run with discipline and efficiency. In 1833 he was given three months holiday to help recovery from an illness and in 1836 he retired on a Company pension of £200 a year.

His successor was the Reverend Henry Mackenzie. Educated at Pembroke College, Oxford, the headmastership was his first appointment on coming down and it cannot be said to have been a wholly successful reign. The son of a City Merchant fallen on

45

hard times, and well connected in the City, he was an evangelist in the Dr Arnold mould. It is hard to say why he did not expend his undoubted energies on Bancroft's; the committee of the time were particularly efficient and keen on improving the school. He soon realised that his calling lay in another direction – in the growing suburbs of London. He became involved in building churches in Mile End and resigned as Head Master in 1840 to dedicate his life fully to that mission. The Company generously donated money to his appeal for the ten churches and he dedicated a book of sermons to them in 1842. He went on to be a famous rector of St Martin's in the Fields and finally in 1870 became Bishop of Nottingham, dying in 1878.

The life of the boys during this period appears to be inextricably linked with the series of outbursts and riots which occurred at regular intervals, especially in the eighteen twenties and thirties. As has been stated above Bancroft's was not exceptional in this: before Vaughan's headmastership of Harrow it was said to be unsafe for people to pass the school as they were liable to be pelted with stones, and militia once had to be called to Winchester to suppress a rebellion.

Politically, this period began with riots so serious in Westminster that the King was unable to open Parliament and ended with the Great Chartist Marches, the intervening period including the Peter's Field riot in Manchester in 1819 and the burning of Bristol in 1831. Boys so close to the Capital, with many of them living there during the holidays, could not but fail to be susceptible to such events. Perhaps the most important point, noted in 1840, was that the boys had no organised games or activities outside the school hours and time weighed heavily on their hands. From the beginning a number of boys had run away from school and entries such as, 'John Venables expelled for running away', 'James Prior expelled for running away' and 'Alfred Slater given a second chance', appear regularly in the minutes of the Court of Assistants. In 1819 Richard Rowsell was expelled for the simple reason that Peché found him unmanageable.

The first serious outburst of trouble was in 1821, when the Visitors reported that several boys were guilty of theft, absenteeism, running away and general insubordination. An investigation was made and several boys were expelled. Sporadic expulsions for running away were made in the next few years and discipline appears to have declined under Mackenzie. On 24th July 1838, when Dinham took over temporarily in Mackenzie's absence, the boys seized the school room and barred it. This incident is well described in the report of the investigative committee:

'Mr Dinham, thinking it necessary after the departure of Mr Mackenzie on Wednesday morning to address a few words to the boys by way of caution to the Idle and exhortation to the School generally, accordingly did so before dismissing them at twelve o'clock, it being a half-holiday. He entreated them to pursue a course of attention and diligence and give him as little trouble as possible, as they must be aware that the whole charge of the establishment was to him a very anxious charge. In what he said he particularly called on the monitors to discharge their respective duties faithfully, for by so doing they would relieve him of much of this anxiety and personal labour. What was said appeared to have the desired effect; all went on well and quietly; the boys attended Chapel duty as usual at half past four.

'But between 5 and 6 o'clock, about a quarter past five, Mr Dinham had occasion to go to the School, and found to his astonishment the doors and windows effectually barricaded and secured, and upon enquiry understood that several boys, *viz.*, 18, besides 9 others who were detained there against their inclinations, but were let out through one of the windows after the lapse of an hour or more, were within, and that he (Mr D.) was refused admittance. Mr Dinham, in order to give them time for reflection and to consider what they were doing and hoping that they might offer terms of submission without obliging him to proceed to extremes, thought it prudent to leave them in possession, but no submission occurred. Some boy discharged a firework.'

The ringleaders were flogged and later appeared before the Court of Assistants, when several were expelled and Dinham was reprimanded for failing to keep better control. A year later Mackenzie reported that a number of boys had left the school during his absence and four boys were expelled, a further seven leaving a few months later when 'The spirit of rebellion' was still abroad. The special committee which investigated the disturbances reported in late 1840. They felt that the boys should have

47

someone controlling them in the playground and at meal times, and further that a means of directing their exertion in play hours should be found.

The result of the committee was the appointment of an usher at £30 a year to help keep control and do some teaching, and one of the almsmen as beadle at £10 a year. The Company also gave money for certain toys to be kept in the play shed. Occasional expulsions continued, including two boys for cutting the tail off a cat and another for indecent and improper conduct – though the authorities started inflicting the lesser penalty and perhaps more effective punishment of being deprived of 'Animal Food' for two days a week and made to wear a yellow jacket. No further mass expulsions were necessary until the reign of Symns.

There can be no doubt that the committee's findings were taken as a personal reprimand by Mackenzie and his assistant Dinham. Whereas the latter, with his growing family, could not move on, Mackenzie took his driving evangelical zeal away from pedagogy and used it to propagate the Church Militant, ending as one of the first two suffragan bishops since the Reformation. To his office the Drapers' Company elected the Reverend Richard James Francis Thomas of Christ Church, Oxford, a contemporary of Mackenzie but apparently very different in temperament. A classical scholar of The House, he published a number of books during his lifetime including a book of sermons and of mathematical tables.

The aftermath of the 1838 riot was still noticeable at the school and Thomas' first task was to restore discipline. In this he was aided by the Bancroft Committee. He was an advocate of that well known educational doctrine, so rarely heard today, of 'spare the rod and spoil the child'. Discipline was restored and in 1849 the Company forbade the flogging of boys and also refused to build a remedial room for recalcitrant boys. Thomas' relationship with the Drapers' Company soured in the last few years of his headmastership. They declined to appoint him Rainey's lecturer when Peché died in 1849 and he refused to deliver the annual Founder's Day sermon, an action which caused the Court of Assistants to write informing him of their displeasure. This was also the time when the inadequacies of the syllabus – the fault of the Governors and the sacrosanct status of the Will rather than of the Head Master – were being discussed, and when in 1855 Thomas wrote to say that he had become rector of Yeovil in

Bancroft's Hospital, Mile End, *c*.1880

The Rev. Henry Mackenzie, Head Master 1836–40

The Rev. John Entick, Master 1737–54

Gravestone of Charles Dinham,
second master 1818–51, at Mile End

SACRED
TO THE MEMORY OF
MR CHARLES DINHAM,
33 YEARS SECOND MASTER OF
BANCROFT'S SCHOOL,
DIED OCTOBER 26TH 1851,
AGED 57 YEARS.

AND OF HIS INFANT DAUGHTER
LAURA LECAMUS,
DIED JANUARY 21ST 1830,
AGED 21 MONTHS.

ALSO OF
MR THOMAS HACKETT,
HIS FATHER IN LAW,
DIED MARCH 27TH 1835,
AGED 78 YEARS.

The Rev. Richard Thomas, Head Master 1840–55

The Rev. John Symns, Head Master 1876–1906

The Rev. William Hunt, Head Master 1855–76

Somerset few tears were shed at Drapers' Hall.

While riot and insurrection occurred the welfare of the boys had to be ensured and the Bancroft School Committee were keen that the boys' lives should be as tolerable as possible within the rules of the Institution. In 1813 jersey breeches replaced the experimental leather ones and the quality of cloth was closely examined by the Committee, who also ordered handkerchiefs for the boys in 1839. In 1824 the practice of boys sleeping two to a bed was stopped but to contain laundry bills the sheets were changed once a month rather than once a fortnight, though a reversion to fortnightly sheets was made in 1839 when each boy was also given his own hand towel.

The boys' health was the province of the housekeeper, Mrs Chamberlain, a popular and efficient lady whose portrait was painted by order of the Court; when she was ill in 1829 they sent her a case of 'Mountain Wine'. She retired aged eighty-nine in 1837, to be replaced by Mrs Amelia Fortescue. During her brief stay a boy, Frederick Neale, died and his parents complained of his treatment at the school when an inquest was held. Juvenile death at the time was not uncommon and no condemnation of the matron or the school came from the coroner; the case, however, was reported in the newspapers and the Drapers' Company held an enquiry after which it was resolved that Mrs Fortesque was 'Unequal to the discharge of the various and laborious duties attached to her station'.

The domestic staff, which had increased to six women, was reduced to four, the laundry being sent to a local workhouse at a shilling per dozen articles, and Mrs Strong became matron. In 1829, Samuel Byles, liveryman of the Drapers' Company, was appointed surgeon and apothecary to the school at £40 a year which was increased to £60 four years later when he agreed to visit the almsmen daily.

The health of the school had been good but from 1838 when there was an outbreak of scarlatina the school was subject to regular epidemics. The form was always the same: the boys' 'Friends' were asked to take them away, the building was disinfected and whitewashed and the boys returned from their unexpected holiday. The problem with the site was that it was badly drained and simply not large enough for one hundred and fifty people. Dr Byles and his successor Dr Self, appointed in 1856, were forever pressing for improvements. The environs also were changing and the large population in what was almost London's East End was placing a great strain on the water and sewage systems. Furthermore, the placing of the Mile End Workhouse immediately to the north of the school, with whom there were constant boundary squabbles, did little to improve the atmosphere of the school grounds.

Another outbreak of scarlatina occurred in 1840 when one boy died. Following this the Court ordered a daily glass of beer for each boy and some almshouses were converted to sickrooms. In 1841 almsman MacKenzie was given £2 for lodging the Hill brothers while they had smallpox. Several outbreaks of ringworm in 1841 and thereafter caused boys' heads to be rigorously examined at the beginning of term and infected boys were returned to their homes. Later in the year a boy contracted typhus and the Christmas holiday began early, Dr Byles complaining in the strongest terms of the school drains.

A less sympathetic case was the boy sent home that year for incontinence. 'It appeared evident that the punishment lately inflicted had not had the desired effect of correcting this pernicious habit.' Even in that age, deprived of child psychologists and social workers, the punishment seems rather harsh and coincided with complaints by some parents about Thomas' use of the 'cat'. More sympathy was given to Boulton who was 'acting in a very strange and excited manner for which no reason could be assigned, except the possibility of the late warm weather having affected his brain'. He was sent home, to be followed a month later by the rest of the school when nineteen boys contracted a bad fever, one boy dying.

In 1850 a boy died of typhus and again Byles complained to the Court. After inspecting the Bill of Fare, it was stated that the diet was 'much more liberal than in most other public schools' and compared favourably with Christ's Hospital and the other London schools. It was, however, decided to add more green vegetables to the diet and to give more milk and butter. The problems were only solved in the end by the removal of the school to Woodford, and the unhealthy site must have been an important consideration in determining that move.

A more notable victim of the environment was Mr Dinham who died in 1851 after suffering from stomach pains. His income had risen to £150 in 1835 on condition that he gave up private pupils, and his wife became matron in 1847, following the death of Mrs Strong. The Company allowed her to continue as matron and added a pension of £50 a year until the youngest of her nine children left home. They also granted one of their charities, Pennoyer's Gift, to her son, to be apprenticed to Dr Byles and to two of her daughters to become schoolmistresses, a third marrying Dr Byles' son. Mrs Dinham was a popular and efficient matron, finally retiring in 1874 on a pension.

Since 1840 there had been an usher in the school to assist the masters. Prior to that a senior boy, called a preceptor, had helped for a nominal sum and the last of these, George Harrison, was given £25 to attend Central Training School. It was from that school that the ushers came. The first, Oakeshott, appears to have been the most satisfactory in teaching but had to be dismissed in 1843 when a petition from the head monitor and senior boys complained of his nocturnal behaviour. His successor Marshall lasted a year and resigned because of the constrictive nature of the job, and his successor Gilpin was dismissed after two months for failing to keep discipline, and the next usher, Biggs, who was assaulted by one boy's elder brother, survived until 1852, when he was given £20 towards the cost of emigration. The office disappeared in the reorganisation that followed.

The charity income continued to grow during the first half of the nineteenth century, thanks largely to the increase in value of the London property, the Holborn houses in particular seeing a rise in income to £335 a year when the leases were renewed in 1838, and The Poultry rent rose to £130 a year in 1830. At the same time the farmland rents dropped during the depression following 1819, and in 1830 leases were granted annually 'until the country is more settled'. The loan returned by Lord Selbourne was placed in consols as was the regular surplus made on the account.

In 1829 the Court ordered that in future the trust must bear all charges made against it, and despite the fall in farm income the trust was making a regular surplus of £1,000 a year. By this time a Royal Commission had been established to investigate charities and found on examination that all was not well with some of the Drapers' Company trusts, as will be mentioned below. The Bancroft Trust shared ownership of a property with the Company in Basinghall Street and its share of the income was raised from £9 to £15 8s 6d in 1838.

51

The Company had to decide on what to do with the surplus; amongst the suggestions was one to extend the trust, presumably within the same buildings, to the education of girls. In view of the radical change envisaged, an appeal was made to His Majesty's Solicitor General for an opinion. The answer appeared to be yes.

'I think that under the clause at page twenty of the printed copy of the testator's will the Drapers' Company will be warranted in applying the surplus funds in the establishment and maintenance of a school for girls. I come to this conclusion upon consideration of the ample nature of the discretion conferred on the trustees by the clause in question and the apparent reasonableness and usefulness of the course which they propose to adopt and the strict resemblance which it bears to the application of the Funds directed by the Testator. Altho' however this is my opinion yet I strongly feel the force of the observation contained in the opinion of the Attorney General taken in 1796 that it is very difficult to tell Trustees that a case depending so entirely on the discretion of the judge they can with prudence act on any professional opinion. It may be further observed that the testator has in this case made provision in both branches of the charity for males only, and it may perhaps be contended that this circumstance sufficiently indicated that the establishment of a school for girls would not be consistent with the testator's views. I do not think such reasoning to be sound still it may not be prudent for Trustees wholly to disregard it. On the whole therefore the advice I would give to the Company is to get two respectable persons to present a petition under Sir Samuel Romilly's Act stating the views of the Company and that the establishment of a girl's school would be a useful measure and praying the sanction of the court to its adoption. Upon such a petition the court would direct a reference to the Master and I should think there can be no doubt that the intentions of the Company would be approved and sanctioned and they would thus be saved from all responsibility.'

R. M. Rolfe
Lincoln's Inn
29 May 1835

The decision was postponed until the next meeting when the Court tied eleven all on the proposal, the master casting his vote against the motion, the second time such a vote had tied on this issue in fifty years.

During this time the wall to the Jewish burial ground was rebuilt for £110 and continual repairs made to the draining of the playing areas. In 1827 substantial repairs had been carried out costing £5,650, more than the school had cost to build, for which £3,000 of bonds were sold. The school's drains were greatly improved in 1847 when the main sewage system was joined for £456. Water closets replaced the privies, cisterns were put in the dormitories and almshouses and fires were provided in the dormitories for the first time in 1841.

The almsmen as usual were causing problems through drunkenness and immoral living. Their incomes rose by £1 in 1829, then by a further £5 to £26 a year in 1835. It was firmly established that no one would be entered below the age of 60 and despite the new almshouses the number of almsmen was allowed to drop to twenty-four again. By 1841 the combined cost of constructing new buildings and repairing old ones had driven the account into a regular deficit and all bills had to be forwarded to the Hall for inspection before payment. Notwithstanding this position new facilities were built in 1848. The Head Master's house was extended to accommodate him, his wife and five children and two servants and behind the dormitory the Trust built a new dining hall, turning the old one into a third classroom. It was clear to the Company that Bancroft's must change and expand if it were to survive and the Drapers' Company proved equal to the challenge.

BANCROFT'S HOSPITAL.

Report of the Conduct and Progress of _Reilly_

For the Half Year ending July 29th, 1858.

Character for Diligence _Very Good_

Conduct _Moral Conduct good; but he is very childish & playful in school._

Remarks _Has leave to "stay over"_

Signed, _W Hunt._

Head Master.

☞ The Holidays end on Tuesday the 24th of August, on which Evening the Names will be called over at Seven o'Clock, when every Boy is expected to be present, unless his Friends have PREVIOUSLY sent to the Head Master a Medical Certificate accounting for his absence.

Charles Reilly's report, 1858

B H .

BANCROFT'S HOSPITAL.

CERTIFICATE OF CHARACTER.

This is to certify that _Charles Reilly_ has been a Scholar

of this Institution for the space of _5 ¼_ years; that he has made _very good_ progress

in the various Branches of Education taught in the School; and that he leaves the Hospital with

an excellent character, _having gained a conduct medal & several prizes the latter chiefly for Writing & Drawing in which he excels._

Dated this _25th_ day of _February_ 185 _9_.

William Hunt M.A.

H. Master and Chaplain.

Charles Reilly's leaving certificate

54

CHAPTER V
Reform

THE DEMAND for reform following the French Revolution led to the Reform Act of 1832 which abolished the worst excesses of the old Parliamentary system and gave the vote to the growing middle classes. At the same time the enormous growth in the population and its movement from country to town placed an intolerable strain on the services which town and parish had heretofore provided.

Successive governments throughout the nineteenth century recognised the need to place more and more facets of everyday life under the aegis of Royal Commissions and Parliamentary Committees – not that this idea was new: England had enjoyed a centralised government since Henry VII and before, authority being exercised locally through JPs and the Quarter Sessions. The increasingly complicated mechanisation, however, intensified a process which has never abated. The enfranchising of the urban artisans in 1867, held up by Lord Palmerston and finally granted by a Conservative Government, led to the cynical comment that the new masters had to be educated, so education became the subject of a series of Commissions and Acts of Parliament, culminating in the Act of 1902.

Although money was granted from the Exchequer in 1833, the great problem facing all ministries was that of Church versus Dissent. The majority of schools – for pupils up to about twelve years old – were run by either of those two groups and the non-conformists and Utilitarians objected to government aid being granted to Anglican schools, one of the effects of the Forster Act of 1870. This, the most important of the Acts, established the notion of education being a public duty with local boards having the power to build elementary schools, financed by grants and a rate levy. Attendance became compulsory in 1880 and free in 1891, and it was from these schools that the reformed Bancroft's of 1886 drew its ablest scholars.

55

The notion of national secondary schools came about in 1902 but, before that, the existing schools were subject to two Royal Commissions resulting in the Clarendon and Taunton Reports. They investigated the many grammar schools and ancient foundations existing in virtually every English town. These ranged from great foundations such as Eton and Winchester – the Public Schools – to many consisting of a master and a handful of boys. Geographically there was a great concentration in or near the City of London, with none at all in some new towns, especially where the nucleus of an old market town did not exist, as in Liverpool. The new middle classes seeking a good sound education for their children did two things: they founded new schools on the lines of Arnold's Rugby reforms, the so-called 'Proprietary' school such as Marlborough and Cheltenham, and they clamoured for the reform of the old endowed schools.

Compulsory reform had been in the wind for some while. The Charity Commission was established in 1853 though its predecessor, a section of the Court of Chancery, had made a systematic investigation of the nation's charities and their trustees. The Clerk of the Drapers' Company had gone before it and it was discovered that the property of the Company and its Howell's Trust had become intermingled. The Court ordered the Company to reimburse the charity, at the same time converting it from its original purpose of providing dowries for the founder's kin to the establishment of two girls' schools in Wales, one in the South at Llandaff and one in the North of the Principality at Denbigh. This is a very early example of the 'modernisation' of a trust and was to set a precedent.

At this time there was a very critical report from a Royal Commission on the City's Livery Companies suggesting that they be abolished and their funds pooled and put to better use, the fate which befell the City's parochial charities a generation later. The argument was that the companies, mainly small, no longer had a valid purpose and their funds would be better used in the furtherance of education. Such a charge could not be levied at the handful of great companies such as the Drapers, who had long concerned themselves with good works beyond their own members, but all the companies were included together in the general criticism. Nothing came of the plan, but it encouraged the livery companies to extend their philanthropic activities to ward off future criticisms, especially when the incomes of some rose greatly during the property boom of the eighteen sixties and seventies.

Between 1850 and 1880 the income of the Drapers' Company rose threefold enabling them to make in the 1880s three annual payments of £16,666 from income to build the Woodford school, a figure larger than their total revenues in 1850. It was during this period that the livery companies, like those Dukes fortunate enough to own London real estate, ceased being comfortably off and became truly rich, enabling them to make great gifts to numerous good causes, and so, in the eyes of a world greedy for their wealth and caring not for the traditions of such ancient foundations, they justified their existence.

The Commissions enquiring into the endowed schools were more successful in seeing their recommendations implemented. The Royal Commission of 1861 chaired by the Earl of Clarendon investigated 'those Chief Grammar Schools of the country known collectively as the Public Schools', namely Eton, Winchester, Westminster, Harrow, Shrewsbury, Rugby, Charterhouse, St Paul's and Merchant Taylors, the last three being in the City and closely linked with City institutions. The Report resulted in the Public Schools Act of 1868 which abolished the more gross abuses of the foundations and reformed their governing bodies and the syllabus. A second Commission chaired by Lord Taunton began in 1865 and investigated the 572 endowed schools who enjoyed a gross income of £183,066 with a further £13,897 a year in exhibitions for university education for former pupils.

The schools differed enormously in wealth and stature, Bancroft's with its £5,000 a year being second only to Christ's Hospital in income amongst the London schools. The report resulted in the Endowed Schools Act of 1869 which established three permanent commissioners to draw up new schemes for the 572 schools and a host of other educational trusts and foundations enjoying an income of £600,000 a year. The work of the Commission took years to complete but by the time they had finished the destiny of many schools, including the large majority of present day Head Masters' Conference Schools, was firmly laid.

The Drapers' Company had already considered implementing changes at Bancroft's. It was on the death of Dinham in 1852 that the suggestion of reform was first made by the Court. A special committee commented that the standard of education was poor, inferior in some respects to that given to sons of labourers and artisans in the National and British schools. There was no mental arithmetic or linear drawing. Latin and French were, however, taught to forty-five boys whose parents paid two guineas extra for the privilege, and music and science were taught to the older boys, though the lack of equipment hindered the last.

A record of the last pre-reformation days has been left by A. G. Browning. He was one of four sons of a doctor in Leadenhall Street who were all educated at Bancroft's through the influence of one of his patients, Thomas Greenaway, Master of the Company in 1887 – one suspects a not untypical mode of gaining admittance to the school. Browning left the school in 1848 and went to Charterhouse. He reappeared in Bancroft's circles, a Fellow of the Society of Antiquaries, at the dinner in 1900 and sent a description of his school life to *The Bancroftian* in 1904.

The whole syllabus was geared still to Bancroft's Will, namely to provide literate apprentices for the City, with a grounding in English and accounts, though a little history and geography were also taught. The gift of toys in 1840 allowed the boys to play single wicket cricket in the covered playground called the Pillars. On the Wednesday half holiday they played the full game, 'Our Pillars edition was expanded into a kind of edition-de-luxe, the same page but with wider margins, on Gardner's Field beside the school'. Rounders was played 'behind' – the name for the assy* at the rear of the school.

Browning's memories of the domestic staff were full of affection, 'The goodness of [Mrs Strong, the matron], a motherly woman, especially to the little chaps and those who were "down" in the sick room, must surely have been stored in the memories of all who came under her influence'. The other staff too were popular, including Mrs Anderson who washed the boys and Anne Pratt who combed their hair, lacquering it with a mixture of warm lard and oil of almonds.

The dormitories, though cold, were hospitable and the beds incredibly comfortable. A game often played was to place a cherry stone under each leg and leap from bed to bed, skipping one each time, from one end of the dormitory to the other,

---

* See Glossary

returning on the previously missed ones. 'The crisp report of the crushed cherry stones was as exhilarating as the rattle of musketry and to our young ears as loud as any detonation from rockets and bombs.' Clearly the strict discipline supposedly imposed in the school was allowed within reason to lapse.

Browning made no reference to the masters, except for one incident when the usher's spectacles were seen peering through the door glass and a boy crept up and slammed the door in his face. He does not mention Thomas or Dinham, and his comments on the education given at the school are the same as those made by the committee of 1851. He ends his article by praising the new school and congratulating the boys on the excellence of the new building and curriculum.

Changes were effected immediately with the appointment of Cornelius Laycock to replace Dinham. There were fifty-two applicants for the position and Laycock, a master at Dalston Commercial College, was elected on a salary of £120 a year. Through his long service and continued connections with the school in retirement, he was the oldest tangible link between the old order and the Woodford school and his later pupils were to provide some of the founding members of the Old Bancroftians' Association. His sons were born and educated at Bancroft's and one taught Latin at the school temporarily during the vacation from Oxford. Laycock was a capable artist and wrote in a copperplate hand.

An affectionate tribute was made to him by F.W. Humberstone (1854–60) in *The Bancroftian* of 1902. He says that the drawings executed by the boys under his tutelage were first rate but that, especially with the mechanical subjects, something was lost owing to the ignorance of the boys as to the objects' use. He was a gifted arithmetician, teaching the boys mental arithmetic, with seemingly complicated problems being solved by means of arithmetical progression, a skill always shown to good effect on Visitation Day. Although he freely used the rule as an implement of punishment he appears to have been kindhearted, and the few words of farewell given to each boy on his leaving were usually sufficient to melt the strongest heart. His favourite biblical text was I Samuel 15 v. 22, 'Behold, to obey is better than sacrifice, and to hearken than the fat of rams', on which he would hold forth as the boys were retiring for the night. In his later years he wore his stove-pipe hat in the corner of the big school room to

59

protect himself from the draught while he taught. He very reluctantly retired when the school moved from Mile End, the Court of Assistants formally recording their gratitude for his long devotion to duty. He died in 1902.

The sudden resignation of Thomas in 1855 allowed the Company to appoint the Rev William Hunt as Head Master. There were some nineteen applicants for the post and the Bancroft Committee recommended the election of Hunt, a master at Queen's College, Birmingham, and a former scholar of Corpus Christi College, Cambridge, where he was 17th Wrangler in 1846. It was an auspicious choice; not since Peché had the school been ruled by a man devoted to it and seeking its development and improvement, seeing the position of Head Master not as a stepping stone but as an end in itself. The Drapers' Company appreciated this, increasing his salary gradually to £500 a year by 1867 and giving him Rainey's lectureship in 1858. On several occasions they ordered his sermons to be published and eventually he became rector of St Michael's, Cornhill in 1875, a position he held till his death in 1887. He seems never to have enjoyed good health and the health problems at Mile End no doubt exacerbated his weak constitution, so the rectorship of St Michael's was probably equivalent to an early retirement award for his sterling work in the headmastership. His reign of twenty years saw some important changes which, though overshadowed by the revolutionary changes of his successor, should not be underestimated, for they saw the birth of the new school. The two most important developments were the imposition of specific entrance qualifications and external examinations. The members of the Court still exercised their right to present boys to the school and the pupils continued to come from all over the country, some even from abroad, but a majority, as always, were sons of people living in or near the City, who knew a member of the Court.

The social mix of the boys had always been great but it is probable that, as the middle classes moved their homes from the City and the Tower Hamlets, so the school drew its pupils more and more from the poorer classes whose educational training before school would have been inferior to that of boys from more affluent homes. To counteract this trend the Company decreed that boys must come from good homes and have respectable

'Friends' and in 1873 a single entrance examination based on the three Rs was introduced.

The school syllabus also was improved. A part-time French Master, Mr Mayer from Stepney Central School, was appointed on £50 a year in 1863 and his successor, Mr Graillot, added German in 1871. Mr Laycock continued as second master with a succession of ushers* to help him, and was joined by Mr Ranker in 1865, who was replaced by Mr Phillips to teach Latin and Mr Williams as a fourth master in 1874, both on £150 a year.

The Bancroft Committee had some problems keeping lesser staff, especially the Oxford and Cambridge graduates who could no doubt easily find equally well paid jobs in more pleasant surroundings, for the health of the old Mile End site was not good. The higher standards soon showed in the new annual examination, conducted by an external examiner appointed alternately by the Vice Chancellors of Oxford and Cambridge Universities, commencing in 1866. The examiner stayed at the school for a week and conducted a series of written and oral examinations from which he prepared a report and a class list. The week culminated in Visitation Day when the examiner was expected to conduct a general *viva voce* examination of the whole school in accordance with Francis Bancroft's Will. The Company were reluctant to break the old rule, despite complaints from the examiners, one of whom refused to comply.

On a lighter note, it is recorded that an elderly member of the Court, failing to grasp the significance or purpose of the previous week-long tests, congratulated the examiner on coaching the boys in the answers to the oral questioning in such a short time. The old practice ended with the demolition of the Mile End building, as did the catechism, for, although the school remained and remains an Anglican foundation, it was decided in 1864 to admit non-Anglicans.

In 1873, following a series of good examination reports, a number of boys were first admitted for the local examination board exams., the predecessor of the old Matriculation and School Certificate, and did remarkably well in them over the next thirty years. In 1875 six Bancroft's boys entered the Oxford local exam. All were placed in the first class, each being presented with a silver medal by the Drapers' Company, and the

---

* See Glossary

ADDRESS

Delivered at their Annual Visitation of Bancroft's Hospital,

BEFORE THE

MASTER, WARDENS, AND COURT OF ASSISTANTS,

OF THE

WORSHIPFUL COMPANY OF DRAPERS.

JULY, 1866.

GENTLEMEN,

The happiest of days has again come round, and once more our hearts are gladdened by your presence. We give you hearty welcome, and hail with great delight the opportunity of thanking you for the favors we have received at your hands.

It has fallen to me to address you on this occasion, as the spokesman of the School, and with the greatest satisfaction do I undertake the task, assured that you will look with favor on a child's humble efforts.

Since your last Visitation, numbers of our Schoolfellows have entered the "World's broad field," and begun to reap the fruits of the education conferred on them by your generous patronage And, I trust, we who still remain are not altogether unmindful of your kindness in placing us under able and good Instructors, who treat us as their own children, and who do their utmost to promote our welfare here and in after life.

We almost always on these occasions have some special favor to thank you for. This time we are called upon to acknowledge the greatest boon ever conferred on this Institution within our remembrance. I allude to the privilege of remaining an extra year under your protection. This extension of our stay at school will not only be a great present relief to our parents, but will tell vastly on our future prospects. It will be our own fault if we do not make good use of the opportunity thus placed within our reach for qualifying ourselves for getting on well in the world. I am sure, Gentlemen, that all now present, both the boys and their friends, feel sincerely and deeply grateful to you for this inestimable kindness.

Permit me to thank you also, in the name of the whole School, for giving us an opportunity of passing a higher and more searching Examination. By appointing a stranger to test our progress, you have given us a fresh stimulus to exertion ; and I can truly say that we never felt so much inducement to work, as during the past Quarter. We are delighted to find that our Examiner thought well of us, and that his report is likely to give satisfaction to you and to our Masters.

We are now going to meet the dear ones at home ; and what a happy meeting it will be to those whose consciences tell them they have done their best to sustain the character of the School ! We cannot all win prizes, but we can all earn good reports, and so make our parents' hearts rejoice, and render our holidays more delightful.

We separate this time with the pleasing hope that not one familiar face will be missing when we return ; for by the great favor you have lately conferred, none of us will leave this Institution for some time. Indeed, with only two or three exceptions, we may all look forward to competing in another examination, and gaining then, if we do not now, some token of your approbation.

Having thanked you, our kind Governors, I would now affectionately and very gratefully acknowledge the kindness and zeal of the Teachers you have set over us. They labour most assiduously to promote our moral and religious improvement, and they deserve our most sincere and heartfelt thanks.

Nor would we forget our kind Doctor and Matron ; whose skilful care and tender nursing have done very much towards making the school so like the happy homes to which we are now returning with glad and eager hearts.

Gentlemen,—permit me to conclude my address with hearty wishes for the prosperity of your ancient and honorable Company.

Visitation Day, 1866; Head Monitor's Address

BANCROFT'S HOSPITAL.

VISITATION DAY, 1866.

PROGRAMME.

Subject and Order of the Speeches.	Authors.	Speakers.
1. The Omnipresence of God	*Hutton*	WHITING.
2. Scene from the "Andria"	*Terence*	TEARLE. RUDDUCK. GREEN. WHITING.
3. A Lawsuit	*Cowper*	CLARK.
Song by the Choir.		
4. The Homes of England	*Mrs. Hemans*	NOYES.
5. Scene from "The Merchant of Venice"	*Shakespeare*	HARDING. RUDDUCK. DAWSON. GUERNSEY. TAYLOR. UNDERHILL.
Song by the Choir.		
6. The Spider and the Fly	*Mary Howitt*	STEVENS.
Duet.		TEARLE. GREEN.
7. Monsieur Jourdain et ses Maitres	*Molière*	HARDING. DAWSON. RUDDUCK. TEARLE. GREEN. BLOGG. ROWELL.
8. The Astronomical Alderman	*Horace Smith*	BLOGG.

EXAMINER'S REPORT.

DISTRIBUTION OF PRIZES.

Address to the Governors by the Captain of the School ... HARDING.

Visitation Day, 1866; Programme

successes at this level continued after the move to Woodford.

During this period also, the Drapers' Company made it possible for Bancroft's boys to go on to other schools where they could train for University entrance. Derby School and Malvern College were especially popular, though other boys went to Winchester, Harrow and University College School, the last especially founded to prepare boys for London University Matriculation. It is probable that Bancroftians had gone on to other schools and then to University in the past – such as Browning, mentioned above, who went on to Charterhouse – but it now became a regular practice. Soon reports began to arrive of University success, again often made possible by the Drapers' Company's largesse. It was to be some years before a Bancroft's boy went direct from school to university but the school was, at least, providing the sort of academic groundwork necessary for such an education, which doubtless encouraged the Company to stand by the trust when it stood threatened by Victorian legislation.

The life of the boys under Hunt became, one suspects, a little less harsh, although rules of silence were still maintained at meal times and in the dormitories. Hunt's reign began with a minor disturbance, the cause of which is unexplained. One morning in chapel, shortly after Hunt had taken up his appointment, the boys maintained complete silence during the service and later that day forty of them locked themselves in the school room. Hunt forced the door and the ringleaders were beaten and later several were expelled, but this did not quell the riotous spirit of the boys, for another was publicly birched and expelled for throwing an inkwell at the usher.

In 1856 two boys were expelled for forgery and absence, after which peace seems to have been restored, and from 1860 a series of drill instructors was appointed to exercise the boys and help maintain discipline. The men were usually competent at their work, for which they received a guinea a week and an almshouse, though one was dismissed for getting drunk whilst supposedly taking the boys to Victoria Park.

The boys were encouraged to remain smart – the uniform was similar to that of a naval cadet, complete with shako hat – by the annual grant of a guinea to the boys who kept their uniform looking smartest. It was from this period onwards that an *esprit de corps* began to appear amongst the boys and the Old Boys which

64

led to the foundation of the Old Bancroftians Association after the move to Woodford, and under Hunt it seems the boys present and past began to feel a pride in Bancroft's. Indeed, an attempt to found an Old Boys' club was made during this period, but was unsuccessful.

It would be wrong to exaggerate the change in the area about the school in the mid-nineteenth century. There was no heavy industry nearby and the docks were a mile away. The school had a fairly large plot with a field on one side and the Jews' Cemetery on the other, and some of the development nearby was a planned suburban system, especially around Tredegar Square, and as late as the 1870s a boy's father described himself as a gentleman farmer from Bethnal Green. Nevertheless, the great expansion of London during this period created health problems for the whole area and Bancroft's with its old building was prone to epidemics. Dr Byles and his successor Dr Self were forever urging alterations in the diet and trying to improve the buildings.

In 1851 it was agreed that all boys would be vaccinated against smallpox and the incidence of that disease was rare, usually involving one or two boys after the vacation. They would be put in an almshouse and tended by an almsman who had had this disease until they had recovered, the almsman receiving a gratuity for his services, though in 1872 the holiday was extended when smallpox broke out in Mr Laycock's house. In a boarding school any disease will be prone to spread amongst the boys and references are found to measles in 1862 and scarlatina in 1867 and 1874 when a boy died. The other problem persistently occurring was ringworm, which usually resulted in the infected boys being sent home.

A far worse fear came from the outbreak of cholera in the area. Although the Metropolitan Water Board had been established in 1865, giving London a centralised sewage system, the demands of an ever growing population caused such a strain on the supply of water that cholera outbreaks became common. In 1866 'Friends' were advised to remove their boys as cholera had broken out in Mile End and in 1869 an epidemic again occurred in the district and affected the school. The remedy for such outbreaks was to give the boys brandy, whitewash the rooms and hang disinfected blankets everywhere.

Throughout this period the medical officers warned about the condition of the building. In 1853 Dr Byles recommended the

65

building of an infirmary and new baths but the trust could not afford the cost. The dormitories were considered too crowded by Dr Byles who feared a visit by a Government health inspector. The words of Byles and his successor Self were ignored until 1875 when a third dormitory was built. Fortunately for the boys another suggestion of the medical officer was taken up in 1865, when it was resolved that the 'beverage of the boys should be something more generous than water'. It was felt that a half pint of beer a day and better milk would help avoid chilblains and cutaneous eruptions.

The health of the staff was no better during this period. Both Hunt and Laycock had to be sent on holiday in 1868, and the ill health of Mr Ranker, the third master, in 1865 was solely attributed to his cramped, ill-aired room. The sanitary arrangements at the school, though vastly improved since its building, were insufficient to cope with a hundred and fifty people. New urinals and baths were built in 1867 and the almsmen's privies were replaced by water closets, but the whole fabric was beginning to show its age.

Throughout the 1850s and 60s the trust income was barely able to meet the normal expenditure of the foundation and there was simply no money for extensive repairs. The income from the three farms began to fall during the agricultural depression of the 1870s and was never to recover. Although this was partly offset by rising rents from Holborn and Godliman Street, £590 and £45 per annum respectively, the bulk of the trust fund remained in Government bonds and war loans and continued to render the same income year after year. Fortunately food prices were falling and there was little inflation, though the masters' salaries rose, as did the number of masters. It was obvious to the Bancroft Committee that the trust income could not maintain the school forever and the moment of decision coincided with the Endowed Schools Act.

Mention has already been made of the dismay of the Drapers' Company at the passing of that Act and it placed them in a quandary. There was no special bank account for Bancroft's, the clerk paying the bills from the Company's cash and reconciling the balances for each Company trust at the end of each year. This enabled individual trusts to go into deficit without anyone realising until the year's income and expenditure were calculated prior to the annual audit. The Bancroft account was in deficit to the Company for £571 in 1856. Certain economies were made and it was back in surplus by 1860. The fund was not able, however, to build up a surplus to carry out structural improvements, and in 1867 the Company ordered the sale of stocks to pay for repairs and to reimburse the Company.

Clearly, such a sale could only solve short term deficits and in the long run make the situation worse by reducing the trust's income. The Company's attitude was that, if the State would not allow it to run its affairs, there was no reason why it should use its own money to subsidise a school whose control it was about to lose, and more stock was sold in the following year. At this stage the Company began to feel that perhaps all was not lost and it was resolved that the Company would maintain the fabric of the school until such time as the future of Mr Bancroft's charity was resolved, giving £2,200 for a new classroom. As late as 1877 extensions were made to the school when a new gym was built in the school yard and four almshouses were converted into an infirmary. This last, however, was known to be a temporary measure, for the days at Mile End were numbered.

The decision to move Bancroft's was taken neither lightly nor abruptly, and even after the Company had resolved to spend money on the foundation it remained undecided for some while as to whether or not the school would move. The first contact between the Company and the Taunton Commission came in 1868 when they were ordered to provide full details of the syllabus 'with a view to ascertain whether the education is suitable to the requirements of the age'. Hunt submitted details with plans for reform.

The Endowed Schools Act became law and the Company established a special committee to decide on how to treat with the commissioners. The Company were asked to submit plans for all their schools before February 1st, 1870, and the Bancroft Scheme was submitted on that day. It suggested that the school should admit two hundred day boys, the new buildings being paid for from certain redundant charities in the Company's possession, originally used for the benefit of Drapers imprisoned for bad debt. The boys would be charged two guineas a quarter each and the Company would retain complete control of the school. There was no suggestion that the school should move, nor was it planned to abolish the almshouses.

An answer acknowledging receipt of the letter was received,

stating that the three commissioners responsible for agreeing new schemes for over seven hundred charities would take some while before they decided on the educational needs of East London and would inform the Company in good time when they were so ready. It did, in fact, take them ten years, by which time they had been changed into a new Charities Commission – the Company had opposed the Charities Act too. There was the inevitable lull following the production of the Company's proposals, though the matter was not forgotten and, on August 4th, 1874, the following resolution was passed:

'Notice being taken that it may be found desirable to remove Bancroft's Hospital from its present site, it is resolved that the Company's surveyor report.'

A site was recommended at Ealing at an early stage but the Company bided its time. It was during the 'seventies that the Company's income grew to an extent which they found mildly embarrassing and they established a committee to discuss what to do with the extra money. The future of Bancroft's became instantly linked with another Drapers' foundation, Drapers' College in Tottenham. The college was established in 1865 for the sons of Drapers in need of education. The scheme was extended to grandsons but the demand for places was never great and the Company regrettably came to the decision to close it, transferring the property to the Company's school for orphan girls, Elmslea, nearby. It would therefore be possible to educate the sons of poor Drapers at Bancroft's instead.

In 1875 a report on the future of Bancroft's had recommended the abolition of the almshouses and the building of a new school on the site which would cost about £40,000. The old buildings were now in such a state that they would not long survive in a fit condition to be used as a school. The site was valued at about £15,000. If the new school were to be attractive to members of the Company, a move might be necessary, although the various committees appointed to investigate such a possibility still hedged on the matter. The Company were still unsure whether or not they could keep control of the school and the resolution passed on December 20th 1878, which ultimately led to the new scheme, has an air of urgency in it: 'In view of the possibility of a Scheme being proposed by the Charity Commissioners under the Endowed Schools Act for the management of Bancroft's School a special committee be appointed to consider and report whether any and what measures can be adopted to retain the exclusive control of this ancient foundation in the Drapers' Company'. To spur them on the Education Board requested further details of the running of the school.

The report of the special committee set up in 1879 to consider means of using the Company's surplus income was presented on June 18th of that year. It dealt largely with Bancroft's and, after giving a description of the trust's history, described the current hospital, the school's syllabus, and the eleven remaining almsmen, the last taking up £1,300 of the trust's annual income of £5,000. The report gave details of the formal recommendation of the Court to the commissioners in 1870, further explaining that the debtors' charities had been converted into a general educational fund in 1875. Whilst no definite plan had come from the Commission they had written in the broadest terms raising certain criticisms of the Company's plans. In particular they wanted the Head Master to have more say in the running of the school, with outside bodies represented on the governing body. They also wanted admission on merit alone, the establishment of exhibitions to facilitate university education and provision for educating girls.

The Committee had taken these points into consideration and were anxious that, when the commissioners eventually came to consider Bancroft's, the Company would have the initial advantage by having a detailed scheme prepared. They therefore recommended that the Company pension off the almsmen from Company funds and build a new school on the Mile End site, comprising a school building for one hundred boarders, eighty educated, clothed and fed at the expense of the trust and the remaining twenty paying £25 a year each, with one hundred and sixty fee-paying day boys and forty day scholars.

The site, only four-and-a-half acres, was deemed large enough to take a boarding school and cricket field. The boys were to be of good social standing and of the boarders sixty were to be appointed entirely at the discretion of the Company, with sons of freemen given priority; this to compensate the freemen for the loss of the almshouses. The Committee also recommended a series of exhibitions which would cost the Company £1,000 a year from its income. Most importantly they recommended that the Company give £50,000 for the new buildings and also close down Drapers' College.

Their schedule of costs for the running of the new school was calculated as follows:

Income	£	Expenditure	£
20 Boarders at £25	500	School	850
160 Day boys at 8 gns	1,344	Boarding costs	2,200
Endowment	5,006	Staff (Head &	
		13 masters)	3,700
		Books	100
	£6,850		£6,850

The Company agreed with the proposal, made arrangements to set aside £16,666 from income for three years to create the necessary endowment, and wrote accordingly to the Charity Commissioners.

There followed a series of letters between the Clerk and the commissioners, in the first of which the commissioners urged the Company to move the school away from Mile End, presumably because there were several schools in the area – Cooper's, Parmeter's, Stepney Central Foundation, Sir John Cass – and they could foresee the need to have such schools in the growing suburbs. Paradoxically, they insisted on the poor of London retaining a right to the foundation scholarships. Over the next two years it was agreed that, as the Company were building a new school for £50,000, they would remain sole governors and have sole discretion in nominating twenty foundationers. Thirty fee-payers were to be admitted on an examination, as were the remaining fifty scholars who were to be pupils from Board Schools within the Bills of Mortality of London, thus retaining the original intention of Francis Bancroft's Will. The new scheme was agreed by Her Majesty Queen Victoria in Council in 1884 and in many respects remains the same as the current instrument by which the school is administered, Her Majesty appointing herself Visitor of the foundation.

The choice of Woodford was one of luck. The Company considered the Patriotic School at Wandsworth but thought it too near London. They therefore advertised for a site of ten acres on the outskirts of London on a high rise, presumably for fresh air and good drainage. The replies brought several promising sites,

70

including one in Muswell Hill, but they proved disappointing. Their agent saw the site of Woodford Manor for sale in a newspaper and the Company bought it from the Earl of Mornington, Lord of the Manor of Woodford, for £9,000, the exchange of contracts taking place on 1st April 1885. Mr Arthur Blomfield's firm won the tender for designing and building the new school and plans were set afoot.

The last days at Mile End saw an intentional running down of the school by the new Head Master. The appointment of the Rev John Edward Symns to replace Hunt in 1875 was a sign of the Drapers' Company's goodwill towards the School, for a man of his great ability no doubt obtained assurances as to the school's future when offered the appointment. The son of a schoolmaster, he was 23rd Wrangler in 1858 and also an exhibitioner and prizewinner of St John's College, Cambridge. He taught very briefly at Forest School before being master at Chudleigh Grammar School in Devon. From there he moved to become Vice-Principal of the Collegiate School in Bath before devoting the last thirty years of his life to Bancroft's.

A tall, bearded man in the mould of so many Victorian divines, Symns created the school at Woodford, setting it on a sure footing so that the next chapter of this book is the proper place to describe him; he did, however, make his mark on Mile End. He persuaded the Company to allow all boys to stay at school till sixteen as of right, with the brighter ones remaining a year more. The local board examinations continued to be dominated by Bancroft's boys and the entrance examination was stiffened to include algebra and simple French for older applicants. The teaching of boys was still by one master for all subjects, the Head Master taking the oldest boys, Mr Laycock the next age group down and so on, the boys being in six classes. The syllabus had expanded but still it did not teach all subjects, the absence of Greek being a distinct disadvantage for those hoping to take Holy Orders, Bancroft's having several clergymen's sons at this time. To emphasise the growing need for high academic studies, one boy was expelled in 1881 simply because he was too stupid to keep up with the other boys.

The same year saw a number of boys, including all the monitors, expelled following an investigation into dormitory bullying and ragging. Their number was not made up, nor were any new boys admitted, so that by 1883 there were only fifty boys at the school. The almsmen, five only, were pensioned off, their long brown coats being assigned to history, along with the annual pilgrimage to St Helen's, Bishopsgate. In their last years there were few problems with the almsmen, just the occasional drunkard, but they had been an integral part of Bancroft's for a hundred and fifty years and their passing, as much as anything else, symbolised the end of the old era. That was regretted by many, especially local people who, comparing Bancroft's most favourably with its neighbouring schools, petitioned the Company to keep it where it was: that, however, was not to be. Another disappearance during this period was that of Bancroft's Tomb in St Helen's Bishopsgate. The nineteenth century was a great time for 'restoring' Medieval churches and St Helen's was so treated during the long incumbency of Rev Dr J. E. Cox, rector 1849–87, and completed during that of his successor John Airey. Apart from ripping out eighteenth century pews and even earlier panelling, Cox sought a Faculty from the Bishop of London to remove all bodies from their tombs in the church and churchyard. This was agreed by the Bishop and the remains of the various corpses were removed. It was at this stage that the rector discovered the existence of the previous Faculty granted to Francis Bancroft in 1723, giving him a freehold within the church of a plot eight feet square, to belong to him and his heirs forever.

Cox approached the Drapers' Company for permission to remove Bancroft's coffin and re-inter it with the other bodies at the new City of London cemetery at Manor Park, at the same time destroying the tomb which Cox regarded as being ugly and out of place in his 'restored' church. The Court were most reluctant to act in this way as they felt they owed a duty to maintain the tomb; indeed, the Will specified that the first charge on the properties in London and Middlesex was the upkeep of the tomb. The Company therefore refused. The new rector, John Airey, continued the work of his predecessor, re-arranging the screens and reredos, the old pews from the Lady Chapel, and the remaining tombs. He approached the Company in 1891 and again the following year when, at the Court held on April 7th, 1892, his request was again declined.

By July the tomb was destroyed and Bancroft's body interred below the original site, the crypt having been sealed. Why the Company changed its opinion so drastically remains a mystery.

Possibly they were advised that the original Faculty could be reversed, although the Bancroft Trust might then have claimed compensation. No doubt both sides were anxious to avoid an embarrassing public squabble, and so a new agreement was sealed by the Company and the Church wardens. It is still binding on both sides, and acknowledges the Company's ownership of the plot which was paved over and surrounded by a brass border bearing the description: 'The plot of ground bounded by this strip of brass is the property of the Worshipful Company of Drapers of the City of London as Trustees of the Will of Francis Bancroft deceased having been purchased by him of this Parish in MDCCXXIII for the interment of himself and his friends only which purchase was confirmed by a Faculty from the Dean and Chapter of St Paul's London. His remains lie buried in a vault hereunder in accordance with the instructions contained in his Will dated the 18th day of March 1727'.

The plot and memorial raised on the wall above were to be maintained at the expense of the parish, and the Company retained the right to erect a barrier around the tomb on the anniversary of Bancroft's death – March 19th – and to have access to the crypt.

All that remains of the fine tomb designed by George Dance the Elder is the Arms incorporated in the memorial tablet.

It is the hope of this work that the reader will understand not only Bancroft's varied past but also appreciate it within the context of its time. The Bancroft's of 1737 and of 1887 were as fine in their ways as that of 1987 and each makes up a continuous story of which all her sons can be proud. We do not know of the adult paths taken by most of the boys before 1889 because there was no Bancroftian magazine to record achievements great and small, but no doubt some achieved greatness – one was reported to have become Lord Mayor – and the majority simply did their duty as best they could. The Company occasionally received letters from parents expressing their thanks for the way their sons had been educated and one of those dated 1861 makes a suitable swansong for Bancroft's Hospital:

'Gentlemen, as parents of George Ernest Spice, who has this day left Bancroft's Hospital, we beg to express our gratitude for the excellent education he has there received through your benevolence. At the same time we wish to bear our humble testimony to the unwearied care and attention he has received

73

from the masters and the matron. We sincerely hope that his conduct through life will be such as to do credit to the good principles in which he has been so carefully trained. We remain, Gentlemen, your obedient and respectful servants,
J. H. Spice and E. Spice,
25, Georgiana St., Camden Town,
November 13 1861'.

GOSPEL OAK, N.W.

September, 1886.

DEAR SIR,

Our old friend, CORNELIUS LAYCOCK, ESQ., is retiring from BANCROFT'S SCHOOL at Michaelmas next, after a service of thirty-five years; and it is the earnest wish of his colleagues and pupils, past and present, to present him with a parting Testimonial.

For the furtherance of this object, a meeting was held in the Vestry of ST. MICHAEL'S CHURCH, CORNHILL, on TUESDAY, 31ST AUGUST; when the following gentlemen were appointed to act as a Committee, with power to add to their number:—

REV. J. E. SYMNS, M.A., The Grove, Tottenham, N. (Present Head Master.)	REV. W. HUNT, M.A., St. Michael's Church, Cornhill, E.C. (Late Head Master.)
H. BLYTH, Esq., Pantheon, Oxford Street.	C. REILLY, Esq., 23, St. Swithin's Lane, E.C.
H. M. GRELLIER, Esq., 17, Abchurch Lane, E.C.	T. G. STARK, Esq., Receiver and Accountant General's Office, General Post Office.
G. H. HAMMOND, Esq., Drapers Hall, E.C.	
H. LAWRANCE, Esq., Teynham House, Half Moon Lane, Herne Hill.	F. J. STEVENS, Esq., New Park Road, Brixton Hill, S.W.
J. H. MANN, Esq., Commercial Union, Cornhill, E.C.	H. J. SUDELL, Esq., 10, Mark Lane, E.C.
H. F. MOORE, Esq., Atherton House, Bedford Hill Road, Balham, S.W.	T. C. YATES, Esq., 24, John Street, Bedford Row, W.C.

At the request of the Meeting, the REV. W. HUNT, M.A., kindly consented to act as Treasurer, and I, with great pleasure, undertook the duties of Honorary Secretary.

If you are disposed to contribute, kindly forward your subscription to the Treasurer, the present Head Master of the School, or to me.

I shall esteem it an additional favour if you will communicate the addresses of any " Old Bancroftians " you happen to be acquainted with.

All subscriptions will be duly acknowledged upon a printed form of receipt.

Faithfully yours,

CHARLES E. YATES,

Honorary Secretary.

Testimonial appeal for Mr Cornelius Laycock

74

CHAPTER VI
Pastures New

THE CHOICE of A. W. Blomfield as the school's architect gave it the services of one of the leading architects of the day and the other three on the shortlist – R. W. Edie, J. L. Pearson, E. C. Robins – never achieved his eminence. Born in 1829 the son of the Bishop of London, he specialised in ecclesiastical architecture and was a strong proponent of the gothic revival, of which Bancroft's is a fine example, and he was knighted during the building of the school. Blomfield was appointed in May 1885, and detailed plans were laid before the Court in June. The scheme provided for a building around a spacious quadrangle consisting of a Great Hall for five hundred boys, eight ordinary and two double classes, two laboratories, a prep. room, a library, a study for the Head Master and a common room for the masters, a woodwork shop, a bath and gymnasium with six fives courts, a lecture hall for two hundred people and a chapel. The dining hall was to seat two hundred persons with ample domestic quarters including a housekeeper's rooms, a surgery and rooms for twelve maids. A large day room was provided and also dormitories and baths for a hundred boys with eight resident masters' rooms.

Most of the plan was agreed, but the lecture hall on the site of the eventual chapel was sacrificed as an economy, as Blomfield's plan would have exceeded £50,000 and the Company were eager to maintain the costs within a £42,000 limit.

Work began immediately to prepare the ground and the Company approached the Prince of Wales to lay the foundation stone. His Royal Highness was unable to oblige but his elder son Prince Albert Victor, later Duke of Clarence and Avondale, KG, was able to perform the ancient ceremony. The Prince, whose dissipated lifestyle and general lethargy were a great worry to the Queen, died of pneumonia in 1892, his younger brother becoming heir apparent and, eventually, King George the Fifth.

75

The worst critic of the Drapers' Company would allow that when it puts on a special show it does so with great style and the foundation laying bears testimony to that. On Saturday 16 July 1887 a special train took the entire school from its temporary home in Tottenham via Liverpool Street to Woodford, where they were conducted up leafy Snakes Lane and down a High Road undisturbed by motor traffic to the new site. There, marquees had been set up and a guard of honour provided by the Essex Regiment – Her Majesty's loyal Forty Fourth Regiment of Foot – in which many Bancroftians were later to serve with distinction. A separate train brought the entire Court of the Company and numerous dignitaries who greeted His Royal

6 Montagu Place.
Montagu Square.
London. w.
Octr 8. 1890

The worshipful Company of Drapers
to Arthur W. Blomfield A.R.A.
Architect. –

	£	s.	d.
Architects commission on cost of works. –	2300	0	0
Travelling expenses Self and assistants	15	0	0
	2315	0	0
Received on account	2150	0	0
Balance due –	165	0	0
	£ 150	–	–

Sir Arthur Blomfield's account

76

Highness. A loyal address was delivered by Mr Sawyer, the Clerk of the Company, and in his reply the Prince congratulated the Company on their sterling works of philanthropy. Luncheon was then served in the various marquees and the young Bancroftians drank of champagne.

It is said that, when the Prince visited the boys' tent, they were slow to stand up, and a member of the Court made comment of the fact at the dinner held that night at Drapers' Hall, causing Mr Symns to make an impromptu speech, strongly defending his boys. The Head Master hated making a speech and spent days of agony before Visitation Day and similar occasions, which gives even greater poignancy to his words on that particular evening, showing the great regard in which he held the school and its pupils.

The work progressed with remarkably few problems. The old Woodford House was demolished, rather than converted for the use of the Head Master, and a new residence built for £2,500. The rent charge and tithes on the land were redeemed and the school moved in to the new buildings, complete save for paths and grass, in the Autumn of 1889. The final cost of the buildings was:

	£	s	d
A.W. Blomfield	45,847.18.6.		
Architect	2,292.8.0.		
Clerk of the Works	556.18.7.		
G.M. Hamor fittings	739.7.6.		
Storey & Triggs furnishing	258.0.9.		
B. Collyer & Son blinds	155.19.4.		
Treloar & Son mats	12.0.0.		
G. Spencer gym fittings	100.0.0.		
W. Holmes – grounds	600.0.0.		
	£50,562.12.8.		

Blomfield would have no difficulty in recognising his building were he to enter the School today and one hopes he would approve of the various extensions which have been added since 1910, for to their eternal credit, the Governors have always made the new buildings of similar red brick to the original structure, and it takes a seasoned eye to differentiate the phases of the school's development.

The School stands on a long high ridge between the Rivers Lea and Roding, one of the highest points in Essex. The ridge has long been a roadway, probably pre-dating the Romans, and it passes the School proceeding in a north by north easterly direction on its way to Epping and the pleasures of Cambridge and Newmarket beyond. Between the road and the School boundary is a broad grass verge, part of Epping Forest where the freeholders of Epping still graze their cattle. On the opposite side of the road a row of ancient horse chestnuts and a slope hide leafy suburban roads which have grown up on the old Buckhurst estate of the Buxton family. Climbing one of these roads, The Glade, one sees the School appearing on the horizon, the view gradually expanding in size as one reaches the crest of the ridge. The Glade, an old right of way, faces the school tower in an alignment no doubt arranged by Blomfield.

One sees the tower, similar to one at Hampton Court, its high double gates, surmounted by three storeys of mullioned windows and topped by battlements and two smaller side towers, one containing the spiral staircase. On either side of the tower the buildings rise to three storeys, the second floor, originally the dormitories, having five high-gabled dormer windows. Each end of the block has a slightly jutting wing with three storeys of well lighted rooms and a fourth small window lighting a room entered only by passing from the tower via the dormitory ventilators. In front of these buildings and separated from them by a broad drive is a hedgerow, and the tower gate is approached through the Memorial Gates, their pillars bearing the names of those Old Boys who died in the Second World War. To the left of this main block is the Head Master's house, a residence befitting such an eminent position, and to the right the 1940 service block. Before entering beneath the tower a few steps to the right will reveal the foundation stone, laid by Prince Albert Victor of Wales, K.G.

Within the gates one sees a door to the left with the plaque to Mr George Haines, B.E.M., on it and ahead lies the quadrangle. Not as large as Tom Quad or Trinity Court, it has a very spacious look to it, helped by the centre of the opposite side having been left open, the railinged arches giving a view towards Chingford and beyond. The principal buildings of Blomfield's

78

design are arranged around the quad. Turning back to see the tower, not so prominent as from the front, one sees Francis Bancroft's supposed arms and the school clock, both saved from Mile End. Passing clockwise, one sees the reverse of the front block which contains a ground floor corridor (cloisters until 1974) with offices, once classrooms, facing on to the High Road. In the corner is a staircase, as solid as those at Montacute in Somerset, rising to the long first floor corridor, with its classes facing east to the High Road, and then to the second floor where classrooms have been created from the old dormitories.

The south side is dominated by the five great windows and high roof of the old Great Hall. This was entered through the south cloisters, now closed in, and rose from ground floor to its hammerbeamed roof. The ground floor has had a varied history since 1937 and is now classrooms. Above them four of the five bays light the library with similar windows on its other side facing the head master's garden, the full glory of the great hammerbeamed roof still dominating the room. In the south corridor is the Remembrance Tablet to the Old Boys who died in the Great War.

Still turning clockwise, one sees in the south-west corner a smaller staircase containing on the first floor the original art room and laboratory with a lecture room, its tiered floor still surviving. These rooms are now the history department. The ground floor rooms in this corner were originally an open space entered from the field bank and quad 'assy'. It was bricked in to become changing rooms in the 'twenties and part was later a sea scout store but is now three classrooms. Passing the open arches one comes to the Chapel, furnished with oak pews facing each other in 'college' fashion, the walls containing several brass memorials to Symns, Playne and Sangster Simmonds amongst others. Towards the altar above the left hand stall a cherub holds the Bancroft family arms while a similar cherub on the right holds the Drapers' Company arms above the Head Master's stall. To the left in an alcove, which some might call an apse, is the organ, rebuilt several times, most recently in 1964. A door leads to the vestry. The altar, about which controversy arose, is simple in the Anglican fashion, modelled on Mile End. A portrait of the Virgin and Child, after Bellini, the property of the Drapers' Company, is a fine altar-piece, and the stained glass window above it is a memorial to Mr Symns.

The Chapel has always held an important place in the memories of generations of Bancroftians and it is always a delight to return there for the O. B. Day service: it has proved a sad but poignant venue for memorial services to prominent Bancroft Old Boys and members of the staff.

On the north side of the quadrangle, occupying most of that range, is the Dining Hall with yet another fine roof. It contains portraits of George Haines and Sir Frederick Warner, F.R.S. and a bust of Sir Harold Saunders. The doors at the east end, similar to the screen of a medieval hall, have above them a mural executed by Miss Playne, whose grandfather was Head Master from 1906–31. The north-east corner contains another solid staircase and the buildings between it and the gate used to contain the junior day room on the ground floor, once the common and prep. room for the whole of the school house, with the senior dormitory, 'the bunkers', on the first floor. The boys privileged to live in that dormitory enjoyed a certain amount of privacy, their beds being within partitions. It is now classrooms and the day room is the Masters' Common Room.

The best view of the school is attained by walking to the tennis courts at the far corner of the school field and looking back and up to the marvellous array of buildings, the glorious mingling of red and white centred on the Chapel with the old great hall and tower behind it. From here one can see most of the new buildings added since Blomfield's time. On the far left is the new swimming pool built in 1973 on the site of the World War Two air raid shelters. It is of Olympic length and behind it lie the gymnasium and squash courts with the 'swappers' or changing rooms on the site of the old gym and bath. Moving one's gaze rightwards, beside the pool windows can be seen the new great hall, its great windows and high walls fitting in well with Blomfield's buildings. It is joined to the quad by a cloister and inside it has a gallery and a stage, making it a theatre with a seating capacity of 900. Here the annual Visitation is held on Vis. Day, lacking the *viva voce* of olden days but still following the spirit of Francis Bancroft's Will. Here also in 1945 Mr and Mrs Churchill became freemen of the Borough of Wanstead and Woodford; for many years the great hall of Bancroft's was the only large assembly room in the borough. Its foundation stone was laid by the Earl of Athlone on Visitation Day 1937 and records his name and many decorations.

Pupils at Tottenham, 1887
The figures in gowns are, from left: Messrs Hall, Symns, the examiner,
Messrs Darby and Winterton

Mr Winterton's sitting room at Woodford, *c*.1904

Bancroft's School, Woodford, from the High Road, *c.*1900

School Staff at Woodford, *c.*1900

Visitation Day, *c.*1904

Mr G. W. Williams,
Chairman of Governors 1920–35

Mr Herbert Playne, Head Master 1906–31

Sheltered by the great hall cloister is the Adams Building, given by the Drapers' Company in 1964 to mark the 600th anniversary of their first charter, and intended as boarders' common rooms. Today it is the music block and chaplain's rooms. Again glancing right-wards, past the Chapel and quad one sees on the right the three stages of the science block. At right angles to the main school is the 1910 science block containing its original high laboratories, one each on ground and first floor, with several smaller rooms. Linking it to the main building is the bi-centenary block erected by the Drapers' Company in 1937. It too contains science rooms and in a block jutting out at right angles to the old great hall along the bottom of the head master's garden, the 1937 block contains a ground floor woodwork room with a spacious art room above it. Between it and the Head Master's house is a long narrow room built as a day boy locker room in 1964, now partly converted to classrooms.

The final building, just seen behind the 1910 block and entered through it, is the 1969 science block erected with a gift from the Drapers' Company. Built on stilts it contains two laboratories on each of its first and second floors. It was opened by Lord Zuckerman O.M., the scientific adviser to H.M. Government.

The buildings no doubt have their inconveniences for a modern school, central heating having weakened the ability of teenagers and, more especially secretarial staff, to resist draughts, but the important feature of Blomfield's design is that it is a building of character, the memories of which fill all Old Bancroftians with pride and affection, and we can but thank Heaven that it has survived an age when glass and concrete are worshipped and glorified. When someone reminisces about Bancroft's it is not just a name and the vague idea of a place that comes to mind but rather a specific building of room and dignity whose memory lasts for ever.

Bancroft's spent three years in Tottenham, at Grove House, before Woodford was ready. The old school at Mile End had reached such a state of dilapidation by 1886 that the rent of Grove House – £350 a year – was cheaper than the estimated temporary repairs. The Company had agreed to sell most of the old site to the Beaumont Trustees for £20,000, though the Charities Commission forced them to realise its full value of £22,400, with Bancroft's Trust continuing to own the freehold of the houses in St Helen's Terrace. The Beaumont family had been one of the principal land owners in the Stepney area and had established the trust to benefit local people. By selling the land to that trust the site passed from the trusteeship of the Drapers' Company for two years, returning when the Company decided to give generously to create the People's Palace and East End College, today Queen Mary's College.

Nothing remains of the Hospital *in situ* save for part of the front wall and pillars, the almsmen having been decently interred elsewhere, though several gravestones survive, Mr Dinham's being the most legible.

The Company explored several potential sites for the temporary school, finally leasing Grove House for £350 per annum for three years in 1886 from the Tottenham Lager Beer Company. £600 made it habitable, a further £21 a year provided pews in the nearby parish church, and the field of Drapers' College was provided for the boys' use.

A detailed description of the Tottenham days is given in the 1937 book by R. S. McMinn who began his eighty-six years of devotion to the school at Tottenham in September 1886. On the same day a new employee, George Haines, joined the school as porter, a position he was to hold until 1949, sixty-three years of service in which he rose in the memories of Old Boys to a pinnacle above even Head Masters as the epitome of the school. When one adds G. A. Powell to the school list in 1888, the first known O. B. to receive the accolade of knighthood, one realises the importance of the Tottenham days as a prelude to the great achievements of Woodford.

Grove House was a fine red brick Georgian house dating from the early eighteenth century, to which the Society of Friends made additions during their ownership from 1828 to 1878 during which period a school room and dormitories were added. Lord Lister was the most famous pupil at the Quakers' school. The buildings were surrounded by spacious lawns and separated from Tottenham High Road by tall trees and a high wall: appropriately for a Drapers' Company charity* a mulberry tree dating back to the reign of Charles II grew in the grounds giving

---

* The Company planted mulberry trees at the instigation of King James the First to encourage an English Silk industry, and several still bear fruit in the garden at Drapers' Hall.

both fruit and leaves with which to feed silk worms. The school was large enough for the fifty or so boys, and the grounds more spacious than at Mile End.

The Head Master lived in a separate house while the three masters, Messrs Darby, James Hall and Winterton, lived in. In their teaching they were aided by Dr Teed, borough analyst for Islington, who gave rudimentary lessons in chemistry, and by Messrs Wallace and Martin who taught respectively the practical and theoretical side of physical training in the wooden gymnasium and in the bath, the latter open to the elements, causing the bottom to be caked in mud and decomposing vegetation. Of the three masters Mr Darby was the oldest, Messrs Hall and Winterton being young men preparing for ordination. Darby was approaching retirement and had problems maintaining discipline, especially during evening prep. when a free licence appears to have been given to the boys, in return for which he was liberal in his use of the cane. He retired when Bancroft's moved to Woodford.

The two younger masters were more popular and more proficient in teaching and disciplinary skills: McMinn recalls the custom of making them presentations on Valentine's Day and of Mr Winterton singing in the common room at night to Mr Hall's accompaniment. Both had been 'ushers' in the last Mile End days. On one occasion Mr Hall continued to play the harmonium when reduced to a squatting position by the collapse of his stool. They both continued to teach at Woodford.

The life at Tottenham was regimented and at times hard, which McMinn freely admits. The day began at 6.30 with quick prayers: those too long in their devotions were made to stand out in morning prep. Quick ablutions were followed by study from 7 to 7.30 and breakfast at 8. The school morning consisted of lessons from 9 to 12.30 and these continued after luncheon till 4 o'clock. After a sparse tea came prep. and then to bed at 9.30. A spartan regime but one which continued to produce academic success. The six Bancroftians put up to the Oxford Local Examinations in 1886 were all placed amongst the eleven Class I boys from a total of 240 London entrants and similar successes were gained in the science exams at Kensington in 1888. Boys continued to gain university places via various public schools and the Head Master gained especial pleasure when B. S. Hartley was 19th Wrangler in 1889, following a distinguished career at Queens' financed by the Drapers' Company, who also helped equip W. R. Hart for service in the Royal Navy when he came third in the examination for naval clerkships.

It was clear that Bancroft's was becoming a first rate academic school, especially with the new scholarships drawing the brightest boys from all London. The Head Master had already established that on the move to Woodford all boys would be allowed to stay until seventeen, if he recommended it. The Committee, however, were not keen to expand too fast, since an extra two years of free education would place a strain on the endowment. No pupil of Symns went straight from School to university. Leisure activities at Tottenham were restricted to a few hours after prep. in the evenings and to Sunday afternoons, when they were often taken for walks along the River Lea or to Bruce Castle. 1887 saw Queen Victoria's Jubilee loyally celebrated by Bancroftians with a sports day and a visit to the sea paid for by the Drapers' Company.

One Visitation Day was held at Tottenham in 1887, with a band and a special luncheon. The Head Boy, Barton, delivered a speech of welcome – a reminder of Mile End allowed to lapse thereafter until revived in the 'thirties. Copies of the oration were sold to fellow pupils for 6d though the Master of the Company paid a guinea for his copy. The other Visitation Days were cancelled through the ill health at the School, for Grove House was as prone to disease as Mile End had been and the efforts of the fine matron, Mrs Spurgin, could not prevent mumps in 1886 and a serious outbreak of diphtheria which claimed one boy in 1887 and closed the school early for Christmas. It is not surprising that the committee had insisted on building the new school on high well-drained land.

Tottenham forms a small period in the history of Bancroft's but it implanted itself firmly in the memory of those who were there, especially McMinn and J. H. Thorpe, the well-known illustrator. McMinn makes light of the bullying which existed there and later at Woodford, joking about the 'black hole', a small cupboard where boys were locked by their seniors. As he put it, 'Spartan days that put iron into the blood and fire into the soul with imagination and ambition'.

Drapers' Hall,
Throgmorton Street, E.C.
5th July, 1887

Sir,

I am desired by the Master and Wardens of the Drapers' Company to invite the attendance of yourself and a lady at the laying of the foundation stone of the new buildings of Bancroft's School, at Woodford, Essex, by H.R.H. Prince Albert Victor, on the afternoon of Saturday the 16th instant. On hearing that you propose to attend the ceremony, I shall have the pleasure of forwarding to you the necessary tickets of admission, with railway and carriage passes.

I am to request the favor of an early reply.

I have the honor to be,
Your obedient Servant,

W.P. Sawyer

Clerk.

Invitation to the stone-laying at Woodford

BANCROFT'S SCHOOL.

A Special Train for Guests invited to witness the laying of the Foundation Stone of the New Buildings at WOODFORD, Essex, by H.R.H. PRINCE ALBERT VICTOR OF WALES, on SATURDAY, the 16th JULY, will leave the Liverpool Street Station of the Great Eastern Railway, at 1.40 o'clock in the afternoon of that day for Woodford, where carriages will be waiting to take Guests to the site, about a mile-and-a-quarter distant.

The Band of the Royal Artillery will play a selection of Music in the Marquee, and Luncheon will be served from 2 until 3 o'clock, by which hour Guests are requested to be in their seats.

After the ceremony Tea and Coffee will be served, and Guests returning to town will be conveyed to the Woodford Station, whence a special train will leave for Liverpool Street at 5.30.

The Railway Passes sent to Guests must be produced when called for.

No person will be admitted to the Marquee without a Card of Invitation, which is to be given up at the Entrance.

Attendance instructions for stone-laying

BANCROFT'S SCHOOL.
WOODFORD, ESSEX.

Governors:

THE COURT OF ASSISTANTS OF THE DRAPERS' COMPANY.

BOARDING FOUNDATION SCHOLARSHIPS.

There are one hundred Boarding Foundation Scholars, seventy of whom are provided with board, lodging and education at the school, free of charge; the remainder have to pay a fee of £10 per term.

Fifty of the free Boarding Foundation Scholarships are awarded to boys who have for the three years preceding the award been in attendance at Public Elementary Schools in the Administrative County of London. A competitive examination for filling up vacancies is held annually in November and candidates for admission to it must be less than twelve and not less than eleven years of age on the 31st July following. This examination is conducted by the London County Council, of whom particulars are obtainable on application.

For the other twenty free scholarships and for the thirty pay scholarships there is no such restriction, and all boys considered eligible by the Governors are allowed to enter for the examinations, which are held from time to time for the award of vacant scholarships, but in the case of the twenty free scholarships preference is given to the sons of poor members of the Drapers' Company. At these examinations candidates for admission are examined in Reading, Writing and Arithmetic, History, Geography; also in Elementary Mathematics, Latin and French, as optional subjects.

The age for admission to the School as regards the fifty last mentioned scholarships is from ten to thirteen years. The age for leaving is seventeen and in special cases eighteen years.

Religious instruction is given according to the doctrines of the Church of England. Instruction is also given in the following subjects—viz. :

> Reading, Writing and Arithmetic.
> Geography and History.
> English Grammar, Composition and Literature.
> Mathematics.
> Latin.
> French.
> German.
> Chemistry, Physics and Mechanics.
> Drawing, Drill and Vocal Music.

[P.T.O.

Prospectus

87

CHAPTER VII

JOHN EDWARD SYMNS
1889–1906

THE AUTUMN Term of 1889 began in the new building at Woodford without undue fuss, though the great open spaces and fresh air caused wonder to the boarders, most of whom lived in London, and the new buildings were a great improvement on Tottenham and Mile End. Since 1887 the Governors had been filling the full quota of boarding places in each of the three categories, viz. London foundationers, fee paying foundationers and Drapers' Company nominees. There were eighty-four boarders in the new dormitories, joined by forty-eight day boys making an appearance at Bancroft's for the first time since 1802. The Rev James Hall and Mr W. C. Winterton (ordained in 1902) came from Mile End and were to be the Head Master's staunch supporters until the death of Mr Hall in 1905, shortly before Mr Symns' own death. Mr Winterton continued until 1926, the longest serving master in modern times.

The Masters' Common Room was added to immediately with the arrival of Mr G. L. A. Brinkmann, a Hanoverian who was to stay at Bancroft's throughout the Great War, and Mr R. E. Moyle, with a further two masters in 1890 and 1891. Although they each tended to specialise in a particular field masters taught all subjects to their classes, especially in the junior part of the school. The school ranged in age from nine to seventeen – the Charity Commissioners would not permit that extra year to allow direct university entry – though general entry was allowed up to thirteen and boys started leaving from fifteen onwards, either to go to the City or to another school to prepare for university entry.

An entrance examination was held for the L.C.C. and fee-paying scholarships each year at Drapers' Hall, consisting of English, French, Algebra, Mathematics and a little History and Geography. The boys who won through were of the highest academic standard and formed the backbone of the school's successes until after the Second World War. The twenty Drapers' nominees sat no examination but had to be of a sufficiently high standard to keep up with their peers. Some were the sons of Drapers, others the offspring of clergymen or serving officers or colonial civil servants, namely that class of person whom society decreed should educate their sons in a proper fashion without giving them the income to achieve it and the Drapers' Company came to their assistance. Such beneficence meant that Bancroft's continued to have a broad spectrum of English social life in its dormitories.

The number of day boys grew rapidly during the early years, 133 by 1892, 194 by 1896, 225 by 1903, and they came from a wide area. In those days the Great Eastern Railway branch line ran from Stratford to Woodford where it branched, one part going on to Ongar, the other going via Chigwell and Barkingside before joining the main line again between Ilford and Seven Kings, namely the Central Line Loop as we know it minus the Leytonstone to Newbury Park tunnel. This allowed the boys to come from Ilford, Leyton, Chigwell and Loughton and the villages around. Those from Woodford and Chingford had to come by foot or bicycle, there being no form of public transport, though the School at one time did pay 6s 0d a day for a brake to bring the boys up from Woodford station.

The advent of day boys was treated warily by the boarders and rivalry naturally grew up between the two camps. The distance which most day boys travelled made them nine to four pupils with neither the will nor ability to participate fully in the school's extra-curricular life, dominated by games. Gradually, however, the day boys asserted themselves and by the end of Symns' reign both their weight of numbers, and a tendency for more of them to remain at School till seventeen, allowed them to challenge the boarders' supremacy on the field in the School House versus School competitions.

The re-siting of Bancroft's had a profound effect on the surrounding area, not least for the schools already there. Excluding small schools in Woodford and Buckhurst Hill the nearest rivals were – and remain – Forest and Chigwell Schools. Forest is a nineteenth century foundation at Snaresbrook, founded for the sons of the clergy and in 1890 it was a predominantly boarding school with a famous football side, able to fill day places from the growing suburbs of Leyton and Walthamstow, so not over-worried by our emergence two miles away along the Epping Road.

89

For Chigwell, however, the prospect of a new school infringing on its 'catchment area' was less welcome. An old school, founded by William Harsnett, Archbishop of York, in 1629, Chigwell boasts William Penn as an ex-pupil. During the latter part of the nineteenth century following the Endowed Schools Act, it set about reorganising itself along the lines taken by so many country grammar schools. It expanded its curriculum, its buildings and the number of its pupils without the aid either of a generous endowment or of a munificent benefactor. That Chigwell succeeded where so many similar places failed is a great credit to its governors and one can understand their feelings when Bancroft's appeared, offering day boy scholarships with which they simply could not compete. The governors of Chigwell asked their Bancroft's counterparts to withdraw the scholarships and the School Committee agreed, seeing no advantage in antagonising a neighbour.

In 1894 the Governors of Chigwell wrote to suggest that the two schools should merge, Chigwell continuing as a classical school, Greek still being forbidden to Bancroftians by the Charity Commissioners, and Bancroft's being a 'modern' side. Such an arrangement on a more modest scale had originally existed at Chigwell. The School Committee politely but firmly declined the suggestion. No advantage could be seen in it for Bancroft's and the prospect of renegotiating the settlement with the Charity Commissioners was daunting even for the Clerk of the Drapers' Company. A year later the chairman of Chigwell's Governors, Mr G. Savill, again wrote suggesting that the Company take over the running of Chigwell School, which offer was also declined.

Chigwell School survived and flourishes and the cricket match against Bancroft's is our oldest continued fixture – the soccer matches predated it, commencing in 1892 but were of course discontinued in 1926 when we changed the shape of our ball. The author dines as a guest each Summer at Chigwell School with one of their Old Boy societies and should comment be made concerning the relative antiquity of the schools in Essex, enjoys relating how Chigwell only survived through the action, or inaction, of our Governors. May our neighbour continue to flourish.

The School Committee gave more thought to the proposals made by Essex County Council, a body created by Act of

Parliament in 1888 and given control, amongst other things, of education which previously had been the prerogative of the parish. The new councils were not slow in asserting their authority and made it clear, in the nicest possible way, that they regarded Bancroft's as an Essex school over which they had certain rights. The Committee had no more intention of arguing with Essex than they had with Chigwell and agreed to the County taking up scholarships at the school for day boys, though declined them for boarding scholarships. Essex County Council could see no point in planning a school of its own in the area if Bancroft's and Chigwell would take its pupils and both agreed, starting a happy and mutually beneficial arrangement that lasted until 1977. In 1893 the Council offered a grant above the level of fees if it could nominate two Governors. Considering the emphasis which the Court had earlier placed on it remaining the exclusive nominator of Bancroft's Governors, it is perhaps surprising that they agreed to this suggestion which was fully backed by the School Committee. The Charity Commissioners, however, refused to agree to the change which was finally implemented – at their insistence! – in 1920. Links with the other 'endowed schools' of Essex were formed when Col. Lockwood MP called a meeting of school representatives in 1897 to put up a united front against the County Council.

Throughout this period of growth the presence of the Head Master dominated the school and it would seem from the eulogies at his death, most of Woodford Wells. It is a fact that the Head Masters of Bancroft's are bought by the yard to give *dignitas et gravitas* to their office. From photographs and the recollections of men who knew him, there can be no doubt that the Rev John Symns had great presence, the long beard hiding his clerical collar, an academic gown his formal clerical suit of clothing. The son of a schoolmaster, it was said that he was born to that vocation.

It seems today slightly strange to combine the Cloth with the slide rule but he succeeded in uniting them and also was a great Head Master. His sheer love of mathematics enabled him to share his pleasure with his less gifted pupils and to put across the theories of Euclid. He knew that, excepting a few clever scholars, his pupils were not geniuses and would never achieve the status of wrangler at his beloved old university. He thought it more important to train in honesty, integrity and all those other

91

Victorian virtues which we now hold up to ridicule, that they might better make their mark on the world. 'I don't care about the scholarship, it's the tone of the school that matters', he would proclaim and his devotion to Bancroft's was great.

Eighty years have passed since his death and yet one can imagine him on Visitation Day in the old Great Hall, extolling the virtues of his pupils. 'Another Bancroft boy' would begin a sentence proclaiming yet another success in university exams or at Darmouth or Woolwich and he had no fear in standing up to the Committee or the Company if he thought the boys were being maligned, as mentioned above, in the incident following the Woodford stone-laying.

One suspects he was the first Head Master whose opinion the Court actually respected. No doubt to his pupils and younger colleagues he was an awe-inspiring figure but no tyrant, and although he had no hesitation in birching boys he found it as beneficial to make the boy feel ashamed of his ill deed by calling him 'a low fellow' and commenting, 'Very curiously brought up at home, weren't you?', rather than inflict physical punishment. The examination results during his headmastership were very creditable, Bancroft's gaining more places in the honours of the local Board Examination than any other school, and when the honours school was abolished, following a year in which his pupils took four of the six top places, he regarded it as a personal victory over the examiners.

A member of the Headmasters' Conference in its early days, Symns much regretted that neither he nor the Court could persuade the Charity Commissioners to allow Bancroft's to take its full place as a public school. Forced to lower his sights slightly he succeeded in making Bancroft's one of the best schools of its type in England. A happily married man who saw his older son enter upon a distinguished career in the Indian Civil Service, he was both a keen gardener and a fly fisherman. During the Summer Term he always delighted to conduct Va, the senior form, around his garden, a shockingly ancient panama replacing his square, and would delight in solemnly asking then to name a particular plant (Southernwood) known as 'Old Man' – his nickname amongst the boys.

Without doubt Symns was a force to be reckoned with. He only once clashed with the Bancroft Committee and that concerned the Chapel. He was formally appointed chaplain in

BANCROFT'S SCHOOL.

FOUNDATION SCHOLARSHIPS, 1891.

ENGLISH HISTORY.

(For boys over 11.)

1. Name the leading statesmen (not more than two in each reign) in the reigns of Edred, William I., Henry II., James I., Anne, and George IV. ; and write against each name the leading measures or actions with which the name is associated.

2. What is the meaning of—*villenage, præmunire, tonnage* and *poundage, assize of arms, benevolences, free trade, orders in council, county councils?* Write a short historical note (not more than four lines) on each.

3. Under what circumstances was the Conquest of Ireland effected?
   Or, Trace the steps by which India passed under the English crown.

4. Write a short life of any three of the following:—Cardinal Wolsey, John Hampden, Lord Burleigh, Archbishop Laud, Thomas Wentworth (Earl of Strafford).

5. Between whom were the following battles fought, and with what issue?—Culloden, Talavera, Towton, Marston Moor, the Boyne, the Nile, Bunker's Hill, Inkerman. Describe *one* of them.

6. Name a great writer in the reigns of Edward III., Elizabeth, Charles II., and George IV. respectively, and name one work of each. Describe shortly one of these works.

7. What changes in the constitution of Parliament have taken place within the last century?
   Or, What possessions has England gained or lost during the same period?

Scholarship examination: English History

1890 and objected to what he considered laymen's interference when the Committee tried to lay down guide lines for the Chapel Service and, more importantly, the decoration of the altar. Symns was, presumably, influenced by the Tractarians in his beliefs and the Committee feared that middle class, nonconformist Essex would object to the trappings of Popery. The Court sympathised with those views though were not willing to enter into a theological discussion themselves, 'being unwilling that the peace and unity of the Company should be disturbed by a debate on theological or ecclesiastical matters as to which conflicting opinions may be found to exist'. A religious authority was therefore sought and, being the Drapers' Company, they consulted the Archbishop of Canterbury.

The Primate of All England replied that he saw no objections in changing the altar cloths according to the season, especially as they had come from the Mile End Chapel, though he agreed to the cross being placed above the altar, on the window ledge, rather than on the altar itself and Symns was allowed to face East when preparing the sacrament, which was an accepted practice. It was agreed that Communion would be held on one Sunday a month and on feast days, that Sunday services would be at 10.30 and 3.30, the first with a sermon, and that the quarter hour daily service was to consist of Introduction, Confession, Venite, a psalm, a New Testament lesson, the Collect and a special prayer. The Archbishop concluded by saying that the chaplain should always consult the Committee who should place all confidence in him.

Compulsory Chapel was just one of the features of the boarders' regimented day which was much the same as at Tottenham except there was more space in which to do it. Outside school hours life centred on the Day Room, a room partitioned in 1973 to create the new Masters' Common Room. Here the boys did prep., spent their few leisure hours and even changed for games. The sixth form were allowed the exclusive use of the Library, the well-lit first floor room overlooking the Head Master's house, and now a classroom. The boys were slow in founding formal societies such as debating societies, and energy was expended on the sports field where the boarders dominated the school team – only occasionally was a second eleven formed, as there were simply too few senior boys. Indeed, the team invariably included several masters, notably Messrs

Hall and Winterton, who were effective full backs.

The Rev James Hall, always an energetic man, ran the sports side of the school. The difficulty arose in finding opposition to play. We first played Chigwell at soccer on October 26th 1892, also a first in that only boys were in the team. Captained by the great McMinn, it was a one-all draw. Transport made away matches difficult and the team of masters and boys played local clubs at Buckhurst Hill, Hainault and Claybury Hospital and a match against a team of Old Boys. As the sixth form expanded, transport was organised to away games and we began playing Brentwood, Forest, Grocers' and Mercers' Schools, City of London, the Royal Masonic School and Trinity College, Finchley.

Cricket, also, was against local clubs in the early years with masters joining the boys. In the Whit Monday match against Woodford Wells in 1892 Mr Charles Page, who stayed only a year at the school, scored 212, a record never beaten at that club. The school team came of age in the early years of the century captained by H. L. Saunders whose propensity for scoring centuries has never been equalled in the school. That he gained an honours place in matriculation and went on to become Sir Harold Saunders and a staunch Old Bancroftian shows him to have been a great all-rounder.

One of the problems was the lack of space on which games could be played. At the time the school field had not been fully levelled, allowing only one football pitch running from Reeds Forest to where the pavilion now stands. The Committee and the Court soon appreciated the significance of this defect and allowed £15,000 if suitable ground could be found. In the meanwhile part of the forest at Riggs Retreat (where Brook Road meets Whitehall Road) was levelled and used, remaining in use till the 'fifties. Woodford land cost £1,000 an acre in 1900, as its building potential dawned upon landowners and, as it was on a ridge, there was no suitable flat meadow nearby that could easily be converted to playing fields. Mr Buxton of Buckhurst who owned all the land opposite, offered some at a reasonable price but it was considered too expensive to flatten it. Eventually six acres were bought from the Monkhams Estate in 1905 and were used until sold for development when West Grove was purchased.

Despite the lack of ground and very rudimentary showers – no hot water – games were an important part of the boys' lives and, though not compulsory, were a useful means for the boarders to relieve themselves of the frustrations of their cloistered existence. Soccer and cricket were the major sports of those days, varied by the occasional paper chase through the forest – imagine such a thing now – and, hare and hounds. The School also had some fives courts, on the site of the present Great Hall, and the game enjoyed a certain popularity. An annual athletics day was started by Mr Hall in the 1890s.

The highlight of the social season, apart from Vis. Day, was the Christmas Concert. The musical skills of Messrs James Hall and Winterton have already been mentioned and new members of staff added their expertise, most notably James Hall's younger brother, Mr J. E. Hall who trained the choirs and orchestra, which won the Stratford Music Festival in 1897, and Messrs T. H. Littlewood and H. H. Horton who wrote, respectively, the music and words of *Carmen Bancroftianum*, first performed in 1892. A typical programme is the concert for Christmas 1897:

Mr T. H. Littlewood	'Cello Solo 'Sample Aveu'	Thorne
Miss Ethel Harrison	'Damon'	Stage
Mr Joseph Leete	'The Vagabond'	J. L. Mallory
Mr Victor Meticolfe	'Violin Solo "Mozacka"'	Bohan
Miss Ethel Harrison	'Should he upbraid'	Sir H. R. Bishop
Mr Joseph Leete	'The Skipper of the Rose'	F. Bevan
F. Goldby	'Singing in de moonlight'	Chandoir
W. H. Walken	'Plantation Song Nancy'	G. Scott Gatty
J. B. Molyneux	'Come where my love lies dreaming'	G.Scott Gatty
Mr. E. H. Livermore	'De Ole Banjo'	
H. J. Stumbles	'Ole Honey'	Ivan Coryle
Mr E. H. Livermore	'Dinah Doe'	J. L. Mollory
E. M. Meredith	'Messa's Wedding Day'	Farrington
E. Howe	'Poor Old Joe'	Coster
F. Goldby	'That Grand Old Song'	Chandoir
M. W. Burkett	'The Torpedo and the Whale'	
	'Carmen Bancroftianum'	
	'God Save the Queen'	

Musical Director: Mr J. E. Hall.   Accompanist: Mr Walter Latter

School plays were confined to Visitation Day except when the more informal mid-term concerts included a one-act entertainment, usually written by a pupil. Vis. Day was then much as it is now: the Master, Wardens and several other members of the Court of Assistants visited the foundation and toured the School. They were no longer making sure that the butter was ordered economically or that the Head Master was not pilfering the petty cash. Instead they came to admire, with just pride, what they had helped to create and the Head Master's speech in the Great Hall, always a terrifying ordeal for him, must have confirmed their feelings. Mr Symns told of 'another Bancroft boy' who had gained a prize at London University or Guy's Hospital or anywhere else that his boys went, for prizes always seemed to fall to them. The Master of the Drapers' Company always presented the prizes, books for those who had fared best in their forms. To these were added in 1892 the first special prize, the Trower History Prize, when Mr Henry Trower, a past Master of the Drapers' Company, gave £300 of Trinidad stock on trust to the Company, to provide a history prize at Elmslea Girls' School and one, or possibly two, such prizes at Bancroft's. The Trower Prize was the first of numerous such small trusts, most of them gifts of Old Boys, which provide prizes for the pupils of the school, a list of them appearing at the end of this book.

A feature of Vis. Day in the first years at Woodford which survived from Mile End was the report of the examiner, the actual *viva voce* being consigned to history. There were no national examinations in those days and the local board examination at which Bancroft boys excelled were seen as a first step towards university. It was therefore considered necessary to hire an outsider from a university to examine the whole school. The practice had started during Mr Hunt's headship and, when the school moved to Woodford, a London University man was brought out instead of the alternate nominees of the Vice Chancellors of Oxford and Cambridge. The practice ceased at the turn of the century when the staff was strong enough for an internally-organised examination, but for the first Vis. Days the examiner reported on the state of the school and the report was invariably good.

The rest of Vis. Day consisted of exhibitions by the boys, especially of drawings and paintings, when the gifted sketches and caricatures by J. H. Thorpe were greatly admired. When not playing first class cricket Thorpe became a regular contributor to *Punch* and other journals, and his valuable Cricket Library was bequeathed to the Drapers' Company on trust for the school. Vis. Day concluded with tea in marquees, the band of the Essex Regiment playing the popular tunes of the day, and there was a cricket match on the school field.

The health of the School remained good during this period, except for an outbreak of diphtheria in 1903 and the occasional bout of mumps. The air of Woodford was undoubtedly good but the School's plumbing was, by our standards, very primitive. The night lavatories were in the basement beneath the junior common room, while during the day the whole school used latrines near the kitchen. Fortunately only a minority of boys played games as there were no proper changing rooms and no showers or baths until the first pavilion was built by the Drapers' Company in 1897. The good health of the school was no doubt partly due to the matron, Miss Spurgin, who retired in 1892 to be replaced by Miss Rimington. She in her turn moved on in 1903 to another school to be replaced by Miss Sheppard, a legendary figure, especially during the Great War, who finally retired in 1929. These ladies were aided by a large staff of maids, cooks, sewing maids and daily helpers, for these were the last days of abundant cheap domestic labour.

The matron was in a class apart with an income of £200 a year and her board – more than most masters – but the others were paid very little, although what they did receive was solely for pocket money. Cook in 1890 was paid £28 per annum, the nurse £22 and the maids five shillings a week. George the porter received an increase of ten shillings a week in 1891, taking his weekly pay to a guinea plus his cottage and, of course, his livery, which cost £5 10s 0d that year, with £1 17s 6d for his little top hat. The gardener, who lived out, received 28s a week, his boy 10s, while Flood the engineer received 30s and a cottage.

The Head Master received a stipend as chaplain of £105, his basic salary being £150 with a capitation payment £3 each for the first hundred boys, £2 for the second hundred and £1 for each boy after that, giving an income of about £876 a year by the time he died, plus his house. By 1900 when there were eleven masters on the staff their total salaries were £1,860: they were mostly young, of course, but all graduates and the highest paid received £230 a year, non-resident. To maintain so many staff at such a price, the fees were raised for the first time in 1902. Apart from a joining fee of £1 to the Sports Club, day boys under eleven paid £3 10s 0d a term, the older boys £4, with the 30 fee paying boarders' fees rising to £30 a year. Day boy lunches rose to £2 a term.

The endowment income remained static during this time.

Farm rents continued to fall; arrears of £500 at Clopton Hall were converted into a 3% loan with the rent reduced to £165 a year and Benton End produced £150, less than it had done a hundred years earlier. The Holborn property was let on a building lease and the other City property continued to yield a good rent each time the lease fell due. Part of the Prittlewell property was sold in 1899 to the railway company and a second house in 1902, the money being invested in more land at Saltcoats Farm. The Chiswick houses, owned by the Bancrofts since the 1640s were sold in 1881 for £3,000, the money being used to extend the Godliman Street property. It was becoming less and less cost effective to collect the rents from such small properties though the general divestment of land was not to come until after the Great War.

The rest of the endowment remained, at the insistence of the Charity Commissioners, in government stock, with income declining in real terms, and the capital face value actually declining as national interest rates rose. It is for that reason that the School's endowment is now so relatively small when compared with the income of 1750 or 1850.

A name which now, alas, is but a memory to a handful of senior O.B.s is that of The Bryn. The demand for boarding places at Bancroft's was so great that the Committee sanctioned the Rev James Hall to rent a house on Woodford Green called Balstock to take boys. That was in 1892, and in 1896 a house called The Bryn was rented in Whitehall Road, the Committee allowing £1,250 for necessary alterations. A house was later purchased outright for £2,400, Mr and Mrs Hall running it with the help of her sister Miss Wedge, which housed thirty boys at any one time. It lay just beyond the Monkham's Ground in Monkham's Drive and adopted the name 'The Bryn'. The idea of such houses, of course, follows the classic pattern of many public schools, where a boy's house was literally the house where he and his fellows lived. The Bryn survived the Great War, Mr Peel taking over from the Rev A. E. Hall in 1920 until it was sold in 1922. Any further extension of this idea had been discouraged when Mr Lydall was refused a house in 1902. The problem probably lay in the lack of space at the school for more day boys, a problem which the school has had ever since.

The boys from The Bryn fell into a no-man's-land between boarders and day boys; they prayed each day with the former but played games for the latter, giving great assistance to the day boy XI. It also made a twenty-four hour job for James Hall. Apart from teaching English he edited *The Bancroftian*, organised the school sports, ran the concert and the choir, oversaw the tuckshop and assisted the Head Master in Chapel. He was also an assistant curate at St John's, Leytonstone where he often cycled, and it was following a hard ride that he suffered a stroke in 1905. He lay ill throughout the Summer holidays, finally dying on 29th September, the feast of St Michael and All Angels, aged forty-six. A youthful looking man with a brown moustache, he was very popular with the boys, especially those at The Bryn, and a twinkle was never far from his eyes. He was forever trying to persuade the authorities to put a gate at the bottom of the field near his house which they refused to do: furthermore the Head Master forbade anyone to enter through the hedgerow. It is not known whether Mr Symns knew that his principal assistant was in the regular habit of breaking this rule but one doubts if he would have approved, especially when, sending a boy to The Bryn for something, Mr Hall added with a wink that the hedge was easily passable at one point. One suspects that such disregard for a pointless and time-consuming rule was typical of this much respected master. His younger brother the Rev A. E. Hall took over his place at The Bryn, marrying his brother's sister-in-law Olive Wedge, and ran the house until 1918. He was the third Hall brother to teach at the school.

It was the spirit of loyalty which Mr Hall and Mr Symns instilled in the boys which gave birth to the Old Bancroftians Association in the form of the Football Club and Annual Dinner. From the first days at Woodford an annual match had been played between the first XI and a team of Old Boys but they were an impromptu team and it was with the circulation of *The Bancroftian* from 1892 that contact between Old Boys was more easily maintained. J. H. Thorpe was the great organiser behind the team formed in 1894. It consisted of some of Symns' best pupils, names that should be honoured as long as Bancroftians gather together; apart from Thorpe they included R. S. McMinn, D. S. Barton, W. D. Van Homrige, A. B. Arnold, G. A. Powell, J. S. Goddard and A. W. Parsons, who played full back for England. It was never easy to get a team together: there was no club or ground and no regular fixtures; such glories lay in the future. It did, however, create an embryonic organisation for other O.B. events and for the eventual Association itself.

The first Annual Dinner was held at the Haunch of Venison in Fleet Street on 23rd January 1896, again organised by J. H. Thorpe: the 4/-d ticket provided a seven course meal, and about forty O.B.s attended. A series of smoking concerts was also held at the Haunch of Venison during the next few years, the dinner moving to the Holborn Restaurant, chaired by the ubiquitous Rev James Hall. An Annual Dinner has been held since, except when their duty took so many Old Boys overseas between 1914 and 1918 and 1939 and 1945.

THE ORIGINAL "ADVERTISEMENT". NOV. 1892.

'THE BANCROFTIAN.'

Edited by the Rev. J. Hall, B.A.

The First Number will appear about the 21st inst. You are reminded of your promise to subscribe to and support the Paper, aud are requested to secure your Copy on the day of publication. With the New Year it is hoped to begin the system of terminal subscriptions; 1/3. paid on the first day of the term ensuring the delivery of the term's numbers (3).

Notice for first issue of *the Bancroftian*

Menu of first Old Bancroftians' Supper, 1896

The event which bound together boys and Old Boys more than anything else was the publication of *The Bancroftian* in 1892. Again Mr James Hall was to the fore, encouraging 'copy' and writing the occasional editorial and creating a format which survived until 1972 when it was a much lamented victim of inflation. It carried reports on school matches, the concerts and Old Boy occasions such as the dinner, and also gave details of pupils' successes and news of Old Boys. The early numbers came out each month during term but it soon became a termly affair carrying articles on trips abroad and long letters from O.B.s in far-off places serving the Empire. Several O.B.s served in the Boer War, none fortunately being killed: the war was keenly followed by the school.

Other events of national importance during these years included Queen Victoria's Diamond Jubilee, witnessed by a group of boys and celebrated with a full holiday, and the Queen's death in 1901. The coronation of Edward VII the following year won a whole week's extra holiday.

The Boer War raised the question of a Cadet Force at Bancroft's; there were several sons of serving officers at the school and one or two boys each year were commissioned into the armed forces, but the demands of the Boer War showed the need for a larger reserve force. The Head Master suggested this idea on Vis. Day in 1903, inviting the support of parents who would have to pay 30s for their sons' uniforms; the army would provide guns and a little ammunition. Nothing came of it, though a scout troop was started under Mr Playne.

The death of Mr James Hall proved a great shock to Mr Symns and some later felt that he never recovered from the blow. He had always declined to enter a pension arrangement despite the Committee's willingness to share in contributions and, determined to die in office, also declined a rich living in the gift of his old college. He celebrated his seventieth birthday in 1905 but discovered that the pains which he took to be lumbago were in fact caused by cancer of the liver, and in the new year he informed the Committee of this fact. He last entered the school in February of 1906 and died in the Head Master's house on May 23rd. The funeral on the 28th was held in the School Chapel, conducted by the Revs W. C. Winterton, A. E. Hall and H. T. Cavell, vicar of Woodford. Numerous Old Boys and pupils attended and he was buried at Buckhurst Hill, near to the School which he loved and served so well. The achievement was great. He created not only a school but a school spirit on which his successors have, collectively, created the present school.

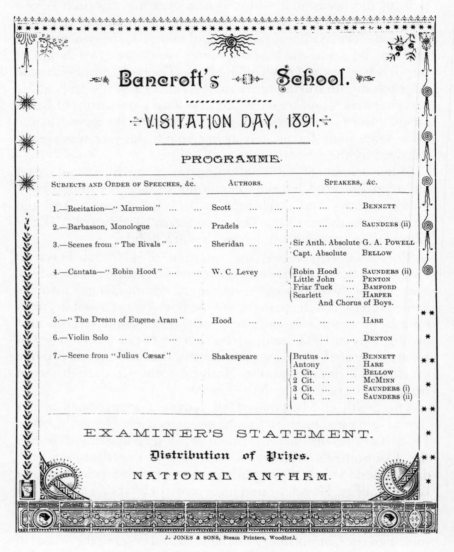

Bancroft's School.

VISITATION DAY, 1891.

PROGRAMME.

SUBJECTS AND ORDER OF SPEECHES, &c.	AUTHORS.	SPEAKERS, &c.	
1.—Recitation—"Marmion"	Scott		BENNETT
2.—Barbasson, Monologue	Pradels		SAUNDERS (ii)
3.—Scenes from "The Rivals"	Sheridan	Sir Anth. Absolute	G. A. POWELL
		Capt. Absolute	BELLOW
4.—Cantata—"Robin Hood"	W. C. Levey	Robin Hood	SAUNDERS (ii)
		Little John	PENTON
		Friar Tuck	BAMFORD
		Scarlett	HARPER
		And Chorus of Boys.	
5.—"The Dream of Eugene Aram"	Hood		HARE
6.—Violin Solo			DENTON
7.—Scene from "Julius Cæsar"	Shakespeare	Brutus	BENNETT
		Antony	HARE
		1 Cit.	BELLOW
		2 Cit.	McMINN
		3 Cit.	SAUNDERS (i)
		4 Cit.	SAUNDERS (ii)

EXAMINER'S STATEMENT.

Distribution of Prizes.

NATIONAL ANTHEM.

J. JONES & SONS, Steam Printers, Woodford.

Visitation Day, 1891

104

house v School 12 0.

DATE.	OPPONENTS.	GROUND.	RSLT	GOALS	
				FOR	AGST
1903.					
Sat., Oct. 3rd ...	Woodford Albion F.C.	School ...	...*Lost*		
Wed. ,, 7th ...					
Sat. ,, 10th ...	Old Finchleians	School ..	*Draw*	1	1
Wed. ,, 14th ...	Grocers' Co. School...	School ...	*Won*	3	0
Sat. ,, 17th ...	*Forest Albion* ...	*Riggs*	*(Won)*	5	0
Wed. ,, 21st ...	*Strand School*	*School.*	*Lost*	5	7
Sat. ,, 24th ...	St. Bartholomew's Hospital ..	School	*Won*		*scratched*
Wed. ,, 28th ...	J. H. Thorpe's XI. ...	School		*scratched*	
Sat. ,, 31st ...	London Hospital	School	*Won*	6	0
Wed., Nov. 4th ...	Chigwell School	School	*Won*	16	0
Sat. ,, 7th ...	Chigwell F.C. ... X ...	Chigwell X	*Won X*	*Scratched*	
Wed. ,, 11th ...	Claybury Asylum	Claybury	*Lost*	3	5
Sat. ,, 14th ..	Old Finchleians	School	*Draw*	2	2
Wed. ,, 18th ...	City of London School ...	Beckenham Hill	*Draw*	4	4
Sat. ,, 21st ...	St. Matthew's F.C.	School ...	*Draw*	1	1
Wed. ,, 25th ...	*N. Kudlingbury's XI*	*School.*	*Lost*	3	4
Sat. ,, 28th ...	Mercers' School ...	Shepherd's Bush...	*Won*	6	5
Wed., Dec. 2nd ...	*Thorpe's XI*	*School*	*Lost*	3	6
Sat. ,, 5th ...	University College	School	*Won*	2	0
Wed. ,, 9th ...					
Sat. ,, 12th ...	Old Bancroftians' F.C. ...	School ...	*Lost*	2	11
Wed. ,, 16th ...					
Sat. ,, 19th ...	H. L. Giles' XI.	School ...	*Won*	11	2
1904.					
Sat., Jan. 23rd ...	St. Andrew's F.C. ...	School	*Scratched*		
Wed. ,, 27th ...	Claybury Asylum ...	Claybury ...	*Lost*	2	6
Sat. ,, 30th ...	University College	School ...	*Scratched*		
Wed., Feb. 3rd ...	Chigwell School	Chigwell ...	*Won*	10	1
Sat. ,, 6th ...	St. Bartholomew's Hospital ..	School ...	*Won*	7	1
Wed. ,, 10th ...	City of London School ...	School ...	*Won*	7	0
Sat. ,, 13th ...	Mercers' School	School ...	*Won*		*Scratched*
Wed. ,, 17th ...	London Hospital ...	Higham's Park ...	*Lost*	1	4
Sat. ,, 20th ...	Woodford Albion F.C. ...	School ...	*Won*	9	3
Wed. ,, 24th ...	Battersea Grammar School ...	School ...	*Won*	4	3
Sat. ,, 27th ...	Forest School	Walthamstow ...			
Wed., Mar. 2nd ...					
Sat. ,, 5th ...	H. L. Giles' XI.	School ...	*Won*	4	1
Wed. ,, 9th ...	J. H. Thorpe's XI. ...	School ...	*Won*	4	3
Sat. ,, 12th ...	St. Matthew's F.C.	School ...	*Won*	6	0
Wed. ,, 15th ...	*Strand School*	*School 1st Eleven Park*	*Draw*	3	3
Sat. ,, 19th ...	Old Bancroftians' F.C. ...	School ...	*Lost*	2	5
Wed. ,, 23rd ...	Grocers' Co. School... ...	Edmonton... ...	*Lost*	0	1
Sat. ,, 26th ...	Chigwell F.C.	School ...	*Won*	8	0
Wed. ,, 30th ...					

School house v School *School house Won* 12 0

SECOND ELEVEN.					
1903.					
Sat., Oct. 10th ...	Woodford Ferndale F.C. ...	School ...	*Lost*	0	6
Wed. ,, 14th ...	Grocers' Co. School, 2nd XI.	Edmonton ...	*Won*	2	1
Wed. ,, 28th ...	*Mellows XI*		*Lost*		
Wed., Nov. 4th ...	Chigwell School, 2nd XI ...	Chigwell ..	*Won*	14	0
,, ,, 11th ...	Central Foundation School ...	Wood Green ...	*Lost*	3	6
,, ,, 18th ...	City of London School, 2nd XI...	School ...	*Lost*	1	3
Sat. ,, 21st ...	Boys' Brigade	School ...	*Lost*	0	6
1904.					
Wed., Feb. 3rd ...	Chigwell School, 2nd XI. ...	School ...	*Scratched*		
,, ,, 10th ...	City of London School, 2nd XI. ...	Beckenham Hill .	*Lost*	2	3
,, ,, 24th ...	Central Foundation School ...	School ...	*Lost*		
Sat., Mar. 19th ...	Boys' Brigade	School ...	*Lost*	1	2
Wed. ,, 23rd ...	Grocers' Co. School, 2nd XI. ...	School ...	*Won*	8	1
Sat. ,, 26th ...	Woodford Ferndale F.C. ...	School ...	*Scratched*		

School Football Club fixtures, 1903-4

105

GENTLEMEN,

I beg leave to offer myself as a candidate for the Headmastership of Bancroft's School, and will state concisely particulars of my education and experience.

I am a Graduate of the University of Oxford, and my name is on column B of the Register of Teachers.

I am married, and am thirty-five years of age.

I was educated at Clifton College from 1881 to 1889, and went from there as Mathematical Scholar to University College, Oxford. At Oxford I obtained 2nd Class Honours in Math. Mods., and 1st Class Honours in the Math. Final Schools.

Since September, 1893, I have been an Assistant Master at Clifton College, and have had experience of teaching in all parts of the School, from the Preparatory upwards.

At the present time I am in charge of the Mathematics of the Military Side, and Form Master of the Military Middle Fifth.

I represented Clifton College on the Committee of the Mathematical Association for the improvement of the teaching of Elementary Mathematics.

Besides Mathematics, I have had some experience in teaching Elementary Science and Classics; I have also been responsible for the religious instruction of my Form for several years.

For nine years I was "House Tutor" in Mr. W. O. Moberly's Boarding-house, and at the present time am House Master of North Town.

Although not an expert at games, I have been able to take my full share in them and other pursuits of the School. I have served in the Cadet Corps, and was President of the Scientific Society for five years.

I forward copies of seven recent testimonials; and will only say in conclusion that it your choice should fall on me, you may be sure I shall do my utmost for the good of the School.

I remain, Gentlemen,
Your obedient servant,

HERBERT C. PLAYNE.

Mr Playne's curriculum vitae

CHAPTER VIII

HERBERT CLEMENT PLAYNE
1906–1914

IT MAY be said of Herbert Clement Playne that, like his predecessor and successor, he was appointed for a specific purpose by a governing body determined that the school's progress should continue. Mr Symns had established Bancroft's as a leading place of learning but sights were now set higher than local board examinations, though their importance was still recognised.

The new Head Master had attended Clifton College near Bristol, one of the 'proprietary' public schools of the mid-Victorian period. After reading mathematics at University College, Oxford, he returned to Clifton to teach and keep a house, and it was this background which attracted the governors, who hoped that he would turn Bancroft's into a school of similar type and reputation.

He was a large, hirsute man aged thirty-five whose sparkling eyes stand out in early photographs. Shy and retiring, even remote to younger boys, he was a man of great energy – his son compares his departure for school down the drive to an angry blackbird – he also grasped the importance of administration for a school. A skilled mathematician, he delighted in the classics, which he occasionally taught, and was a keen naturalist and ornithologist. He was most at ease on his boat, a converted oyster sloop, kept on the River Crouch, and some senior boys were invited to the yacht for summer cruises.

His reign saw the Head Master's house fully used for the last time, for the Playnes had six children – and the Airedale Jim – and kept a full staff of butler, cook, maids and nannies, the salary of £900 a year being supplemented by private means.

Whatever preconceptions he may have had of Bancroft's, he soon realised that it was not just another charity school of a rich livery company but had traditions and loyalties every bit as strong as those at Clifton, with a longer pedigree. He wisely nurtured these forces rather than attempt to squash them, this period seeing the foundation of the Old Bancroftians' Association and the School Mission. Such developments are, however, incidental to the great changes which he instigated at school.

The system inherited from Mr Symns was of thirteen forms taking boys from nine to seventeen. Jumping forms often gave pupils an arbitrary grounding in some subjects such as French and Latin, so Mr Playne's first step was to reduce the number of forms to eleven, with parallel fourth forms, allowing boys to pass through each form from I to V. Teaching was still on a form basis, the master being expected to teach all subjects, specialising in one or two subjects which he would teach to much of the school.

A more memorable and lasting change was the construction of the house system. Day boys, with Bryn boys to the fore, had become a growing force on the School field but now all day boys were divided into East and West Houses depending on which side of the High Road they lived, the boarders being divided into Odds and Evens for sporting purposes. Games remained voluntary, learning to swim being the only compulsory exercise, though the new house system, the Monkhams ground, new swappers and an improved Riggs Retreat increased the quality of play and induced more involvement by day boys.

It had been clearly recognised by the Governors for some while that the school had to have a healthy sixth form if it was to compete fully with other schools and gain admission to the Public Schools Year Book. The only block to this had always been the objections of the Charity Commissioners and the Board of Education. Thanks to the efforts of Sir William Sawyer and his successor as Clerk to the Drapers' Company, Mr Ernest Pooley, those two bodies agreed to a new scheme in 1912 allowing each boy to stay on till the Summer after his eighteenth birthday.

A growing number of boys took advantage of this extension and it allowed scholars to pass direct to university, by-passing other schools and exempting boys from preliminary examinations. The first Bancroftian to enter Oxford or Cambridge direct from School was F. S. Higson who won a mathematics scholarship at King's in 1914. The date was ominous: like so many of his contemporaries he fell in the mud of France and it was his successors of the 1920s who took full advantage of the new system.

The School continued to nurture scientists, who were given new laboratories by the Drapers' Company in 1910. Originally the Company agreed to lend the money to the school, interest free, to build the labs. but the loan was converted to a gift when it became clear that the school's finances could not afford to repay the money – £4,000 for the building and a further £400 to fit it out. The first Bancroftians to take advantage of this were C. B. and D. T. A. Townend whose scientific grounding led to distinguished careers in industry and in the Second World War, and both were awarded the CBE.

As the Master of the Drapers' Company pointed out, rather patronisingly, at one of the pre-war Vis. Days, the station of most Bancroftians did not make them leading men of society but rather they were the backbone-of-the-nation type filling important jobs in town and city. This ignored the fact that little was known of Old Boys from the Mile End era, and that the crop of O.B.s who were to bring credit to the school – Saunders, Cunningham, Self and the Peppiatts – were as yet on the bottom of their career ladders. A. H. Self was Mr Playne's first head monitor. From London University he gained a high place in the Civil Service examination, along with his contemporary P. J. Bennett, and went on to take external London University degrees in mathematics and divinity. A man of strong convictions, a founder of the Association and Mission, his career culminated with high office in the Air Ministry during the 1939–1945 war and he ended his career with three Knighthoods: KCB, KCMG and KBE.

Other O.B.s of this period were leading distinguished academic lives. Chrystall took a first at UCL and became a lecturer; N. L. Mackie took firsts at London and Oxford and had commenced a teaching career at Manchester in jurisprudence when the Great War began – he fell in 1915; and Sladden was a Christ Church exhibitioner in natural sciences, while at Cambridge S. Maugham took a first in the same subject and W. W. R. Hooker was twentieth Wrangler of 1908 – Mr Symns would have been especially delighted. Another prize winner was A. C. Wood at London, who won both the Goldsmith's prize for English and a prize for Anglo-Saxon. There were others, many of whom were dead by 1919, who were adding lustre to the school's academic prowess.

Amongst more senior O.B.s, reports came of progression in a variety of careers in all corners of the world. D. Buxton, head monitor at Tottenham, and G. W. Swann were successful engineers in Canada, and *The Bancroftian* travelled to India, Africa and the Far East, to those vast territories of the Empire where one hopes the sense of decency instilled in them by Mr Symns made them good ambassadors for their race and their school.

The school staff of those days – few in number, nearly all from Oxford or Cambridge, without teaching qualifications – either came and went quickly or stayed for thirty years. In the latter category Mr Playne inherited Messrs Winterton, Brinkman, Littlewood, Collins, Kislingbury, Chapman, Blyth, Lucas and Raven, with Sgt Major Skillan for PT. There were no important retirements during the period, though amongst important appointments were the Rev A. E. Hall, third of his brothers to come to Bancroft's, who was put in charge of The Bryn, and Messrs Sifkken, Bowmar-Porter, Richards and Guthkelch. The last was at Bancroft's for only two years before he went to King's, London, to teach, but made a lasting impression with his erudition, and made a determined attempt to civilize the boys. Another brief appointment, Mr Wilding, founded the Literary Scientific and Debating Society in 1908 (today pupils would make much of the initials) and he encouraged day boys to participate in the debates which took place after school until tea time. In Autumn 1910 the programme included:

Oct. 13   'That this House is in favour of the payment of Members of Parliament by the State'

   20   'Shooting Stars' by F. S. Higson

   27   'That this House would favour the construction of a Channel Tunnel between England and France'

Nov. 3   'The Peasants Revolt of 1381' by L. C. Benns

   10   'The World before the Deluge' F. Holt

   17   'That this House considers that the better education is that afforded by a classical as opposed to a non-classical education'

   24   'English Humour' Rev A. E. Hall

Dec. 1   'That this House views with alarm the growing halfpenny Press in Great Britain'

   8   'Some French Cathedrals and Ripon Cathedral' with slides by Rev. C. O. Raven

Plus ça change . . .

Mr Symns had attempted to form an OTC following the Boer War but had little support, and it took the energy of a new master Mr P. G. Blyth to instil martial skills and discipline into Bancroftians with the formation in 1909 of a troop of Sea Scouts. The body was popular with the boys, succeeding in uniting the boarders and day boys and giving the former yet another outlet for their energies. The troop was known was the 4th Epping Forest Sea Scouts and the first camp was held at Marshwood, near Southampton in the Summer of 1909 and became a regular and eagerly anticipated side of school life, with other camps in Knighton Woods near the school, the Buxton family, as always, being good neighbours and friends of the school.

The school field during this period gradually became flatter as the natural slope from the Chapel assy to Whitehall Road was levelled, a process financed by tuck shop profits. Only one pitch was available for soccer or cricket, the lesser matches being played at Monkhams ground or Riggs Retreat. The Monkhams ground – the site of the present Tudor Close off Monkhams Drive, the public right of way from Monkhams Avenue demarcating the West boundary – was purchased by the Drapers' Company in 1905 for £2,000 from Mr Twentyman. Although his son (or a near relative) was a pupil at the school, relations were not always happy and occasional writs and injunctions were issued with regard to drainage and rights of way. There were no changing facilities, boys travelling to and from the pitches already kitted out.

The increase in the School's size during this time, the tendency of boys to stay on longer in the VIth form and the greater participation of day boys in sports all enhanced the standard of school sport, allowing it to compete against larger London-based schools, though travelling was by no means easy in the days before the char-à-banc. Apart from schools and O.B. sides, the cricket club in those days played local clubs and Claybury Hospital (one assumes the staff) and Essex Club and Ground. Boys also found their way into Essex Public School sides to play Essex. Other games, apart from soccer, were supported. Fives was encouraged though the courts were used rather for informal fisticuffs than for the intended sport, and athletics was an alternative to cricket during Spring Term, though the great days of that sport began after the war.

In 1912 the Old Boys founded a Cricket Club. A match

111

against the School had become a regular feature of the season since the 1890s but now there were sufficient keen and able O.B.s living near Woodford to form a side each weekend. A. H. Self was the first captain, with elders such as J. H. Thorpe and J. S. Goddard giving their support. The tiny figure of A. V. Cooper, who played for several years in the school XI, was soon to the fore of the O.B. team, scoring 730 runs and taking 88 wickets in 1913, with R. C. Davies proving an adept bowler.

Matches were against Essex and North London sides (most Old School sides already belonging to a league) and in the years before the war a second XI was formed. Home games were played at the Leyton ground of East London College, by courtesy of the Drapers' Company. Tennis and squash flourished there just before the Great War.

One other sporting achievement of O.B.s must be mentioned: the fencing skill of Chalker and A. H. Corble. Both fenced for their country and Corble became a leading authority on the history of the sport. With his brothers he was a bastion of the two new organisations, each in its way symbolic of Bancroft's maturity: the Old Bancroftians Association and the Bancroft's Mission.

An attempt to found an organisation had been made in the 1860s but had come to nothing, and it was the move to Woodford which gave the scheme its impetus. The founding of the Football Club in 1894 and, of wider appeal, the holding of an annual dinner and 'Smokers' from 1895 provided a nucleus for the founding of the society. Many Old Boys subscribed to *The Bancroftian*, so addresses were available for Bancroftians back to 1890 and some veterans of Mile End were known. Both Mr Playne and Ernest Pooley, the Clerk of the Company, realised the advantages of a flourishing Old Boys' Society and gave the project their strong support.

The founding committee comprised W. J. Saunders, J. C. L. Sharman, R. S. McMinn, E. Swanson, J. S. Arkinstall , J. S. Goddard, N. L. Mackie, D. McKichan, W. H. Peppiatt, P. M. Phillips, A. J. Rayment and H. L. Saunders, and met in Goddard's offices behind, appropriately, the Drapers' church, St Michael's, Cornhill, on Michaelmas Eve 1909. It was decided to call the organisation The Old Bancroftians' Association and W. J. Saunders, Rayment and McKichan were charged with the

HRH The Duke of York inspecting the O.T.C. 1921

HRH The Duke of York at the unveiling of the War Memorial tablet

School Chapel, 1920

Junior Day Room, 1920

Old Great Hall

Dining Hall

Chemistry Laboratory, 1910 Science Block, *c.*1920

The School from the air, *c.*1920

task of writing the rules. An inaugural meeting was called for Friday 26th November at Drapers' Hall, 430 letters being posted and over 100 O.B.s attending, to enjoy the first of many teas provided by the Company. The constitution was agreed, Mr Playne becoming first President, followed in successive years by McMinn, G. A. Powell and the Rev W. C. Winterton, one of only two assistant masters to hold the office. The first Secretary was McKichan whose great capacity for hard work increased the membership from an initial 50 to 213 at the outbreak of war. Sadly he died of 'Spanish flu' in the last year of the war.

Early days were not always happy days. One parsimonious O.B. pointed out that his 5s membership gave him precisely the same as his previous 1s subscription to *The Bancroftian* and a more generous one suggested an all-in price of 10s to include the Annual Dinner. The Association has flourished ever since and has found most favourable mention in the various visitations of HM Inspectors of Schools. An early example of the O.B. A.'s usefulness was in the formation of the employment bureau: O.B.s wrote articles on their professions in *The Bancroftian* and guided school leavers towards the right type of job. The Old School tie (not to mention blazer, hat band and cravat), as first chosen, caused confusion with that of Malvern College, so a thin light blue stripe joined the claret one running between the black and blue in 1925.

No finer example can be found of the generosity and good work of all things Bancroftian than the Bancroft's Mission in Custom House. The link began in 1911 when an Old Boy, the Rev A. F. Fletcher, a curate at St Matthew's, suggested to certain O.B.s that it would be a good thing for Bancroftians to do charitable work with the youth of the parish. Such schools as Eton, Repton and The Leys had their missions, and Bancroft's joined their ranks in 1911. The inevitable committee was formed, chaired by Mr Playne with G. G. Corble as treasurer, Messrs Winterton, Littlewood and Richards from the staff, with Mrs Playne and Miss Sheppard, and A. J. Rayment and A. H. Self from the new O.B. A. From the beginning it was Self who worked hard for the project, drilling a dozen or so ten to twelve year old boys, preparing them for the local cadet battalion of the Essex Territorials. His combination of great physical fitness, a burning Christian zeal and a brilliant administrative mind created the Mission, expanded it, and raised funds to build the

113

Bancroft Hall, an annexe to the church vestry, by 1913. The Drapers' Company, as always, helped out with a £150 grant and funds were raised by subscriptions, donations and the takings from an annual concert at the school. The Mission continued for most of the war, helped out following the dreadful Silvertown explosion in 1917 and expanded after the war.

All this activity was good for the morale of the school and places were keenly sought for both boarding and day places. The Governors were reluctant, however, to expand too quickly since the extra fees (£4 a term) would not meet the salaries of the extra staff required. The finances were not in a healthy state because costs rose, but endowment income, especially from farmland, was not keeping pace. The Governors were opposed to raising fees and wary of becoming too closely associated with the Essex County Council. Plans were prepared to reduce the number of free boarding scholarships and make parents pay for clothing except in cases of extreme need.

While these discussions were taking place, five of HM Inspectors of Schools visited the School in December 1913, stayed a week and eventually produced a report: the ever-wary Mr Pooley advised the Company that they were not obliged to accept recommendations. In fact the report was most flattering, especially of the Governors and Head Master, whose generous salary of £1,000 a year the Inspectors acknowledged to be suitable for his position. They found the boys bright and promising and very able for their years, though the dullness of the classrooms and inadequacy of the heating system were regarded as detrimental to the boys' well-being, and the inspectors were critical of some masters, 'There appears to be a lack of initiative and brightness in their work; they are all too hard-worked'. They also felt that the Head Master spent too much time teaching.

Their recommendations to increase the staff and send some masters on courses added to the financial uncertainty of the school. The Finance Committee reported to the Court of Assistants of the Company the perilous state of affairs, for which no solution seemed possible from the Bancroft Trust alone. The Court decided on two things: that a grant of £1,000 be given for a new heating system, and that 'it was beneath the dignity of the Company to accept Government aid for one of its principal charities'. They would reimburse the Bancroft fund for any deficit incurred, as well as paying off the current debt of £2,000. This state of affairs, the only time when Bancroft's became a permanent liability on the Company's finances, was to exist until time or circumstance restored the School to a sure financial footing. The announcement was made public on Visitation Day 1914.

The Summer of that year is known to history as one of glorious weather, the old world basking in sunshine for the last time. The tragedy of the following years is not that that world went for ever – post-war Vis. Days were just as grand – but that so many of Sgt Major Skillen's young gymnasts, and the boys receiving books from the Master of the Drapers' Company, did not see the year 1919.

It can be argued that the first six or eight years of a new administration are the crucial ones and will show both the aspirations and success of the new man. If that is so, then the brief spell 1906–1914 saw a growing confidence amongst Bancroftians in themselves and the School, and Mr Playne's plans proved an admirable blue print for the great success and advances of the post-war years.

BANCROFT'S SCHOOL.

Class Lists, July, 1907.

GOVERNORS.

THE COURT OF ASSISTANTS OF THE DRAPERS' COMPANY.

HEAD MASTER.

H. C. PLAYNE, M.A., Late Scholar of University College, Oxford.

ASSISTANT MASTERS:

REV. W. C. WINTERTON, B.A., University of London.

G. BRINKMANN, Graduate Göttingen University.

T. H. LITTLEWOOD, M.A., B.Sc., Late Scholar of Corpus Christi College, Oxford.

T. B. COLLINS, M.A., Late Exhibitioner of Christ Church, Oxford.

W. C. KISLINGBURY, M.A., Late Scholar of Queen's College, Oxford.

P. G. BLYTH, M.A., Late Scholar of Queen's College, Cambridge.

R. S. LUCAS, M.A., University of London.

C. O. RAVEN, B.A., Late Choral Scholar of St. John's College, Cambridge.

L. H. POND, B.A., Trinity College, Cambridge.

A. C. L. GUTHKELCH, M.A., University of London.

REV. A. E. HALL, B.A., University of London.

W. J. DOBSON, B.A., Late Scholar of Exeter College, Oxford.

————————

J. J. CHAPMAN, Instructor in Woodwork.

SERGEANT-MAJOR SKILLAN, Instructor in Gymnastics.

————————

The Holidays will end on FRIDAY EVENING, SEPT. 20th. The names of Boarders will be called over at six o'clock, when every boy must be present, unless his friends have previously sent to the Head Master a Medical Certificate explaining the reason of his absence.

DAY BOYS will return the following morning, SATURDAY, SEPT. 21st at the usual time.

List of masters, 1907

116

CARMEN BANCROFTIANUM.

H.H.Horton, B.A.   T.H.Littlewood, M.A.

Floreat Ban-crof-ti-a!

Floreamus pu-eri! Vivat et me-mo-ri-a Fundatoris nostri!

CHORUS.

Nobis in ae-ter-num Magni sint ho-no-res. Floreat Bancroftia! Floreant rectores!

Adsit amor patriae,	Absit ignorantia;	Adsit amicitia;
Adsit et parentum;	Absint et spernenda;	Sodales et amemus;
Amor sit scientiae,	Absint nobis omnia	Absit avaritia;
Vitae ornamentum.	Quae sunt contemnenda.	Honesta resonemus.

Carmen Bancroftianum, the school song

117

CHAPTER IX

1914-1918

THE GREAT WAR saw Bancroft's coming of age and the School and its Old Boys were not found wanting at their country's call to arms. It is not for us to question the motives, the passions, of millions of people throughout Europe in 1914, nor can it be within the scope of this work to comment on the carnage and slaughter which wiped out the best of our manhood, except where Bancroft's was directly affected. The two World Wars are treated in their own special chapters, recognising the overwhelming influence of those two events on our country, our school and its pupils and Old Boys. They caused social change which still affects each of us today. The two wars were, of course, very different and were entered into with different feelings – we wanted to fight in 1914, we had to fight in 1939 – feelings which were in evidence at the School, and it is the change which occurred in thoughts about the War, as well as in material things, that concern us in this chapter, along with a description of the great war service of Old Bancroftians.

Bancroft's was a perfect microcosm of Britain at war: the increase in the price, and decline in the quality, of food, the disappearance of domestic help, were all problems which faced the School and the Bancroft's Committee. Equally, the gradual increase in the number of Old Boy deaths, especially from late 1916 onwards, shows the growing importance of the British forces on the Western front, as the French army, bled white by constant fighting, collapsed into apathy and mutiny.

The assassination at Sarajevo passed almost without notice towards the end of the Spring term, 1914 – such things were always happening in Eastern Europe – and the boys broke up in July to enjoy the balmy Summer, one of the hottest on record. The mobilization of European armies in late July, the declarations of war by Hapsburg, Romanov and Hohenzollern, and Britain's entering of the conflict to honour 'a piece of paper' seventy-five years old, all occurred during that holiday, and by the time School reassembled on 9th September, the first battle honours had been added to the colours of the British Expeditionary Force. The School was undoubtedly filled with the same patriotism as the rest of the nation and immediately asked itself: what can we do to help the war effort?

The School Committee had already decided that Bancroft's would continue its normal routine as far as the war allowed, and when Messrs Elliott, Sifkken and Simpson enlisted, agreed to make good any loss in salary and keep their places open for the duration, and several Belgian boys were admitted as temporary free day boys. (One, J. Lequim, headed the class list in the Remove in 1916.) When not encouraging their sons to enlist, the major concern of the English in those early days of war lay with the Belgian refugees who poured into England as their tiny country was overrun by so called 'baby-bayonetting, nun-raping, pickel-haubered' Prussians. Many refugees were billeted on families, or in country houses – including Valentines, near Ilford – and a vast number were sheltered at the Earls Court Exhibition Hall under the aegis of G. A. Powell, whose brilliant organisational skills found and overcame a worthy challenge.

The boys' lives were hardly affected as yet in any material way and their efforts were limited to making arm cushion rests for wounded soldiers under the supervision of Miss Sheppard and Nurse Woods, two much-loved ladies. The boys twisted pieces of paper which were stuffed inside envelopes made of cloth remnants sewn together by the maids. They were sent mostly to No 2 General Hospital, Lincoln, where Miss Sheppard's sister was matron. Several of the more nimble-fingered boys were taught to knit balaclavas and socks which were dispatched to the Essex Regiment at Warley. Otherwise, normal life continued. That first term of war saw football matches against Chigwell, City of London, Parmiter's, Grocers' and Kensington Central College, and boys continued to take Matric and enter the professions, though the universities had all but ceased to function. England had never been obliged to field armies of schoolboys and, though many attempted, and some succeeded in joining up under age, it was Old Boys who fought and so Old Bancroftians will figure prominently in this chapter.

Thanks to the Association, *The Bancroftian* and the never-ending efforts of Miss Sheppard, as close a track as security allowed was kept on the School's sons with the colours. The second war-time *Bancroftian* records 163 O.B.s who had joined up, of whom fourteen were regular officers, and letters were received from O.B.s. at camp and, soon, in France. Several were involved in the siege of Antwerp and two were captured, while two more were interned in Holland, and a number of O.B.s participated in the charge of the London Scottish at Ypres.

Not only O.B.s in Great Britain answered to the call of war: the Rev F. C. Frost tried several times to become a Canadian Army Chaplain and eventually enlisted as a private. Before gaining a commission towards the end of the war he was awarded the DCM as a stretcher bearer. Before Christmas – when the war should have been over – the first two names were placed on the Roll of Honour, Seton killed on board HMS Formidable sunk by a mine, and W. H. Peppiatt, private in the London Rifle Brigade, whose two younger brothers were to bring such distinction to the School both during and after the war. A letter from Gray records the celebrated Christmas Day truce when his colleagues exchanged rum and cigars with the Saxony regiment in the opposite trench.

As 1915 began the pattern of trench warfare was established throughout the western front and everyone prepared for a long war. It was proposed that the School should form an OTC and a letter in *The Bancroftian* of February 1915 made comment on the small percentage of serving O.B.s who held the King's Commission, a deficiency which would be corrected by an officers' training corps. The letter produced a terse reply from Mr – or rather Sgt Major – Sifkken who deplored the intimation that only by a commission could Bancroftians contribute to the war effort. The foundation of the OTC went ahead, 60 boys being attached to the Woodford platoon of the 4th Battalion the Essex Regiment, transferring in 1916 to the Public Schools battalion of the same regiment, under the command of Mr H. Jones, a new master. At the same time the O.B.s at the front began to receive commissions as the average life span of a subaltern dropped to a matter of weeks.

Captain C. T. Ewald won the DSO in February 1915 and F. A. Knight was the first Canadian to fall at Neuve Chappelle. Other casualties mounted. There had been three Nash brothers at School, all popular sportsmen, and their contribution to the war effort is all too typical of so many families. F. L. Nash ran off to the war when under age, leaving his mother this poem:

With a gift to the Princes' National Fund
And a map hung up on the wall
Do you think we've done our duty
And answered our country's call?

No! It's men we want, and men who'll die
To oust the Kaiser's plan;
And it's better to die on the battle field
Than to live a cowardly man.

When this horrible war is over
And our sons that are spared come home
Oh! how lovely to be amongst them
And to know our duty's done.

He fell in April. His brother H. M. Nash, was killed in December, his death being recorded as follows:

'Another London man named Nash stood out above the German trench flinging his grenades with the utmost gallantry. He was a fine cricketer and did not throw his bombs in the orthodox way, but with the overarm swing of a fast bowler. So now he played his last game as though he were practising in the nets, and kept the enemy back until they lobbed one of their bombs at him and struck him on the head.'

The third brother V. Nash joined the army straight from School in 1916 and was reported missing in 1917 but later turned up as a prisoner.

By the end of 1915, 380 O.B.s had enlisted, of whom thirty had died. Reports came to *The Bancroftian* from all parts of the world, for the frontiers of the Empire still had to be protected. G. Holt was killed by his own men in a seldom-mentioned mutiny in Singapore, and, later on in the war Oscar Corble helped to stem German intrigue in Sudan. Towards the end of the year Tossetti, a fine cricketer, and Bessell each received the MC as did N. L. Mackie, a most distinguished scholar who passed through London and Oxford Universities and was a Professor of Law at Manchester when the war began. He fell in October. The war was beginning to affect every family in the realm, though the slaughter for Britain had hardly begun.

At home, the boys kept track of the war by subscribing to the *Daily Telegraph*, *Daily Mirror* and *The Nation*, while Miss

121

Sheppard recorded the movements of O.B.s on a huge board in the common room. Miss Sheppard was a most popular matron who quite literally wore herself out serving the school. Any O.B. writing to her could be sure to receive a reply and news of other Old Boys serving in his theatre of war. Parents, too, kept in touch with Miss Sheppard and any O.B. back from the front would, after shaking George's hand, head straight for her prim sitting room entered by her own front door, for a chat over a formal tea drunk from dainty bone china cups and served by hands showing increasing symptoms of arthritis. Miss Sheppard also had the School to run in gradually deteriorating conditions. 'Boots' joined up and the domestic staff was diminished so the boys had to help out in the kitchen, the monitors slicing and buttering – with margarine – the great 4lb. loaves whose price rose steadily from 4d in August 1914 to 7d in March 1915. Meat also increased in price and deteriorated in quality, with fish pie replacing the inevitable beef or mutton on two days a week. Vegetables meant potatoes and swedes, except for a few greens grown on the field and in the Head Master's garden.

Curiously enough the standard of food improved, presumably because it needed that much more effort to prepare, though the boys became more susceptible to disease. German measles sent the boarders home early in 1916 and a continuous outbreak of boils and impetigo persuaded the authorities to allow a breakfast ration of bacon. It took a great war to provide meat breakfasts at Bancroft's, an irony not lost on the boys.

The nights were enlivened by air raids on London, the Zeppelins flying along the Epping–Woodford ridge, guided by the reservoirs of the Lea Valley. On one early raid in 1916 Mr Freeman, a new master, followed the fall of bombs on his bicycle, returning to calm the awakened boarders by assuring them that it was only fireworks being set off. On another occasion a Zeppelin was brought down by the great gun on Pole Hill – a greater danger to the school than the German bombs – and souvenirs were eagerly sought; the Head Master's edict forbidding this sent up the price fourfold.

No danger seems to have been felt by the boys from these raids, though the Governors took them seriously and implemented the various Board of Education directives sent them on the subject. The problems of running the School in war-time were a great strain on the Head Master. Too old to fight, he helped out at the

Army remount centre, being a skilled horseman. As staff joined up – Messrs Hughes and Porter joined up in 1915, Mr Blyth in 1916 and Mr Freeman the year after – replacements were harder to find. The School finances, in a sorry state when the war began, deteriorated in several ways. Numbers dropped as fathers on army pay were unable to meet fees which were increased to £4 10s 0d a term in 1916. Although the income of the Trust's farmer tenants doubtless increased during the war, rents remained the same, while those on City property fell – Holborn from £1,340 to £1,130 a year when leases were renewed in 1916. Also, salaries rose, the masters' bill being £3,844 a year in 1917, and domestic help and food were more expensive.

Throughout, the Drapers' Company met the deficit and even planned for the future. In 1915 the Bancroft's Charity Scheme was altered, formalising the plans prepared by Mr Playne in the years of peace and allowing an expansion of the school sixth form and curriculum, giving those loyal O.B.s yet another reason to press for victory, though the price in lives was rising with each issue of *The Bancroftian*.

As the British Army prepared itself for the bloodbath known today as the Battle of the Somme, almost five hundred O.B.s were amongst their number, including J. H. Thorpe who, despite his age, joined the army in 1916, and O. H. Corble 'found an opportunity of rendering more direct service to the cause of war. Anticipating his destiny for the next year or two, he walked into P. J. Bennett's office one day and dumped a kit bag at his feet containing all the appurtenances of the office of Secretary to the Association, not excluding petty cash and the inevitable IOUs forming part of the same'. The Association maintained the same officers throughout the war and ceased all social and sporting activities. When Corble was commissioned in the RNVR, Bennett ran the show almost single handed.

The Mission, also, had problems during the war, at a time when its facilities were greatly needed. Several of its keenest helpers had gone to war and its activities were necessarily curtailed. Though the club house survived damage, Limehouse was near the scene of the horrifying Silvertown munitions explosion in 1917. The explosion was heard at Woodford, during evening prep. on a still Summer's evening: 'Suddenly the hall door rattled and the curtains silently floated out and fell again. There was a long, uneasy pause, broken at last by a most ugly

123

roar far away. No one needed to be told it was a disaster. Prep. ended and as we were shepherded to the day room we could see a light in the sky over East London'.

The School helped the local vicar, Mr Evans, well known to them through the Mission, as much as it could. Seventy people were killed and many badly injured, left yellow by the gunpowder.

From the front, 1916 brought both a growing number of awards to O.B.s and an increase in the Roll of Honour. An interesting letter from Captain R. C. M. Keefe to Mr Littlewood talked of his 'wonderful good luck out here, as I have been through three attacks on the Somme, apart entirely from the other trench warfare, and so far I have only had a slight wound which didn't get me even to hospital'. He goes on to talk of shooting geese and partridge from the trenches. Awarded the MC, he was killed the following year. Another MC was awarded that summer to E. G. Smith who rescued a man from a burning tank in what must have been an early use of that instrument of destruction.

The Bancroftian of June 1916 mentioned fourteen deaths and the toll continued to grow throughout the year and during the desperate fighting of 1917, culminating in eighteen deaths in the October *Bancroftian*: in fact, of the 166 O.B.s who died on active service, a half fell in the last fifteen months of the war. The October issue names included the two Compton brothers, Guy who won the MM and DCM before being commissioned into the Royal Sussex Regiment, and Rex, a Lieutenant in the Essex Regiment, who fell on 12th August, a fortnight after his brother – a 'clean kill' on this inglorious twelfth, a machine gun bullet passing through his head. A third brother, R. Compton, was awarded the MC and, surviving the War, died in 1985. Three of the other deaths in that issue involved men in the Royal Flying Corps, the excitement and challenge of which seems to have had a fatal lure for Bancroftians.

By now boys who had been at School when the war began were amongst the casualties and the hand of death fell most often on those who had left school between 1910 and 1917: of the eleven incumbents of the Committee Room between 1911 and 1914, five died, two lost a limb each and another was seriously wounded. Similarly, of the five day boys who gained the London Universities Intermediate Arts Examination in 1914 two were

124

killed and two seriously wounded. One loss was F. Higson the first monitor in 1912–13, who 'had been perhaps the outstanding character at school throughout his last three years there. Brilliant at games, the winner of an open scholarship at Cambridge, one of the earliest and most willing helpers of the Mission, he was a true representative of the best type of boy whom the School produced and his winning of the MC after only a short period of service had almost been expected'.

With record of deaths came also the distinctions, the commissions and the promotions, and an Old Boy finally achieved the highest military award of all, the Victoria Cross. Pte. R.E. Cruickshank had been at the school for only a short period 1903–4 but he had kept in touch with his contemporaries and the whole Bancroft's community rejoiced in his achievement. The citation in the London Gazette reads:

'For most conspicuous bravery and devotion to duty in attack. The platoon to which Private Cruikshank belonged came under very heavy rifle and machine-gun fire at short range, and was led down a steep bank into a wadi, most of the men being hit before they reached the bottom.

'Immediately after reaching the bottom of the wadi the officer in command was shot dead; and the sergeant who then took over command sent a runner back to Company Headquarters asking for support, but was mortally wounded almost immediately after; the corporal having in the meantime been killed, the only remaining NCO (a lance-corporal), believing the first messenger to have been killed, called for a volunteer to take a second message back. Private Cruickshank immediately responded and rushed up the slope, but was hit and rolled back into the wadi bottom. He again rose and rushed up the slope, but, being again wounded rolled back into the wadi. After his wounds had been dressed he rushed a third time up the slope and again fell badly wounded. Being now unable to stand he rolled himself back amid a hail of bullets.

'His wounds were now of such a nature as to preclude him making any further attempt, and he lay all day in a dangerous position, being sniped at and again wounded where he lay. He displayed the utmost valour and endurance, and was cheerful and uncomplaining throughout.'

125

He survived the war and lived in London where he was much involved in the Boy Scout movement.

Bancroftians were always meeting at the front – Miss Sheppard kept people in touch – but no meeting could have been more poignant than when Capt K. O. Peppiatt, MC, 7th London Regiment, handed over command of a section of trench to Capt L. E. Peppiatt, MC, of the same regiment. The two brothers' careers contain many remarkable coincidences: with their brother who fell in 1914, they joined up in August, were commissioned at the same time into the same regiment, wounded in the same battle and received a bar each to their MCs in the same 1919 Gazette, and both retired as Majors. After the war, L. E. became Sir Leslie, President of the Law Society, and K. O. was made Sir Kenneth when, as Chief Cashier of the Bank of England, his name appeared on bank notes. Two loyal, distinguished Bancroftians who became the most celebrated survivors of that lost generation.

As the last year of the war dragged on, the school began to feel the effect of the long years of privation. Bread, the staple diet for breakfast and tea, had been reduced to three slices a day and the scarcity of meat made day boy lunches impossible. The head boy, Newton, was called up in 1917 under the Derby Scheme and other boys acted as army messengers and special constables, much to the Head Master's concern and annoyance. Air raids by Gothas occurred throughout late 1917, with the occasional dog-fight seen from the school as our aircraft took off from Ponders End. The only damage to the school was from falling English shrapnel which could be heard falling on the dormitory roof.

The school continued in as near a normal fashion as times allowed. The Head Master took to typing and cutting stencils for the school exams while trying to run the school with an ever changing staff. Apart from those who joined the army, Messrs Littlewood and Collins retired in 1917 and Mrs Hall quit The Bryn after twenty years. The Rev A. E. Hall's resignation in 1917 brought to an end that family's long association with the school. One new member of staff, unique until 1969, was Miss A. L. Clarke, 'with pince-nez and the flowing gown, too feminine to be impressive and much at her ease, soon known to everyone as "Laura". She was a very successful teacher. There was competition for her tea parties and when she left, soon after the war, the monitors called on her, perhaps too formally, to make their adieux. "Laura" struggled to find words, but failed, and bursting into tears, ran to the library and locked herself in. It was a sad day.' The impression on Miss Clarke was clearly a strong one for, some sixty years later the school received a bequest of £1,000 to mark the courtesy she had received from Bancroft's and its boys, an award which perhaps says more about, and for, the school than all the medals and baubles of the State awarded to its Old Boys.

The OTC continued under Mr Byrne, a new appointment, who confused the boys no end by issuing cavalry-style manoeuvres. A man with many stories, he hinted at a romantic, aristocratic Irish origin and the school no doubt lost a character when he left in 1920.

To the usual list of schoolboy diseases, 1918 added a most terrible one, influenza. The epidemic, of which Spanish 'flu was the worst form, swept through the peoples of Europe exhausted by war and weakened by malnutrition. Amongst the millions killed on the eve of victory – or defeat – was Donald McKichan, one of the founders of the Old Bancroftian Association and secretary-cum-treasurer in its early years. The school was twice affected and the boarders were sent home in early November 1918 when half their number was incapacitated. Consequently, it was mostly day boys who gathered in Great Hall on 11th November to be informed that an armistice had been signed. A half holiday was granted and rockets fired from Woodford Police Station.

There was national rejoicing, the King appeared on the balcony of Buckingham Palace and bonfires were lit, but the occasion did not have the jingoist spirit of Mafeking night or even of the triumphant relief of VE Day, twenty-seven years later. Everyone was just thankful that the slaughter was over. War was no longer glorious, it was dirty and degrading and no one group was more glad of peace than the boys at school in their late teens. Curiously, the letters in *The Bancroftian* from the men at the front remained cheerful and one suspects that all the horrors of trench warfare seem worse to us, witnessing them from afar, than they did to those who fought and lived in them. The organisational might of the belligerent nations assured that the men they sent to the slaughter were better fed and clothed and received better medical treatment than in previous wars; it could be argued that a soldier of Haig was undoubtedly better treated than one of Wellington or Marlborough. What distinguishes the sieges – for that is what they were – of the Great War is the vast number of men involved, more than in all the previous wars combined, fought with great bouts of intensity, again made possible by the efficiency of the great wheels of bureaucracy. It was the realisation of that fact that made the survivors determined that the war must never be repeated.

The final toll of Bancroftians was not known for some time – indeed the Roll of Honour in the South cloister remained incomplete until 1983 – and the names of dead O.B.s continued to become known. A letter from Mr Beeching described how he had lost two sons, one fighting, the other as a prisoner-of-war. 'As a prisoner-of-war he was brutally starved and died of heart failure on September 12th 1918. With a refinement of cruelty that only demons could be guilty of, he was only allowed to send two or three cards and only one letter all with false addresses purporting to come from distant parts of Germany whereas he was compelled to work immediately behind the German lines in France'. Stories of bravery and luck and tragedy were becoming known each week.

One Old Boy, A. J. Mantle, who at nineteen held the DFC, was with the British Force in South Russia and spent a brief period as a prisoner of the new Bolshevik regime. O.B.s had served in all theatres of war and the final Roll of Honour was a grim tribute to the years of slaughter.

The bare statistics, as far as known, run as follows: 834 Old Boys enlisted in the armed forces, equal to two-and-a-half times the school's entire population in those days. Of those, 166 plus three former masters made the final sacrifice. As one would expect, they were of all ranks, of all types of men and one in fourteen of those serving received a major decoration from the King. The VC has been mentioned, there were also six DSOs, two DSCs – one with two bars – no less than 34 MCs – three with bars – a DFC, three DCMs and 14 MMs. 27 O.B.s were mentioned in dispatches and numerous foreign orders and medals were awarded. G. A. Powell received honours from the Kings of Italy and the Belgians and a CBE from his own sovereign for his work for refugees at Earls Court, though no doubt the long petition of thanks with numerous small gifts, from the refugees themselves meant as much to him. It was a record of which the school could be proud and plans to make a commemoration had been under way since 1917.

The War Memorial Committee drew its members from every interested party: the staff, the governors, the OBA, parents and the head boy. Suggestions were made to increase the size of the Chapel to hold the entire school but the great cost precluded this. Instead, Sir Reginald Blomfield, Sir Arthur's nephew, was commissioned to design a memorial for the centre of the quad. The governors rejected a plan to fill in one of the arches between the quad. and the Chapel assy with a tablet giving the names of the fallen. Instead it went on the wall of the South cloister near to the entrance of the then Great Hall.

The names appear in chronological order of death with no distinctions of rank or honour, although the last three names are later additions and one is not an Old Boy at all, but the brother of one.

The memorial was unveiled in 1920 by HRH the Duke of York KG, Citizen and Draper, who later became King George VI. It was the second time that a member of the royal family had visited Bancroft's and curiously both princes were second in line to the throne. That day was a fine one, the prince was greeted by the Master of the Drapers' Company and the Head Master, and following a speech in which he praised both the Company and the exemplary war service of the school, His Royal Highness unveiled the union flag-draped memorial. The custom has since arisen that no civilian hat has been worn in the quad. as a mark of respect to the glorious dead.

The final peace was declared by Royal Proclamation in June 1919 and an unprecedented week long holiday was granted. The OTC was on duty in Constitution Hill for the victory parade and the school resumed its activities without a threat of bombs or the constant worry of a brother or a father at the front. The O.B. Committee also resumed normal activities, the football club resuming in early 1919 and on 23rd May at Anderton's Hotel the Victory Supper was held. Old Bancroftians are not known for their aversity to a good dinner with choice wines and it is doubtful if there has ever been a dull O.B. Dinner, but the feasts held in 1919 and 1945 were something apart.

For the 1919 Dinner *The Bancroftian* reports that long after the tables had been cleared and the chairs stacked noisily thereon by impatient waiters, the floor space was patterned with kaleido-

129

scopic groups of men who for four years or more had been making history in all parts of the world. One hundred and forty O.B.s attended, including the 'veterans' of the Association – MacMinn, Bennett, Corble G. G. and O. H., Powell, Saunders H. S. and W. J., the Head Master, the Revs J. Hall and W. C. Winterton – but it was more an occasion for the young O.B.s who had survived: L. E. Peppiatt, Evans, a colonel at twenty-seven, and Middleton, a hero of the new RAF. The speeches – there were a dozen – were amusing and light-hearted as the occasion demanded – but the serious undertone was there. 'When we separated at long last with "Auld Lang Syne" and "Carmen" drumming through our heads, there was a smile on our lips and hope in our eyes. But I fancy the thoughts of most of us returned more than once to that solemn moment when, with glasses raised and hushed voices, we stood communing with our noble dead.'

Cricket Group 1913

Your forthright stare is corporate and sane
from eyes that sifted not our chancy stars
to hope one summer might bé given again,
one golden morning at the decent wars,
one last, long night to tell them. For the years
have turned to fantasy your heart – whole then;
and we, to credence grown such mutineers,
mistrust that quiet in the glance of men.
So I, who passed you daily on your wall
your corporate stare, from what far hope derived,
Of what unearthly age memorial? –
How should I know that you were men who lived,
till someone, pointing, 'you and you' he said,
'and you and you and you and you are dead.'

D. C. R. Francombe

ANNUAL GENERAL MEETING,

MONDAY, JANUARY 31st, 1916.

The President, G. G. CORBLE, Esq., in the Chair.

AGENDA.

1. Read Minutes of the last Annual Meeting.

2. Submit Report of the Committee and Balance Sheet for the year 1915.

3. Mr. J. S. GODDARD will move:—

   " That, in view of the continuance of the War, the resolutions passed at the Annual Meeting, held on the 29th January, 1915, for the suspension of parts of Rules 4 and 5, respecting the re-election of Officers, be extended to apply to the year 1916, and that accordingly the existing President, Vice-Presidents, Secretary and Treasurer, Auditors and Committee, be respectively re-elected for the year ending 31st December, 1916."

4. Mr. D. McKICHAN will move:—

   " That, in view of the continuance of the War, the holding of the Annual Dinner for the year 1916, should be postponed *sine die*, and that so much of Rule 15 as directs a Dinner to be held annually, be altered by suspending the same accordingly."

5. Mr. R. S. McMINN will move:—

   " That, as under present circumstances, it is unnecessary that meetings of the Committee should be held frequently, so much of Rule 6 as directs that such meetings shall be held at least once a quarter, be altered by suspending the same during the continuance of the War."

6. Any other business.

Agenda for O.B.A. A.G.M., 1916

DEAR SIR,

All Bancroftians will desire that there should be a worthy memorial of the sons of the School who have fallen in the War.   There are already over 90 names on our Roll of Honour, and no doubt others will have to be added before War is over.

The matter has just been discussed by the Staff of the School, and by the O.B. Association.   It was generally agreed that there should ·be some memorial in the chapel; but, as only a small proportion of the boys are able to attend the chapel, it was considered desirable that there should also be a memorial, evident to all, which should be a source of inspiration to future generations of Bancroftians.

It is not proposed at the present time to decide the form of these memorials.   This will need careful consideration in the future, when the available funds are known.   Meanwhile it is important that we should make preparations now and issue an appeal for funds.   For this purpose a committee has been formed of representatives of the School and the O.B. Association.   The Court of Assistants to the Drapers' Company has expressed approval, and wishes to be associated with this appeal. It is hoped that a sufficiently large sum may be obtained to make it possible to erect memorials worthy of the School and of those whom we desire to honour,

The Committee therefore asks you for your generous support.   Subscriptions should be sent as early as possible to the Rev. W. C. WINTERTON, Bancroft's School, who has consented to act as treasurer.   Lists of subscriptions received will be published in " The Bancroftian."

F. C. LOVEDAY,
E. B. GARDNER,
J. S. GODDARD,
W. C. WINTERTON,
H. C. PLAYNE *(Chairman).*

Letter concerning war memorial

BANCROFT'S SCHOOL.

Unveiling of War Memorial

by H.R.H. the Duke of York,
Saturday, May 28th, 1921.

The following hymn will be sung immediately after Prayer by the Bishop of Colchester :—

O valiant Hearts, who to your glory came
Through dust of conflict and through battle-flame;
   Tranquil you lie, your knightly virtue proved,
Your memory hallowed in the land you loved.

Proudly you gathered, rank on rank to war,
As who had heard God's message from afar;
All you had hoped for, all you had, you gave
To save Mankind—yourselves you scorned to save.

Splendid you passed, the great surrender made,
Into the light that nevermore shall fade;
Deep your contentment in that blest abode,
Who wait the last clear trumpet-call of God.

O risen Lord, O Shepherd of our Dead,
Whose Cross has bought them and whose Staff has led—
In glorious hope their proud and sorrowing Land
Commits her Children to Thy gracious hand.

Buglers will then sound the Last Post and The Reveille.

You are requested to remain in your place until H.R.H. The Duke of York has left the quadrangle.

The band and buglers are present by kind permission of Lieut.-Col. C. E. Johnston, D.S.O., M.C., and Officers of the 7th Battalion, The London Regiment.

Programme for unveiling of war memorial

133

CHAPTER X

HERBERT CLEMENT PLAYNE
1919-1931

THE WAR had done little to change the fabric of Bancroft's. Her buildings, just beginning to mellow, were sufficiently unkempt to befit her pseudo-gentility, and pre-war 'standards' were soon resumed. Matron received £150 a year, nurse £90 and the dozen maids ranged from £36 to £22, all found, the daily women receiving £1 per week worked. George received 25s a week plus his cottage, as did the aptly named Flood, the engineer, though they were increased by £1 in 1921. That year Bateman the groundsman received 30s a week and Wilson the bootboy and Porter the hat boy 15s each. On a slightly different level, those masters with degrees received £315 when newly qualified, rising to a maximum of £500, the chaplain receiving an extra £50, while the Head Master received £1,000 a year. The fees were £7 a term for day boys and £15 for paying boarders, with £2 a term for day boy lunches. The whole teaching staff of nineteen cost £7,493.

Mr Playne had aged over the period; photographs show his beard white and the sparkle in his eyes dimmed, though not his aspirations for the School. The post-war world wanted change, a better life for those who had survived the mud of France, and the scene was set for great social change during the coming decade with the emphasis on building houses and hospitals and creating a brighter, cleaner country. A new Education Act was passed in 1918, piloted through by H. A. L. Fisher. Its great aim of part-time education for all until eighteen was never realised, though it encouraged the building of secondary schools and created a new entity, the Direct Grant School.

The schools which entered this scheme tended to be typified by Bancroft's: small, old schools able to maintain their independence through an endowment or an ability to attract a large number of fee-paying pupils or a combination of the two. The Drapers' Company had refused a government grant in 1914 as it would have meant becoming a 'maintained' school – this new scheme however, promised complete independence though with local government nominees on the board of governors. As long as the Governors admitted one quarter of its boys to free places the government would give a per capita grant for each boy taught, thus subsidising fee payers.

The scheme seemed ideally suited to Bancroft's: a quarter of the boys were already receiving free education on the Foundation, and the grant – £2,203 in the first year – made up the deficit in the school's accounts, allowing a repairs fund to be established. The Governors took the government at their word about remaining wholly independent, though interference from the Board (later Ministry) of Education was to grow over the fifty-odd years of the scheme's duration.

The most important legal result of the decision – sealed in 1920 – was that Bancroft's became an independent school, no longer controlled by a committee of the Drapers' Company. It was a cosmetic change only: Mr G. W. Williams, long the chairman of the committee, became first Chairman of Governors, the other Drapers being Canon Dalton, sometime tutor to the King, Sir William Ellison-Macartney, Mr George Gardner, Mr Ernest Pooley, the Clerk of the Company, and Mr E. de Q. Quincey, Master for the year. The Drapers' Company were to appoint five governors, the Court making three-yearly appointments, and the Master was to sit ex-officio during his year. These six Drapers were joined by two Essex Council nominees, the Rev G. M. Bell and Mr Samuel Cutforth who had family connections with the School, and the LCC appointed one governor, Canon Swallow. Mr T. W. Kirk, an official at Drapers' Hall, was made Clerk to the Governors. The Company thus retained control of the School assuming its nominees voted en bloc.

The Company remained Trustees, administering the properties and investments as well as the law admitted, transferring the annual income to the School account which now operated as a separate entity at Throgmorton Street with its own account at Messrs. Glyn Mills, the Company's bankers. The Clerk to the Governors received all fees and paid all but the most minor bills, a system which survived until 1974. The rest of the scheme, with certain alterations, remains in force.

The new scheme did not have any apparent great effect on Bancroft's, though it is not known what the result of higher fees would have been: the demand for day boy places grew and the LCC candidates continued to provide three or four excellent scholars each year; Mr Playne, however, rued the day that he had surrendered the right to examine scholars himself. The LCC occasionally put forward a boy on non-academic grounds which Mr Playne rightly regarded as cheating the system. As the LCC became more political so the situation grew worse, and had all but collapsed by 1964 when the new Inner London Education Authority severed relations with Mr Bancroft's charity. In 1920 the other changes forced by the Board of Education were the raising of the joining age from eight to ten and the abolition of compulsory chapel. The former allowed the Head Master to increase the size of the middle school and the numbers rose from 342 in 1919 to 381 by 1923, at which approximate figure it remained until 1945.

To find new classrooms the open covered assy in the south-west corner of the school was bricked in, partly in 1922 and completely in 1925, creating two classrooms and a changing room. Part of the Great Hall was also used for teaching by Mr V. W. Richards, where his anvil made a permanent mark on the flooring, while he made a permanent mark on his pupils in a different sense.

Vyvyan Richards was probably the most influential and memorable master of this period. Although his stay was comparatively short by Bancroftian standards – 1909–22 with a two-year break at the war – he had a lasting effect on many pupils and achieved fine results in his teaching of history with a series of scholarships to Oxford. An individual in many senses, he followed the Vitalist philosophy of Bergson and was the first master to attempt to encourage a love of art amongst those pupils whom he took under his wing. He founded the Arts Club to which admission was by invitation and where he allowed and encouraged complete freedom of expression of a variety of subjects, something which spread to his classes where he nominally taught English and History but where a discussion on the latest paper of the British Association or a piano recital might well fill the forty-minutes. Mr Playne's attitude to this remains unknown, but may have had something to do with Richards' very early retirement in 1922.

The anvil in Great Hall was used to make a new press with which he planned to print a facsimile of a Gutenberg Bible. He enjoyed the acquaintance of several literary figures but by far his greatest friend was T. E. Lawrence – of Arabia – who had been his contemporary at Jesus College, Oxford. The two of them owned a hut on Pole Hill near Chingford, on the site of the old gun battery. It is said that when the local authority objected to a permanent hut Richards and Lawrence painted wheels at each corner, an acceptable compromise in less humourless days.

Invited sixth formers went to Pole Hill to help build a cloister, a bath and a miniature railway and there, and at The Pioneers' camps in Knighton Wood, T. E. Lawrence would often join them for supper. He is remembered as a quiet, remote figure wearing a mackintosh and bowler hat; the *Seven Pillars of Wisdom*, be it the autobiography of a great hero or of a monumental fraud, was written partly at the hut.

The Pioneers were a typically Richards sort of body, combining scouting and OTC skills with acting and serious singing. New members had to make their own metal badges of an axe and a flaming torch, and a uniform of shorts and jacket was worn. Virtually its last activity was a 'Masque of Heaven and Hell' delivered in Knighton Wood to a dinner-jacketed Head Master and Col Buxton, the owner, with their wives and guests. What they made of the occasion goes unrecorded but it was a typical finale for an individual who brought great stimulation to the sixth form of those days, and his retirement to Pole Hill, to write and think, was a great loss to the school. The Library still has his early private edition of T. E. Lawrence's great work, and a presentation copy of his biography of Lawrence.

Mr Richards brought a civilizing influence to the boarding house where the life style had hardly changed since 1802. Not that Bancroft's was different from other schools at the time, except that most of the boys were first generation boarders whose parents did not understand the tuck box system, whereby they were expected to supplement the basic school diet.

The School provided an adequate midday meal which seldom varied and the nicknames for dishes are part of the school lore:

Sunday:	cold roast beef; boiled potatoes; fruit pie ('fly pie')
Monday:	roast beef; rice pudding ('maggots')
Tuesday:	roast mutton; plum duff ('appendicitis')
Wednesday:	boiled beef; bread pudding ('resurrection')
Thursday:	roast beef; jam tart ('stiff dick')
Friday:	boiled fish; treacle pudding ('putty and varnish')
Saturday:	stew; bread and cheese ('Caesar's gravestones')

There are variations on the nicknames, showing that the

imagination of little boys does not change much. Memories differ as to the quality of the food but all are agreed it was pretty simple fare. For breakfast and tea there was simply tea or cocoa ('slosh') and bread and margarine ('busters') though boys could provide their own eggs – they were boiled in the tea – and by custom the top was offered to a less fortunate friend. Similarly, a pot of jam would invariably be finished off in an evening as friends appreciated the luck of the recipient. With their meagre pocket money – 6d a week – certain luxuries could be bought from Mrs Haines in the tuckshop, or a friendly day boy might be induced to go up to the baker's near the Horse and Well to buy a bag of buns for a penny. Apart from these delicacies the boarders had but the one meat meal a day.

An interesting post-script to the war was when the school won a German aeroplane in an essay competition, the subject being the London Aircraft Exhibition in aid of the Air Force Hospitals. The school was never told of the success, but several boxes of 'theatrical scenery' arrived at Loughton Station in September 1918. The boys assembled the craft – a Fokker D7 – in the quad; it was eventually broken up as the cost of maintaining its fragile frame became too great.

Outside school hours the boarders' lives were controlled by a series of regulations designed to occupy their every waking hour. There was morning prep. in Great Hall – cold and gloomy – followed by Chapel, and evening prep. after tea when only academic work was allowed, so boys with no prep. to do had to sit and do nothing rather than read a novel. Mr Lucas, the tall, bearded housemaster, enforced these regulations through the four boarding masters, one of whom was always on duty, and the monitors, the three or four senior boys who ruled their peers from the Committee Room, so called from its use by the Bancroft's Committee for meetings at the school. There was bullying, without doubt, especially the barbarous 'dab day' when miscreants had to crawl beneath the legs of a line of senior boys who hit out at them with canes and towels, and occasionally a 'kid' would take on a senior boy in the fives courts and, even more rarely, succeed in thrashing him. By and large, however, the monitors were a reasonable group who controlled the worst excesses of senior boys on juniors.

In the first year of peace A. Hudson-Davies was head monitor, assisted by P. M. J. Mantle, known irreverently as 'Mutt and

138

Jeff'. Mantle, though short in stature, was a giant in every sphere of school life, with Hudson-Davies running him a close second. They dominated the soccer, cricket and athletics teams, vied with each other in the Literary and Debating Society, to which a Dramatic section was added in their time, and each went on to win a scholarship, Mantle going up to St John's, Oxford, to read history, ending a distinguished civil service career as Head of the Companies Department at the Board of Trade, being appointed CMG, while Hudson-Davies progressed from King's College, Cambridge to a distinguished career in industry, culminating in the accolade of knighthood shortly before his death in 1975. Lady Hudson-Davies was the daughter of the celebrated Russian bass, Feodor Chaliapin.

The majority of boarders outside prep. hours spent their time in the large Day Room, with one section partly partitioned off for senior boys. There were no comfortable chairs, no toys or games for inquisitive young minds and no privacy, perhaps the worst deprivation of all. Excepting the seniors' 'bunkers' with their wooden partitions, the boys slept in the long dormitory which survived until the 1970s. The beds were comfortable and the linen changed regularly though there was only one hot bath a week, otherwise the boys washed in cold water. The lavatories, regrettably placed behind the kitchens, were not ideal in any sense and were probably responsible for the large rat population of those days. In short, the conditions of life were grim and remind one of Evelyn Waugh's comment that the Public School boy always felt at home in prison.

It is the aim of this book always to judge the various phrases of Bancroft's by the standards of its time and school life then was not lightened by the gimmicks and machines known to modern pupils, nor were schoolmasters trained for their profession, except by taking a university degree. Yet the pupils of those days, with some exceptions, acquired an affection for the School in no way diminished by the hardships they endured, and it has been suggested by a master of that time that those very hardships instilled a loyalty and a comradeship which may not be as strong amongst those who have enjoyed a less rigorous schooling.

To show that there could occasionally be some amusement in the dormitory there was the tradition of the 'school ghost'. Its origins are lost in the mists of antiquity and may go back to Mile End, and the name of the hapless pupil who supposedly died –

some dozen pupils have died whilst at Woodford – is unknown but his spirit walked the dormitory on a November evening near to the feast of All Saints. Boys from the bunkers dressed in white sheets and walked along the top dormitory, a frightening sight for new boys. Stories abound about this annual event: of the short-sighted master seizing a mop, thinking it a pupil; of the two ghosts walking together discussing the day's football; and of a young master chasing a 'ghost' the full length of the dormitory. A harmless occasion of fun, now assigned to history.

The mode of school life hardly changed at all during this period, though in the masters' common room there were several retirements, their replacements showing the wisdom of Mr Playne's judgement, for several were to remain at Bancroft's for their entire working career.

The first post-war retirement was of Herr Brinkmann in 1920. He had taught French and German since 1889, when the paintwork at Woodford was hardly dry. A native of Hanover, the war period had been very difficult for him, though it says much for the tolerance of local people that he continued to live unhindered in Woodford Green during a period of xenophobic madness. He was too much part of the School and it, in its turn, was too respected a part of the community for people to question him. Equally, Old Boys returning from the front never treated him as an 'enemy' for he had been too popular in class for a mere war to destroy old affection. And affection there certainly was; he was not a natural disciplinarian and yet the amount of ragging in his forms was minimal.

He never lost his German accent and generations of Bancroftians learned French with a distinct guttural emphasis, causing them to laugh on hearing that language spoken by a Belgian refugee, Mr Brinkmann seeing the joke better than they. His retirement was announced suddenly on Vis. Day 1920, for, characteristically, this short, bespectacled man planned a quiet, dignified exit. It was not to be: the boys bought him a clock and a chair and the cheering on his last attendance at Great Hall was deafening. The Old Boys, most of whom had been taught by him, also made a presentation at the Annual Dinner in February 1921 when he was guest of honour. Coining one of his own dicta, he said, 'Paragraph 125 says the subject and verb must agree. For once they seem to be doing so'. He lived in Woodford until his death in 1930 and regularly attended school and O.B. functions.

A greater wrench with the past came with the Rev W. C. Winterton's retirement in 1926 after forty-three years, a period equal to Mr Barrett's in the eighteenth century and most unlikely ever to be equalled again. Surviving O.B.s from the twenties remember him as a typical school padre, slightly remote and dogmatic in his approach to theology; but such was not the memory of McMinn and his contemporaries who recalled the young athletic man who taught at Mile End during its last days and who breathed life into Tottenham and Woodford. There were memories of him and 'B. D.' Hall singing duets in their sitting room; of his playing in the school XI (his black and blue shirt was copied for the School's colours) and of his help in forming the O.B. A. in 1910 of which he was President in 1913. Mr Francombe is the only other assistant master to have been President. Mr Winterton continued to live in Woodford until his death in 1947 and his son, a pupil at the school, was to be Master of the Drapers' Company in 1965.

The post-war period saw Mr Playne consolidating the good work of pre-war years, increasing the size of the school and, especially, the sixth form. Mantle and Hudson-Davies have been mentioned and Norman Suckling also went to Oxford in 1922 and then eventually to Newcastle College – now the university – where he combined a distinguished academic career with a devotion to music, having his compositions played by the BBC and writing a critical biography of Gabriel Fauré. At Cambridge, M. M. Simmons won the Chancellor's Prize for English verse in 1922 and Sydney Gooding, who devoted so much of his long life to matters Bancroftian, studied mathematics as a scholar of Trinity. On the science side the careful teaching of Mr Peet, aided by Mr Beesley after 1925, was sowing numerous seeds of later scientific distinction. A. H. Mumford journeyed to Mile End to the new East London College and ended his career as Sir Albert Mumford and chief engineer of the GPO; F. E. King also commenced an academic career there which culminated in his becoming Professor of Chemistry at Nottingham and our first FRS in 1954, an honour later attained by Sir Frederick Warner in 1976 and John Dewey in 1985.

F. E. Warner was the outstanding pupil of Mr Playne's latter years, according to surviving masters and contemporaries. A fine sportsman who helped ease the advent of rugby football, he espoused left-wing views in school debates. While at UCL he

141

became President of the Union and later combined a successful professional and academic career as a chemical engineer, never forgetting what he owed the school and the O.B.A. for helping him start his career. He remains an active O.B. One of Sir Frederick's school activities was to lead a band which played at school dances held in Great Hall on Saturday afternoons. Such extra-curricular activities grew during the twenties and helped break down the traditional barriers between day boys and boarders. The growth was encouraged by the various young masters appointed by Mr Playne who genuinely wished to broaden the education received, a fact noted by the school Inspection of 1925.

A choral society under Mr Pole, a gifted musician, performed at concerts, and a chapel choir was run successively by Messrs Raven, Booth, Walker and Francombe. Since 1923 there has been an annual school play, produced in those early years by Mr Wheeller, whose West Country accent guided young thespians through the plays of Sheridan and Shakespeare on a makeshift stage in the old Great Hall. He also did much to improve the comfort of the school library, expanding both the number and scope of its volumes.

The play regrettably destroyed the old school concert, a feature of the end of Autumn term since the 'nineties, and the removal of the Lord Mayor's holiday in 1923 robbed the boys of another chance to make hay. There remained, however, the Mission concert, where the 'Co-Pessimists' and Drury's 'Rhythm Boys' (sic.) showed the growing influence of popular music amongst the boys. There was a gramophone and an early crystal set in the senior part of the day room though John Farmer claims to have been the first enthusiast to build his own wireless inside an old cigar box, allowing him to listen undetected in bed to the broadcasts from Savoy Hill. Mr Richards had taken part in early broadcasting experiments.

Perhaps the most energetic new master of this time was Mr C. J. Beesley, still as energetic as ever and a regular attender of dinners. He founded the photographic society in 1926 in the small room at the top of the southwest stairs. An early programme includes:-

'Flashlight photography'   V. O. Cohen
'Dark room dodges'   Mr C. J. Beesley

| 'Making Natural Colour Slides' | F. E. Warner |
| 'After treatment of Negatives' | D. E. Coult |

It merged with the Scientific Society in 1931, and to-day is a flourishing society in its own right.

A keen athlete, Mr Beesley eventually took over athletics when Mr Ridley left in 1933, but before that aided Mr Adams-Clarke to introduce rugby to the school. The reason for the change in 1925 remains obscure, the debate being started with a letter to *The Bancroftian*. It may have been the wish to emphasise Bancroft's public school stature, though neither Chigwell nor Forest felt such a need. It was probably that the younger masters were rugby players themselves and encouraged Mr Playne to make the change. After much discussion the O.B. football club who had enjoyed tremendous success in the twenties, agreed to follow suit in 1931, encouraged by A. C. Newman and other O.B.s who played rugby for other clubs.

Games were not compulsory in Mr Playne's time though there was a growing encouragement by the staff. A new pavilion was built in 1929 aided by a £2,000 interest free loan from the Drapers' Company. A second pitch was added on the school field, financed by tuck shop profits, and Riggs Retreat was used, but Monkhams was considered too small and, with an eye to its development potential, the governors began looking for a new ground. Col. Buxton, always a good neighbour, offered part of the Buckhurst estate at a reasonable price but the governors reluctantly declined as the ground was too hilly. The Buxtons knew that the days of their estate were numbered. Knighton Wood was preserved, the rest disappeared beneath brick and mortar.

The governors finally purchased the Ray Lodge Fields of eleven acres known to Bancroftians ever since as West Grove, from the road alongside the original entrance which was moved in 1974. The cost was £5,280, the inevitable Drapers' Company grant paying for its conversion to five playing fields. Monkhams was sold for £5,500.

One feature of the old ground was the series of curious subterranean tunnels and chambers down which young boys were led to a pre-arranged ambush, to be initiated into the ancient mysteries of the circular rooms. The rooms were probably old boiler rooms of the Monkhams estate.

143

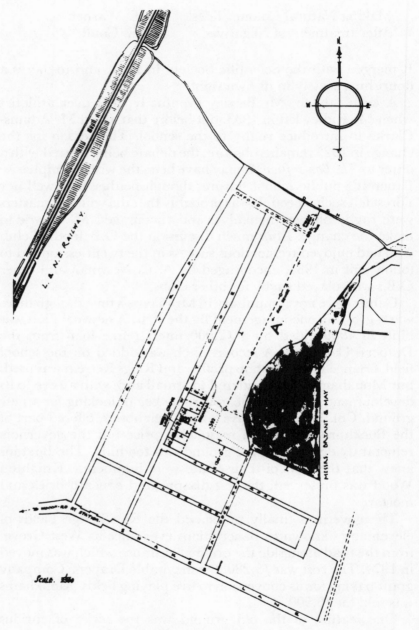

Plan of West Grove

144

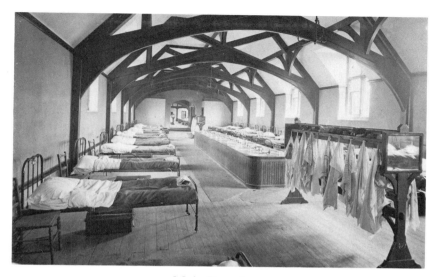

Main Dormitory

German Aircraft, won in an essay prize, *c*.1920

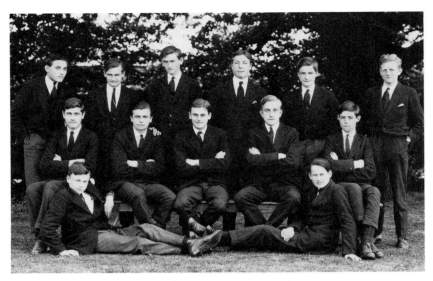

The School Monitors, 1923

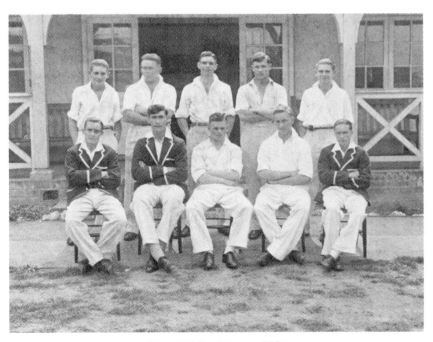

The Cricket Eleven, 1935

Mr Frederick Monro,
Chairman of Governors 1935–50 and 1953–54

Mr Thomas Wells, Head Master 1931–43

Bancroft's School Sea Scouts, with Mr Blyth, *c.*1925

The New Library, 1938

New Great Hall, 1938

Annual Dinner of the Old Bancroftians' Association, Drapers' Hall, 1937

School Staff, 1941

An Old Boys' dinner, Singapore, 1947

Mr and Mrs Winston S. Churchill with Mr Monro and The Master of the
Drapers' Company in the Quadrangle, 1945

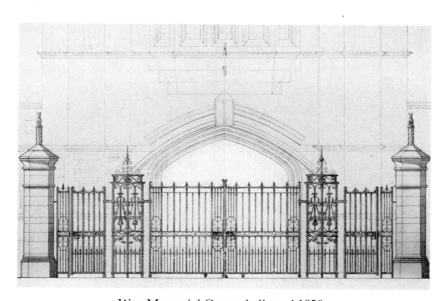

War Memorial Gates, dedicated 1950

The governors continued to oversee the school, ever attempting to improve its standards. To encourage day boys to take higher school certificate, scholarships were awarded at sixteen rather than the previous fourteen and parents were obliged to agree to keep their sons at the school until sixteen, with a £5 penalty for those who broke the agreement. The governors enforced this fine to the point of court action.

Arrangements with local authorities were mixed. Essex scholars were examined by the Head Master and proved adequate to competing with the LCC boys. The LCC itself was proving dilatory in filling its assigned places, which both concerned and annoyed the Governors. At the same time the school declined to take East Ham boys at fourteen, on the grounds that they did not wish the school to become what now would be called a sixth form college.

The financial crisis before the Great War had shifted the burden of clothing boarders from the foundation to the parents. The 'bum freezer' and Eton collar gave way to soft collars and a proper jacket during this period. Clearly some parents, especially widows from the war, needed help to clothe boys, and Mr Pooley the Company's Clerk, made eleemosynary grants to help with the entire costs. Equally, the governors waived fees when a fee paying boy lost his father during his school days.

Bancroft's owes a great deal to Mr Pooley who later received the GCVO and a baronetcy and became Master of the Company in 1944. The Company had always given scholarships to university boys from a fund set up in 1887 but now, with the cost of higher education rising, and more people seeking help, the Clerk arranged for Bancroftians to apply to other Company-controlled charities, most notably Sir Henry Dixon's Trust. This was enhanced in 1925 by the foundation of the Old Bancroftians Exhibition and Loan Fund. The brainchild of the President that year, H. L. (later Sir Harold) Saunders, the aim of the fund was to help young O.B.s at university or while in articles for a professional qualification. In the first year £1,303 was raised, including £250 from the Drapers' Company, with annual standing orders of £62 15s 0d. The Association also agreed to make an annual grant. The capital was invested and the income therefrom with the annual subscriptions – soon reaching £170 a year – was awarded to deserving O.B.s and among the present Fund Committee are several who freely admit the help given them in early days by the fund. It exemplified more than anything also the great co-operation between School, Governors, Drapers and O.B.s.

That other great object of O.B. philanthropy, the Bancroft Mission, continued to develop though the path was not an easy one. The cadet emphasis was dropped in 1920 in favour of a 'ragged boys' club and soon there were classes on four nights a week, with a youth section. H. W. Algar was the great driving force in the early post-war years and the summer camp attracted 50 boys in 1920, with a local man, Mr J. J. Chadwick, helping out and later becoming manager of the club.

In 1923 when Rev E. F. Evans retired, the new vicar made it clear that the Mission was no longer welcome at St Matthew's, so it moved to Ship Road, West Ham, abandoning the Bancroft Hall which Association money had built. Determined that such a setback would not destroy the spirit behind the Mission, a new team of O.B.s including Self, Algar, G. G. Allen and P. M. J. Mantle set about creating a new mission in West Ham. By 1926 the club had three sections, ten to fourteen years, fourteen to sixteen and sixteen to eighteen, the last two affiliated to the National Association of Boys' Clubs. Sunday services were held and a small library established. Football and cricket flourished and the highlight of the juniors' year was an outing in a fleet of O.B. cars to the seaside. The pattern during the twenties was established by this handful of keen O.B.s and grew from strength to strength during the period immediately before the Second World War.

The social life of the OBA still centred upon the Annual Dinner held at the Holborn Restaurant, Connaught Rooms or similar venue. The Football Club held a series of dances and suppers to mark their great successes in the Old Boys' Cup during this period and built their own club house in 1925, gradually converting to a Rugby Club with the demise of soccer a handful of years later.

An O.B. dance was held annually during part of the period and a dinner took place in Calcutta in 1920, eleven O.B.s attending. The largest gathering remained Old Boys' Day, usually the last Saturday of Summer term, when a generous tea would be served by Miss Sheppard, and the President's XI met one from the School.

The O.B.s who had entered the new school at Woodford were

fast becoming middle-aged and it was only a matter of time before a knighthood was achieved, and in 1927 Sir Allan Powell, whose sterling efforts had done so much for the Association in the early days, was so honoured for his civil service work. A steady flow has continued ever since. In 1923 Colonel H. A. Evans became Liberal MP for East Leicester, changing seat and party the following year when he was returned by the burgesses of South Cardiff in the Conservative interest, holding the seat intermittently till 1945 when he was defeated by James Callaghan and was knighted that year.

An O.B. who figured prominently in *The Bancroftian* during this period was the Rev Henry Rogers, who, with his wife Rosa, sailed for Tristan da Cunha where they were the sole representatives of the Established Church, or indeed of the whole Establishment on that remote Atlantic Island, arriving in 1922. His church was sent out in wooden partitions and numerous O.B.s contributed to its cost and construction, he having captured the imagination of his old school fellows. During his three year exile he visited the neighbouring Inaccessible Island, climbed a 7,000 ft mountain, named it Bancroft's Peak and sang *Carmen Bancroftianum*. He returned to England in 1926 utterly exhausted and died during his next incumbency at Leighton Buzzard where the Toc H Lamp is dedicated to him.

The portfolio of properties held by the Drapers' Company as Trustees of Bancroft's Settlement underwent a great transformation during this period and the Company sold much of its farmland. The 96-acre Saltcoat Farm at Woodham Ferrers was sold for £2,200 in 1920, in which year the 260-acre Clopton Hall Farm at Dunmow was sold for £6,150, the Trustees remaining Lord of the Manor. The tenant at Benton End Farm, Hadleigh, Suffolk, persuaded the Trustees to give him time to raise the purchase price – a grave mistake, for the 242 acres fetched only £2,100 in 1936. Of the cottages and town property the small size of most of the sites made it wise to sell, except some of the choice City property. The Prittlewell Cottages were sold between 1899 and 1938, the Chiswick houses, originally owned by John Bancroft, were sold in 1881 for £3,000 and the small share in the Basinghall Avenue property was bought by the Drapers' Company in 1892 for £1,750. The charge on All Saints, Honey Lane, was redeemed, as were most of the Yorkshire and Lincolnshire rent charges.

147

To avoid placing all the Trust's assets in bonds certain additions were made occasionally. Poultry was extended in 1859 for £3,600 and in 1887 Godliman Street – the St Paul's Chain property – was also extended. 62 Cannon Street and 25 College Hill were purchased in 1909 and sold for a handsome profit in 1922 and, most importantly, High Holborn was extended in 1938 for £46,700, a builders' lease being given when the cost was recuperated. 271–277 High Holborn was sold in 1972 at a hugely inflated price and increased the income of the endowment. Today only a new purchase in Cornhill remains, the capital having been reinvested rather than spent on capital improvement.

As the decade drew to its close, so did the careers of several masters. In 1929, the year each master received a £15 a year salary increase, the Rev C. O. Raven retired to the living of Souldern in Oxfordshire. A great eccentric and an old-fashioned master who taught by rote, his retirement was followed by that of Mr Blyth in 1931. An Oxford boxing half blue, he flattened one Mr Stopp, a parent who attempted to assault him in 1919. A keen scout – he later bequeathed £1,000 to the troop – his bored Oxford drawl was easily imitated by the boys to whom he attempted to teach mathematics. In 1930 Mr Kislingbury died. He was a fine mathematician, a great raconteur, a bastion of Woodford Wells Cricket Club whither he retired most evenings to consume bitter beer, and he enjoyed making his subject amusing – 1½ was always 'three teeth' – 'three tooths' being a solecism. The boys respected him. Mr Francombe remembers him seemingly asleep in the MCR yet able to give the precise score of the game of billiards in progress.

That same year J. J. Chapman – called 'Jix' because of his pronunciation of the words 'Jack saw' – retired, handing over to Mr K. G. Clark, an Old Boy. A devout Christian, it was not unknown for him to fall on his knees behind his blackboard before a class began, especially if he had lost his temper, which often involved a certain amount of violence to inanimate objects near to hand.

Mr Raven had served a mere twenty-five years, the other three thirty-one years each, the same length as Mr Lucas who retired in 1932, having seen in the new Head Master. Known as Golly from his great height – short for Goliath – his presence was such that he could stare a miscreant into docility. His life was so well ordered, his behaviour so punctual, that one could check a watch by him, allowing mischief makers to time their deeds around his movements. The fondest memory people have of him is watching him ride his motorbike while sitting bolt upright, a flat cap crowning his solemn bearded face. Five masters with a hundred-and-fifty years service to the school.

To complete the departure of the old guard, Miss Sheppard retired in 1929 after 41 years service. Always very firm with the boys, even those in the sickers – 'This is Mr Playne's strict instruction' – her popularity was always stronger with the Old Boys than with pupils, and she kept up a huge correspondence with the former. Her task of running the School was difficult. Hers was a generation that obeyed instructions to the letter and never questioned authority. The economics of domestic routine laid down when the School moved to Woodford were maintained despite changing circumstance, and she attempted to keep down costs at a time of fluctuating food prices. No doubt a lady of another generation would have tried to improve standards and sought an increase in her budget. Whatever her faults no-one ever doubted her devotion to Bancroft's, the Mission and the O.B.A. of which she was a member.

All of which leads to Mr Playne's own retirement in 1931 at the age of sixty. His quarter century had seen the carnage of war which he had not allowed to interfere with his plans for Bancroft's. There were obvious red letter days: the end of the war; the visit of the Duke of York; Mrs Winston Churchill presenting prizes at Vis Day; the landing of an aeroplane on the school field; the winning by the school of a German fighter in 1919 in an essay competition.

Although a forbidding figure for young boys, Mr Playne's transparent goodness always shone through the aloofness which was a shield for his innate shyness. It is probable that he never quite came to grips with Bancroft's poor scholars and day boys whose fees were met from sometimes meagre incomes, with parents not so devoted to learning as was Mr Playne himself. He could not understand that parents of boys for whom he could guarantee scholarships at university preferred their sons to go straight to the City.

His pattern of headmastership was more that of a housemaster at a great public school. He entertained pupils at his home and allowed the boys to rule themselves, never realising how much bullying went on or that the boys' provisions were so meagre.

149

Like so many reformers before and since he failed to realise that his own changes had become outdated. Notwithstanding the above, most contemporary O.B.s remember him with much affection. His simple, earnest faith, expressed in his occasional sermons, showed the fundamental goodness of his character. Similarly, his love of mathematics, at which he excelled, was always apparent even to his least numerate pupils.

He had inherited from Mr Symns an old fashioned school and handed to his successor one with a thriving sixth form and an excellent record of university scholarship. His choice of staff invariably showed shrewd judgement, his last appointments including Messrs Clark, Francombe, Bellchamber, Stainsby and Houston, sterling men who gave their working careers for the School which Mr Playne served so well.

Members of staff drawn by N. Clark, 1927
Top L To R: Messrs Playne, Kislingbury, Chapman, Ridley;
Bottom L To R: Walker and Raven

150

BANCROFT'S SCHOOL.

DECEMBER 21st, 1927.

"The School for Scandal"

A Comedy by RICHARD BRINSLEY SHERIDAN.

Scene of the Play : London.

Characters in order of their appearance.

Lady Sneerwell	J. LYTTON TEDBURY.
Snake	LEW GREEN.
Servant	WILLIE STEVENS.
Joseph Surface	PAUL MORTON-GEORGE.
Maria	NEWMAN HOOKER.
Mrs. Candour	DOUGLAS COULT.
Crabtree	LEONARD BUSS.
Sir Benjamin Backbite	HENRY WILLIAMS.
Sir Peter Teazle	FREDERICK WARNER.
Rowley	JOCK MILLARD.
Lady Teazle	ERIC PITTMAN.
Sir Oliver Surface	ALBERT WRIGHT.
Moses	HAROLD BERMAN.
Charles Surface	HARRY BONE.
Careless	WILLIAM PIKE.
Gentlemen	JOHN GALLOWAY and
	NOEL ENOCH.

The play produced by Mr. E. T. S. WHEELLER.

Scenery by L. S. BUSS, H. B. WILLIAMS, and V. O. COHEN.

ACT I.	SCENE 1	...	A Room in Lady Sneerwell's House.
	SCENE 2	...	A Room in Sir Peter Teazle's House.
	SCENE 3	...	The same.
ACT II.	SCENE 1	...	A Room in Lady Sneerwell's House.
	SCENE 2	...	A Room in Sir Peter Teazle's House.
ACT III.	SCENE 1	...	The Picture-room in Charles Surface's House.
	SCENE 2	...	The Library of Joseph Surface's House.
ACT IV.	SCENE 1	...	The same.
	SCENE 2	...	A Room in Sir Peter Teazle's House.
	SCENE 3	...	The Library of Joseph Surface's House.

Carman Bancroftianum.

Floreat Bancroftia !
Floreamus pueri !
Vivat et memoria,
Fundatoris nostri !

Adsit amor patriae,
Adsit et parentum;
Amor sit scientiae;
Vitae ornamentum.

CHORUS— Nobis in aeternum
Magni sint honores.
Floreat Bancroftia !
Floreant rectores !

God Save the King.

School play, 1927

151

CHAPTER XI

THOMAS GRANTHAM WELLS
1931–1943

THOMAS GRANTHAM WELLS was undoubtedly the most complex character ever to have occupied the Head Master's house. Like his predecessor he was a remote person, but it was a contrived remoteness, not so much to hide his shyness as to establish what he thought a Head Master's stance should be. This meant that he was never approachable to even his closest colleagues – closeness being a relative term – and ultimately it was to lead to personal disaster.

Mr Wells came to Bancroft's aged twenty-eight from Cheltenham College where he had been a housemaster. He had read Greats at St John's College, Oxford whither he had gone as a scholar from Newbury Grammar School. It was Cheltenham, rather than Newbury, that he took as his model for the new Bancroft's and he knew precisely what reforms he wanted to carry through.

Within a year he had made uniforms compulsory for all day boys, and sports for the whole school. Parents complained about both, as well as a new emphasis on the classics, saying that he was attempting to change the whole character of the School, and a sub-committee of the Governors met their representatives, an unprecedented move. The Governors stood by their man, assuring the parents that Latin and Greek would not overwhelm the syllabus. Mr Wells' only defeat was on an attempt to change the title of Visitation Day to Speech Day; O.B.s rose in revolt and, having the ear of Mr Williams, the Chairman of Governors, made their views known. A compromise made the last Thursday of the Summer term 'Speech Day and Annual Visitation of the Drapers' Company' but everyone, including *The Bancroftian*, continued to say Visitation Day, and Mr Wells eventually surrendered to forces too great even for him to tackle.

His aim, and, one suspects, the aspiration of the Drapers' Company, was for Bancroft's to join the other livery company schools such as Merchant Taylors', Oundle and Tonbridge in becoming a fully-fledged public school, that is, with Mr Wells a

152

member of the Headmasters' Conference. Mr Symns had attended Headmasters' conferences when that body was less demanding on certain features of individual schools' attainments, but Mr Playne had not been elected because of the lack of a sixth form when he became Head Master. It has been said by the late Sydney Gooding, doyen of Bancroftian antiquaries and close to Mr Playne through their shared devotion to mathematics, that the latter declined later advances by the HMC. Mr Wells rectified the situation, the School appearing in the Public Schools Year Book of 1932 as one approved by the HMC, to which body the Head Master was elected in 1937. Some at the time questioned the move, but with hindsight it has assured Bancroft's of independent survival.

The staff was a young one in 1931 and to Mr Playne's excellent appointments of Messrs Beesley, Belchamber, Francombe, Jenkins, Stainsby and Houston, Mr Wells made some equally fine additions. In 1932 Mr Kentfield came from St Edmund Hall, Oxford, to teach modern languages and show prowess on the games field where he conspired with ultimate success to introduce hockey in the Lent term. A year later, and from the same University, came Mr J. B. de C. Emtage, a mathematician-cum-cricketer in the Kislingbury mould and an author to boot, and Mr E. A. Owens, for whom 'no amount of our English indifference has been able to cool the Celtic fire that stokes the vast boilers of his enthusiasm' and who took on the rugby XV.

In 1934 Mr Semple, a distinguished Ulster academic, and Mr G. Cr.. ys-Williams, a member of the MCC, joined the classics department. Mr W. J. H. Earl, scouter and geographer, completed the new intake in 1936, on the retirement in December 1935 of Mr Freeman, leaving only Messrs Bowmar-Porter, Peet and Wheeller and Major Murray amongst the 'old guard'.

Not all the vacancies occurred through 'natural wastage', to use an indelicate modern phrase. The new Head Master had clashed badly with Mr Ridley, a classics master who gained the MC in the Great War at the cost of something less tangible in his personality. His gruff manner and bullying nature, to boys and staff alike, probably protected his mental equilibrium damaged in the trenches. He did not hide his contempt for 'young Wells' and his affected airs, and Wells decided he would have to go. No longer would miscreants be invited to a cupboard in his room to choose a stick with which to be beaten (the favourite was called 'Sweet William').

Forever associated with Mr Ridley was Mr P. L. T. Walker who shared a house with the Ridleys, an arrangement which gave rise to some ribald comment. Totally different to his landlord in character, he was a good junior master and a gifted musician whose Alvis sports car was much envied. He annoyed the Head Master by his inability to arrive in good time for Chapel, where he played the organ. Too often he would walk down the aisle of a packed chapel, impervious to the stares of Mr Wells and the chaplain, Mr Stainsby.

With the full backing of the Governors, Ridley and Walker were told by Mr Wells to resign, which they did, their resignations accompanied by stinging letters to the Governors. They found employment at the Central Foundation School, Stepney, though they continued to live locally. Mr Ridley was killed during the blackout by a 145 bus, his colleague dying recently, having held the office of Mayor of Bishop's Stortford. Mr Ridley's whine and certain catch phrases are curious memorials to him expressed through Bancroftians of that period.

It is much regretted that Mr Wells made no attempt to explain his plans and hopes for Bancroft's to his colleagues, for doubtless they would have shared in many of them. The Governors' minutes show how he supported them at meetings, giving praise where due.

A classic and tragic example of his insensitivity surrounds the death of Miss Evans, the matron. Appointed to replace Miss Sheppard in 1929, it is generally agreed that she greatly improved the standard of boarder food and comforts, helped by the installation of electricity and running hot water to the dormitories during the same period. Lunch improved in quality, though the monotony remained, and teas were more varied, with a hot drink before bedtime, and boarders now came down to cooked breakfasts. All this increased the cost of the matron's budget and Mr Wells became suspicious that pilfering was occurring. The Governors allowed him to act as he saw fit, so he summoned the Head of Woodford CID to his house and an investigation was started.

On 27th February 1935 Miss Evans, her brother-in-law Fuller and the cook, Mrs Booth, were charged and indicted at Stratford Police Court with stealing a pie, a haddock and some dripping

154

and given unconditional bail. The following day Miss Evans committed suicide by taking poison on Wimbledon Common and, in the ensuing publicity, the case against Fuller and Mrs Booth was dropped, the Governors eventually paying compensation to Mrs Booth and Miss Evans' family. The publicity was appalling and Mr Wells was greatly shocked by the whole affair.

That same year His Majesty's Inspectors of Schools visited Bancroft's and, while they had great praise for Mr Wells' teaching of scholarship Latin, they returned a very mixed report, finally printed in 1937. Inspections took place about every ten years during the direct grant period, but it is the 1935 inspection which old masters and Old Boys remember. As no-one save the Head Master and Governors saw it, the document was the subject of much gossip, much of it inevitably inaccurate or without foundation. For the record, the report was very complimentary to the Head Master: 'He knows his school well and has tackled resolutely the problems of school management . . . His response to criticism is of such a nature that any deficiencies will be duly dealt with'. Criticism is made of one or two elderly masters but the rest come out well, though the lack of qualified masters is commented upon. Excepting Geography, all subjects were well taught and Latin, English and Chemistry were highly praised.

The criticisms were mainly aimed at the school buildings, the crowded library and art room and the lack of a music teacher, despite Mr Francombe's 'interest in, and great love of, the subject'. They recommended a full time master, a suggestion fulfilled thirty years later when Mr Bosanquet was appointed in 1968. They also appear to have had a preoccupation with physical training, of which there should have been more lessons, though they drew the line at criticising Major Murray. It was the buildings that needed changing, more space, brighter, better decorated classrooms, cleaner swappers. They did not, of course, explain how the cost of improvements was to be met.

In general, the report was favourable. There was no question of the School losing its grant, and criticisms were more of the Playne school, 'An unwholesome tradition which is in the process of being overcome' based on a common room selected on 'narrow grounds'. Nevertheless, Mr Wells by all accounts was shocked at certain facts brought to his attention, and resolved to answer his critics by action, backed by the Governors.

155

The form structure in 1935 contained – to the modern eye – a bewildering number of IVth forms, though the system worked efficiently, if rather slowly. The main difference between it and the more recent system was that a boy of, say, thirteen could be in one of six forms: were he bright he would be with a sixteen year old in V; were he slower, he could be competing with a ten year old in the Remove, though those are the extremes.

In the main, day boys joined at any age from ten to thirteen, depending largely on whether they attended a state or preparatory school, and boarder scholars came at eleven. There were two streams finally sorted out at twelve and ran thus:

Forms I   II   IIIα – IVβ – IVα – Vβ Vα VI
        IIIA   Remove   IVB   IVA   VB   VA

so that, while slower boys retook general certificate in VA, the brighter boys (the higher stream above) entered the VI form.

The VI under Mr Playne had existed solely to prepare the brightest boys for university, arts candidates for the older universities, scientists for London, and this continuing tendency received the Inspectors' displeasure. Quite simply, most boys left school with their certificate and entered the City at sixteen, not seeing the point of the higher certificate which had no advantage by way of exemption from accountancy or civil service examinations.

Mr Wells had introduced an arts course recognised by the Board of Education in English, History, French and German, but, according to the Report, withdrew an application for a similar science course. Personally, he taught Latin in the sixth form and scored several successes in the late thirties, conspicuously D. H. C. Auburn who gained a distinction in each of English, Latin, French and German, winning a Demyship at Magdalen in 1934. Also at Oxford were D. P. J. Fink at Univ. and S. E. Andrews at St Catherine's Society, while V. Vale went up to Cambridge. Amongst older Bancroftians the early death of R. A. R. Hartridge robbed medieval history of a devoted Cambridge scholar, and H. Potter did sterling work as Dean of Law at King's, London, creating the faculty. A. V. Gardham was elected Hunterian Professor at the Royal College of Surgeons, and G. D. Guthie was awarded a chair in philosophy at Aberdeen.

156

Three O.B.s received the accolade of knighthood during this period: Reader Bullard was appointed KCMG for services as Consul General in Moscow, Henry Self was made KBE and Alfred Cutforth, President of the Institute of Chartered Accountants (and a host at Harlow on the Mission outing) became a Knight Bachelor. The O.B. who received the most publicity was T. Hampson who won the 800 metres at the Los Angeles Olympics in 1932. At School, when he knocked eleven seconds off the School half mile record, the adjudicator assumed his stopwatch must be wrong and he hardly ran at Oxford in his first year. From then on it was one triumph after another for Oxford and the Amateur Athletics Association and finally at Los Angeles. A modest man, he retired from his original job of schoolmastering to help administer Stevenage New Town.

At School, the usual sporting activities were enlivened by Mr Houston, Welshmen Owens and Cryws-Williams, as well as Messrs Kentfield, Belchamber and Emtage, young men whose enthusiasm wore off on some of their pupils, with L. S. Lee and A. R. Millard playing rugby for Eastern Counties Public Schools against Middlesex in 1934. Compulsory games were on Tuesday and Thursday afternoons and some Saturdays, though boarders still dominated the first XV and XI.

The softening influences of boarders' life continued under Miss Whistler as Matron until her retirement in 1938, and Mr Wells suppressed the bullying which had grown in Mr Playne's last years, never minding to lose his dignity by beating a boy. The boarding staff, all young, brought a civilising tone to the establishment and Messrs Francombe, Beesley and Owens, in their time, took the trouble to befriend senior boys who appreciated the liberalising of the new regime. 'Crazy Night' was the successor to earlier entertainments and the boarders at their Christmas party enjoyed a truly delicious tea, the games being better ordered and containing less bullying than in earlier years.

Miss Whistler had a brief but very influential reign at Bancroft's. She had been at Elmslea School, a Drapers' Company school for girls, and was more cultivated than her predecessors. She continued Miss Evans' policy of improving the boarders' food and trying to make School House less of a wrench from home. Her early retirement through failing eyesight was genuinely mourned.

157

Although robbed of the worst excesses of ten years before, boarder life was still regimented, with prep. each evening and Chapel each morning with Evensong on Sundays. The monitors ruled from the Committee Room, though it tended to be a benign dictatorship and, following an incident shortly after his arrival, Mr Wells put an end to much of the bullying which had grown in Mr Playne's last days, at the same time abolishing fagging for middle school boys; fagging for monitors survived until 1970.

Except for senior boys, whose occasional visit to local taverns was tacitly accepted, the boarder never left the school premises unless for sports or for some other specific purpose. The various clubs flourished and political discussion was positively encouraged amongst the senior boys. On the whole both pupils and staff tended to be conservative by nature, but a left wing 'cell' met regularly in Mr Houston's room and purchased works from Victor Gollancz' Left Book Club. Mr Wells made no attempt to stop this society which, one suspects, would not have been tolerated at similar establishments. It ceased to exist with the War and the Russo–German pact of 1939, and many of its members served with distinction during the War, some paying the ultimate sacrifice. Whatever his faults Mr Wells was no hypocrite where the virtues of freedom of expression were concerned.

More adventurous boarders enjoyed climbing the school roof at night – this was not on the curriculum – and some, such as Roberts, claimed to be able to perambulate the quad from roof to roof. Others will remember Joyce, a young maid said to be sympathetic to the pains of growing adolescents. Undoubtedly the Wells era was one of great improvement for the boarding house and new baths were an important feature of the great building work undertaken by the Drapers' Company for the bi-centenary celebrations in 1937. The new WCs were known as 'The Palace' and replaced the previous monastic ablutions.

The date chosen for the bi-centenary was the subject of some discussion. For years, the foundation of the School was taken as 1728, the year of Bancroft's death using the Gregorian calendar. As 1928 approached, however, the Company decided to put it back to 1938, two hundred years after the first boys were entered. Eventually 1937 was chosen, as John Entick and Thomas Downes took their oaths of office on Lady Day 1737.

158

The Company decided to celebrate the occasion with a generous gift of new buildings, spurred on by Sir Ernest Pooley and the new Chairman of Governors, Mr Frederick D'Oyly Monro. Succeeding Mr Williams in 1935, Mr Monro proved as loyal and as enthusiastic an ex-officio Bancroftian as his predecessor. Many will remember his witty, brief speeches at the Annual Dinner, and his going into bat against the School on Vis. Day. Together, he and Sir Ernest persuaded the Company to pay for the new improvements: better art and woodwork rooms, a bigger library and better day and bath rooms for the boarders. It was also decided to build a new Great Hall. Originally it had been proposed to convert the Chapel into a library and the old Hall into a Chapel, though a different plan eventually prevailed. The Great Hall had a false floor put in, with day rooms and a classroom on the ground floor and a library and three day rooms on the first. Beyond the southwest staircase and joining the 1910 science block to the main School, two new science rooms were built with an adjoining art room above a woodwork room. On the north end of the school, the main front was extended with new sickers, matron's rooms and maids' quarters, and new bathrooms were built above the MCR.

The major addition was the Great Hall, complete with stage and gallery and seating for 900 people. The Head Master had already acquired a large number of oak chairs by charging admission to the Christmas play and people were encouraged to donate chairs for a guinea. In 1931 S. E. Andrews ended a prologue to 'She Stoops to Conquer' with:

> 'One change we make (our audience to explete)
> We take your silver when we give your seat,
> That next year, when the Prologue's being spoke
> You'll think with pleasure that you sit on Oak'

On Visitation Day 1937 Queen Mary's brother, the Earl of Athlone, laid the foundation stone with due pomp and ceremony. This was the last but two of the old Vis. Days, with luncheons for boarders and parents in Dining Hall, East and West Houses in marquees and the Head Master and Governors in a classroom. The band played, and the cricket match between the Governors' XI and the School saw Messrs Emtage and Crwys-Williams, wearing MCC colours, face their pupils. A good tea was enjoyed, as were the exhibits of Mr Clark's and Mr Bowmar-Porter's pupils. The food by Ring and Brymer cost 7/6d for Governors' lunch, 2/11d for parents' and 1/6½d for tea, inclusive of tent hire.

The cost of the new buildings was estimated at £42,000 plus fittings, so the Company covenanted £50,000 to the Governors. By the time work was finished England was at war and Mr Wells' reign was approaching its unhappy end.

The Old Bancroftians celebrated the Bicentenary by producing a History of the School and organising a church service. For the History, W. J. Saunders, gentlest and most modest of O.B.s, had been preparing a sketch of Francis Bancroft and the Mile End School for some years, and this author pays tribute to his diligent researching at Drapers' Hall and elsewhere. Sadly, he died before the book was published. Mr Freeman's successors as editors of *The Bancroftian*, Mr Francombe and D. E. Coult, also edited the book; the former's prose style, the dozen word character sketch worthy of Surtees, being far superior to anything which this pen can produce. The Company, School and O.B.A. produced the History with a grant of £100 each.

The Association grew in strength during this period, as the young founders such as McMinn and Powell became respected elder statesmen, a younger generation filling the offices. Colonel French's decision in 1936 to make the dinner a black tie affair received some criticism, but it established a style retained at peace-time dinners ever since. The 1937 dinner, with Goddard as President, was held at Drapers' Hall, and that same October McMinn masterminded a Founder's Day service at St Helen's, Bishopsgate, the first since 1883. A similar service is planned for 1987.

A new society founded in 1936 was the Old Bancroftians' Masonic Lodge, which has succeeded in combining the fraternities of Masonry and Old Bancroftianism to a high degree, and it continues to flourish, open to all masters and Old Boys of the school.

The Dramatic Society, founded in 1924, grew greatly during this period, with A. J. Greenaway becoming Secretary in 1933, a post he has held ever since. Plays in those days were performed in theatres in London, and an annual outing, sometimes to the home of its President, B. Sangster Simmonds, made membership attractive, if exhausting, for O.B. thespians. The production of

Old Bancroftians' Association

Commemoration and Thanksgiving Service

on the occasion of

THE BICENTENARY

of

Bancroft's School
1737-1937

At

Saint Helen's Church, Bishopsgate

WEDNESDAY, 20th OCTOBER, 1937

Preacher:

The Right Reverend The Lord Bishop of Chelmsford

NOTE.

In the North Aisle, bordered by a brass inscribed strip, may be seen the burial place of Francis Bancroft.

The collection will be received in a silver bason inscribed:
"The Gift of Francis Bancroft, Esqr. to Ye Parish Church of St. Hellens, Anno 1728."

Bicentenary service, St Helen's Bishopsgate

serious plays, rather than mere entertainments, has always been the Society's aim, and early plays included *Pygmalion*, *Dear Brutus* and *The Rivals*. Early venues included the Blackfriars and Cripplegate Theatres, and The Drapers' Company have always been most generous in allowing the use of the Hall for rehearsals.

161

BANCROFT'S SCHOOL
1737-1937

UNTO GOD ONLY BE HONOUR AND GLORY

OLD BANCROFTIANS' ASSOCIATION

37th ANNUAL DINNER

HELD AT

DRAPERS' HALL

Friday, 8th October, 1937.

Bicentenary O.B.A. Dinner

That finest of all O.B. activities, the Mission, entered its final phase of existence at the beginning of the war. Bancroft Hall was built on the corner of Prince Regent Lane and Alnwick Road in West Ham, the money raised from O.B.s, the Drapers' company and local and youth organisations. It was opened by Lord Burghley, MP, Citizen and Draper, and was dedicated by the Rev A. Stainsby in May 1939. It was designed by R. W. Lone and built by Colonel French's Company, so it was a truly Old Bancroftian enterprise.

The new building, with its hall, gymnasium, cafeteria, offices and changing rooms and the W. J. Saunders reading room, opened its doors seven days a week. Its activities included: weekly meetings by age Monday to Friday, soccer and cricket on Saturday, and worship on Sunday. Dependent on O.B. generosity to continue, the Mission provided excellent facilities for the boys of Custom House for another thirty-five years, until Newham Council decided that public school philanthropy was no longer appropriate. For several generations of Bancroftians it provided an outlet through which they could repay some of the privileges they had received.

In the last few years of peace, several old masters retired and the war saw the last of the pre-1914 staff go. Mr Freeman – 'Uncle Bum' to generations of Old Boys from the sight of him bicycling away from the school – was a charming little man, rather old fashioned in his ways but beloved by all. He had cycled over most of Europe and beyond, and edited *The Bancroftian* for twenty years. He made it a point to be affable with his pupils, who claim today never to have taken advantage of this. One delightful event, showing his sense of fun, occurred one All Fools' Day. A drawing pin was placed on his chair and, as he went to sit, one boy lost his nerve and warned him. 'Don't be silly, boy,' he said, sitting down, 'I know what day it is.' The boys regretted his retirement more than that of any other during this period: they felt the loss of a friend. In retirement he continued to cycle and also took unto himself a wife.

A sadder parting came when the School Inspectors' Report was issued. R. H. Snape is said to be the finest scholar that Bancroft's has ever attracted. A mediaevalist, his work on English monasteries commands a footnote in Trevelyan's *English Social History* and he published in 1936 *Living History: 1500 to the Present Day*. He was also, for several years, chief examiner for Cambridge University Local Examination Board. For older boys he brought his subject alive, but younger philistines took advantage of his donnish placidity. It was quite clear that middle school teaching was destroying him and also that the history results at school certificate were poor, largely because the staff were so stretched. It must be said that Mr Snape appears almost as a scapegoat in 1937 when the Chairman of Governors – not Wells – took him aside and suggested early retirement. The Report commented favourably on him as a senior master and departmental head and it must have been possible to ensure that he only taught higher classes, leaving younger masters to take on the more ebullient boys. This was not, however, to be the case and Mr Snape went, the Head Master not having the backbone to dismiss him himself, his one action which is quite unforgiveable.

Mr Snape retired to Saffron Walden, between Cambridge and Bancroft's, and he continued to entertain boys there, as he had done at Woodford, dying in 1947.

The other master to retire before the war, after thirty-one years, was Mr A. Bowmar-Porter, the art master. For most of his time he taught in the crowded room at the top of the southwest stairs, only moving to the spacious new room for his last year. A 'below the salt' subject along with woodwork, his gifted pupils came to him out of school hours when he imparted his skills with pencil and watercolour to those who sought to learn. Two years in succession a pupil took the Essex County Art Exhibition, R. C. Russell in 1935 and R. H. Bradshaw the following year. Mr Bradshaw, of course, came back to replace his former master in 1939, although a sojourn abroad in the RAF prevented his taking up his full time appointment until 1945.

It was at this point, with a young, talented, enthusiastic staff, that Mr Wells should have accelerated the creation of the School he wanted, sharing his aspirations with them, but it was not to be. It is conjecture to discuss whether a growing family of his own would have mellowed him, for certainly his family saw a quite different side to his personality. He was married in 1935 to Miss Winifred Harding, the Bishop of Chelmsford performing the ceremony. Several masters attended but there was no breakfast, the bride and groom disappearing immediately after the service. His family grew gradually, a third son dying shortly after birth in 1941. A daughter was born in 1943 and all went well until Mrs Wells caught a chill and died. Her husband was left distraught, though he appeared to carry on manfully, handing over his young family to a wet nurse and then to a local GP.

Mrs Wells, herself a shy, retiring person, was, we presume, the one person to whom he was able to unburden himself. With his young children, also, he ceased to be the unbending martinet. Mrs Francombe remembers entering the nursery of the Head Master's house to find her own young son with the young Wells boys riding on the Head Master's back. D. C. Francombe must remain the only Bancroftian to have ridden a Head Master so. It is a pity that this aspect of his personality was not better known or more greatly shared.

With these personal problems, the growing effects of war cast a shadow over his last years. In the year when the foundation stone of the Great Hall was laid, the plans for an OTC were also prepared, the School eventually opting for an Air Training Corps. The 1938 crisis came and went and the last, curtailed, pre-war Vis. Day was held, the last school-day of peace for six years.

School life during the war and the great service of Old Boys belong to another chapter, though here the retirement of a great character must be mentioned.

Major Murray, DSO, DCM, was a splendid character. His wartime exploits, fighting Boer and Hun, were the source of many tales, supported by numerous scars. A short, quietly spoken man, it is said that two seniors set out to mock him when he first arrived in 1920 by asking if he could box. His reply that he thought he had a knowledge of the first principles of the sport failed to explain that he was a former regimental champion. He floored each of them with a punch, delivered with such precision as to stun them without causing concussion. He never suffered from ill discipline again.

The gymnastic displays of Vis. Day were a highlight of the year and the man left, ostensibly to retire, but in practice to help at the Royal Wanstead School. He combined his position as PT Instructor with that of School Administrator, assisting the Head Master in those non-bureaucratic days.

Mr Wells suffered the long Summer vacation without his wife and prepared for the new term, taking A. H. Barrett for a tutorial on the morning of September 11th. He afterwards retired to the chemistry laboratory and drank prussic acid, carefully washing the glass before collapsing. The inevitable note

165

explained that he could not live without his beloved wife.

A genuinely stunned staff prepared to carry on without him. The tributes neither hid nor excused the faults of his character, but tried to express the successes which he had achieved: that Autumn saw A. H. Barrett go to Worcester College, Oxford, on an open classics scholarship, while A. S. Bennell at Corpus Christi had been awarded one for History, and eight other awards had been achieved. The Chairman of Governors pointed out that the integration of boarders and day boys was largely Mr Wells' work and ended by saying, 'I shall always remember this young man with respect and affection'.

The stigma of suicide, especially during the war, coupled with his austere personality, has long prevented a fair assessment of Mr Wells' headship. Enough has been said of his aloofness. We must compare Bancroft's of 1943 with the last days of Mr Playne's regime. As effectively the House Master of School House following Mr Lucas' retirement, he had largely wiped out bullying and greatly improved conditions. Like Mr Playne, he believed in self government, but insisted that the monitors keep within certain rules and he abolished the privilege of fagging enjoyed by all middle school boarders.

For the staff, Mr Wells was always supportive of his colleagues at governors' meetings, never failing to share in praise for some achievement. His appointment coincided with the economic crisis when the grant was cut and all salaries reduced by a tenth. Within a year Mr Wells had persuaded the Governors to regard Bancroft's as a London, rather than provincial school for Burnham Scale purposes, thus almost restoring them immediately to their previous level. He also obtained payment on a monthly, rather than termly, basis, a system which had seen masters paid in April, July and then in December. His major success was in strengthening the sixth form, helped by some excellent appointments on the staff, and Mr Adams inherited a flourishing academic institution.

Bancroftians of the 'thirties sometimes look back on those days as a golden age and certainly the academic attainments have not been bettered. As Mr Francombe put it, 'Masters came, were appalled, grumbled a bit and stayed on for years and years; and, what was most odd, quite quickly acquired a sort of affection for the place'. The pupils themselves, despite the relative hardships and monotony of their life compared with a later generation,

have remained loyal to the school and the ideas which Mr Wells
tried to instil, surely a worthy legacy.

BANCROFT'S SCHOOL MISSION
BOYS' CLUB

UNTO GOD ONLY BE HONOUR AND GLORY

ORDER OF PROCEEDINGS

AT THE

OPENING OF NEW CLUBHOUSE

By LORD BURGHLEY, M.P.

On Wednesday, 24th May, 1939

Opening of new Mission Hall

Chairman: Mr. J. B. PATERSON

(Chairman of the Mission Committee)

Opening and Speech by
LORD BURGHLEY, M.P.

Dedication of the Building and the W. J. Saunders
Room by
Rev. A. STAINSBY

(Chaplain of the School)

A Vote of Thanks to Lord Burghley proposed by
Mr. F. R. D'O. MONRO

(Deputy Master of the Drapers' Company and
Chairman of the School Governors)

A Vote of Thanks to representatives of Official Bodies
proposed by
Mr. ELMER ASTLE

(President of the Old Bancroftians' Association)

and responded to by
HIS WORSHIP THE MAYOR OF WEST HAM

and
Lt.-Col. S. S. MALLINSON, C.B.E., D.S.O., M.C., D.L., J.P.

(Chairman of the Essex Area Committee of the National Fitness
Council)

CARMEN BANCROFTIANUM

THE NATIONAL ANTHEM

Opening of new Mission Hall

169

10th October, 1939.

Dear Sir or Madam,

Bancroft's School, Woodford.

RE-OPENING

Further to the circular letter dated the 20th September last, I have to inform you that the School will re-open as follows:-

Boarders should report by not later than 4 p.m. on Monday the 17th October next.

Day Boys at 8.50 a.m. on Tuesday the 18th October next.

Dinners for Day Boys will be served as usual. The Governors propose to charge £2.10.0. for the present term, but having regard to the rise in prices that has already taken place, and further rises that may take place in the future, it may be necessary to increase the charge after the present term.

The Governors regret that owing to circumstances beyond their control, this term will be of shorter duration than normally, but endeavours will be made to remedy this during the coming year by lengthening the Spring and Summer Terms 1940, if this is found to be a practical proposition.

It will be a great convenience if all parents will please complete, in the appropriate section, the form enclosed, and return it to this office immediately, so that the Governors may know the numbers of boys returning for the coming term, in order that satisfactory arrangements can be made, especially in regard to food, etc.

Boarders must bring their Gas Masks to the School, and Day Boys must carry them daily.

Yours faithfully,

T. W. KIRK.

Clerk to the Governors.

Letter from Clerk to Governors on outbreak of War

CHAPTER XII

1939–1945

AS IN 1914, the commencement of hostilities against Germany found Bancroft's on holiday, though in every other respect the situation was entirely different from the euphoria of twenty-five years before. As the hope borne by everyone since 1918 began to fade with the rise of Hitler in the 1930s, so Britain prepared again for war. This meant re-armament, an enlarging of the army by conscription in May 1939 and the preparation for a 'home front' war with the civilian population brought into the theatre of war by the mass aircraft bombings of the Luftwaffe. This time there were no illusions about it being a quick, cleanly fought campaign; it was going to be long and bloody, but Britain was going to win.

The problems of war had been concerning the Governors of Bancroft's since the Munich Crisis, and the major question was whether or not to evacuate the School to the country. The decision making was not helped by the inability of civil servants to decide under which category Woodford came: London, which was to be evacuated; country, where evacuees might be received; or neutral, when the decision was to be left open for the time being. Eventually, Bancroft's fell into the first category and definite plans to evacuate were made in 1938 and a year later. In the event, however, the School Governors decided to stand their ground.

It was 16th October before Bancroft's finally reassembled, with 221 out of 286 day boys and 93 out of 100 boarders present. Of the staff, Mr Bradshaw was called up before he actually began teaching full time, the Rev. Arthur Stainsby held an RNVR Commission and Mr Upcott-Gill joined the Essex Regiment. Twelve other masters were within the conscription age limit, but schoolmastering was a reserved occupation, a fact which did not stop younger members of the common room, Messrs Owens, Herring, Beesley and Kentfield, from joining up as the war progressed.

For the boys, life was to continue as usual, government edicts

171

permitting. Air raid shelters were constructed under the junior common room and behind the new Great Hall (where the swimming pool now is) though it was to be June 1940 before they came into daily use. The blackout regulations caused darkness in the classrooms, with some windows painted black – 'lapsing into a Dark Age mentality' – and Evensong was stopped during the winter months, the Head Master being fined £5 by the local magistrates for allowing the vestry light to show after dusk. The regulations also meant that the Great Hall and Library were unusable after dark.

The School being so near London, the Governors realised that the armed forces might need to use it or the grounds, and they had been warned of this possibility in April 1939. The school itself was only used for fire watching and as the base for the school's Air Training Corps, but West Grove was requisitioned for TA use. As it was also crossed with trenches to prevent German landings, its usefulness for games was limited, and they became compulsory on one afternoon a week until the invasion scare abated. Apart from such minor changes, Mr Wells was determined that life should continue. The school play and concert and Vis. Day were stopped for the duration, but classes continued as usual, as did building work; despite both the school surveyor and medical officer being called up, the new sickers and matron's rooms were completed in 1941.

The growing threat of war had caused the introduction of national service in May 1939 and consequently 114 Old Bancroftians were already 'under canvas' in September 1939, 42 holding the King's Commission and eleven being veterans of the Great War. Mr Freeman agreed to keep a tally of war service, which showed that the original number increasing eightfold by 1945. A number of Bancroftians had joined the reserves and territorial units between the wars, and the officers' mess of the 4th Battalion of the Essex Regiment at times seemed like a branch of the O.B.A., presided over by Colonel French. John French, whose family engineering business is still at Buckhurst Hill, epitomised the successful local O.B. A Deputy Lieutenant for the County and the third most senior freemason in the Province of Essex, he had served in the Great War before going up to Worcester College, Oxford. Always a keen TA man, he was promoted Brigadier in 1940 and continued to serve until 1945, despite the loss of a leg in a train accident, ending the war with the CB and CBE. Others in the 4th Essex included Majors Newman and Doyle, Captains Foote, Gregory, Upcott-Gill and Waterman, CQMS Spurrier and Private Nesbitt, while Captain Castle and Lieutenants Barry and Halbert were in other battalions.

The 'phoney war' produced no casualties, though the number of serving O.B.s gradually increased. Although a dinner was impossible, a luncheon was held at the Talbot Restaurant in London Wall in April 1940, the 4/- price being a shilling below the wartime maximum. L. R. Vandome was able to regale those present with his story of being a prisoner on the Altmark, his ship having been sunk by the Graf Spee, and his subsequent rescue by HMS Cossack. It was the only exciting event concerning a Bancroftian up till then, though events in the next few months soon changed that.

There were Bancroftians in the retreat to Dunkirk, some of whom were captured, and there were further Old Boys on the sea and in the air covering the evacuation. By July, the Roll of Honour held its first names: S. L. Morgan was drowned when his ship was torpedoed, and Woods and Perrin were both posted by the RAF as 'missing, believed killed', while R. B. H. Townsend-Coles was a prisoner of war until his mysterious execution by the Germans towards the end of the war. Bancroftians were as attracted to the RAF as that body found them suitable recruits, and the losses during the Battle of Britain were high. All five of the deaths reported in the March 1941 *Bancroftian* were in the RAF as was our first gallantry award, a DFC to J. L. Mitchell. There were now 293 known O.B.s serving, which had increased to 360 by July, and 413 by December 1941.

For the School and the civilian community this period was one of great strain. The School was deemed to be business premises, and fire watchers had to be provided, the boarder masters and boys taking this in turns, while senior day boys took over during the holidays. A branch of the Home Guard was also posted at the school during the period after Dunkirk, Mr Owens being a sergeant prior to joining the RAF.

In January 1941, Mr Wells formed the Air Training Corps squadron – ATC No 638 (BS) Flight – 45 boys joining and six masters applying for reserve commissions. Not surprisingly, Mr Beesley's organisational skills found yet another outlet. The squadron was a great success, gaining more marks than any

173

other during a competition the following year. In more pacific examinations, the work of Mr Wells and his staff produced excellent School Certificate results, 30 out of 31 passing, with 25 Matric. exemptions, and all seven entrants passing the Higher School Certificate. It was decided that boys would in future sit the London University External Matriculation Examination while in VB enabling them to begin the higher certificate a year early and giving masters more time with the sixth form.

The worries for the Head Master and Governors during this period were many and great. Financially, the war was bad for all 'business enterprises', and public schools were no exception. In the general disruption of wartime, families often had to move house, both service and civilian fathers being transferred from one part of the country to another. Similarly, incomes were often subject to great reduction when a man joined up. The Governors resolved to treat each case on its merits, especially where the father had actually been killed, and reduced fees accordingly. There was, naturally, a drop in demand for new places at the School, which the Governors could do nothing to alter. Furthermore, the free LCC scholarships were difficult to fill as primary school pupils were evacuated. The Government gave a special £700 grant, but fees and lunch money had to rise to meet growing costs. Salaries for domestic staff increased – dailies earned 1/- an hour and masters' salaries were raised to help meet the unprecedented 10/- in the £1 income tax. Somehow, the School accounts were kept almost in balance – no repair work was done, no equipment replaced, staff reduced in number – and the account was actually in credit by £1,000 in 1945.

As in the First World War, the boys took on more chores, doing the washing up, helping prepare meals and cleaning their own shoes. The boarder monitors took on more responsibility for supervising prep., being allowed to beat boys – a return, one suspects, to previously exercised prerogatives – with the miscreants having the right of appeal to the Head Master. This led to complaints by some parents of monitor brutality, though Mr Wells declined to alter the new arrangements.

The shelters had been built at great expense by the Governors when they decided not to evacuate the school, but they were built on very watery ground. Consequently they were always an inch deep in water. They were used for two periods: during the Blitz and during the doodle-bug scare. An attempt was made to

174

teach during daylight raids but it was very unsatisfactory.

The boarders slept each night in a specially reinforced cellar beneath the day room in bunks. They were remarkably uncomfortable. During the quiet period after 1942 the boys returned to the dormitories. When the VI and V2 raids began, they went to the shelters for the duration of the raid, taking their bedding with them and returning upstairs when the raid was over, irrespective of the time, rather than being allowed to sleep out what remained of the night.

By 1942, the Blitz was over and Hitler's attention had turned – disastrously for him – eastwards. The boys returned to the dormitories to sleep and parts of West Grove were used again. The only damage so far suffered by the school was from a bomb in front of the Head Master's house which damaged it and some rooms at that end of the school, for which £463 4s 1d was given by the War Damages Commission.

Under the aegis of Mr Francombe the Bancroft Players again performed, with 'St Joan' at Christmas 1941 and 'The Merry Wives of Windsor' the following summer, both in modern dress, with Denis Quilley treading the boards for the first time. As theatrical costumes were impossible to obtain, so was material for school uniforms. Boys were expected to wear dark flannels, a jacket and school tie, and a call for hand-me-downs was made to all parents.

1942 saw the death of Miss Whistler and of Clara Hall, widow of James, two ladies who did much to civilize the boarding house and The Bryn respectively, and the death of Mr Wells' new son triggered a series of events, each more tragic than the previous. Mr Semple, the ebullient, scholarly Ulsterman, resigned his post, as did Mr Earl, to enter the army and navy respectively as lecturers. Academically the year saw D. Hawkes enter Christ Church, Oxford, as senior classics scholar. One of five gifted Bancroftian brothers, he was a shining example of Mr Wells' scholarship and a memorial to him. He continued at The House after the war, becoming Professor of Chinese. N. Ticciati, the son of a distinguished musician of Italian extraction and destined to become a 'cellist himself, went up to Worcester College, Oxford, at the same time. A young man of great latin charm, his occasional absences from the dormitory were tolerated by the omniscient Mr Francombe, but Mr Wells was furious when he discovered what had happened, and was persuaded that neither a beating nor expulsion would be appropriate. His death in his late forties robbed his friends of one of their most colourful number.

The lull following the Battle of Britain saw our country turned into a vast armed camp, at first to serve as the last bastion of freedom in Europe and then as a springboard from which the English speaking United Nations would sally forth and destroy Nazism.

With the exceptions of North Africa and the Mediterranean and our retreating armies in Burma, this was a quiet period for the British army; indeed, it must always be remembered that, until 1944, the majority of the army saw no action, and most O.B. deaths continued to involve RAF members. Not that O.B. soldiers were entirely idle. Several O.B.s were involved in the Crete debacle, Dr N. C. Somerville losing his life while attending the sick, and G. G. H. Pigg was captured. In the Desert Campaign, H. G. Gregory and A. C. J. Van Ammel both won the MC. Later in Italy, Gregory obtained a bar and Van Ammel the DSO, and an MC was awarded to F. J. H. Arnold in Madagascar, and several O.B.s were killed in Africa. When the King visited his troops in that theatre of war his pilot was J. L. Mitchell, DFC, who was appointed MVO.

When Singapore and Hong Kong fell, several O.B.s were captured, including Major J. E. Swyer, Captains J. N. D. Harrison and J. H. Osborne and Lieutenant R. V. Wingham. For them followed three and a half years of humiliation and torture at the hands of the Japanese. Other O.B.s were with the Indian army as it retreated through Burma and, to lighten what was otherwise a grim record, *The Bancroftian* published a letter from Major R. D. Binnie. He and a young Captain, A. G. Waterman, had been playing billiards, the captain winning 6–3.

'Over the cigars and coffee, the talk drifted to England, to Essex, to Epping, to the families living thereabouts, until the name of "French" was mentioned, raising yet another mutual memory. After a pause during which he considered the facts of the conversation the Major said to the Captain, "You did not happen to be at Bancroft's did you?". The Captain admitted that he had and was proud of it too. And that was how 1908–12 met 1924–29. The bar was closed but fortunately Binnie had some awful country-made whisky in his quarters and the two

George. Mr George Haines, B.E.M., School Porter,
1886–1949, by R. H. Bradshaw

Lieutenant Colonel Charles Newman, V.C.,
by R. H. Bradshaw

Mr T. W. Kirk, Clerk to the Governors 1920–51

Mr Sangster Simmonds, Chairman of Governors, 1950–53

Mr A. A. O'Neill, Clerk to the Governors, 1951–73

Mr Sydney Adams, Head Master 1944–65

Old Boys' Day, 1945; open air service

Old Boys' Day, 1945; Messrs Peet, Playne and Adams

hurried there without delay. Glasses, hooch and water were quickly produced and the solemn toast of "Floreat Bancroftia" was drunk standing, the gallant Captain from his great height looking down on the little bald-headed Major. Before the party dispersed for the night a solemn motion was proposed nem con to the effect that both would be present on the first O.B. Dinner after the war. So now two wars go on each night: West v Odds and the other bigger one.'

Major Binnie was dead by the time the letter was published.

The RAF began making raids on Germany as soon as the Blitz was over, and the loss of life was great, the only Second World War service whose loss ratio can be compared with the Western Front of the First. Like all those subalterns at Passchendaele, the RAF fighters were young, carefree and seemingly impervious to the dangers of their task. Bruce Smeaton died rather than bale out of his Spitfire which would have crashed into Castleford, Yorks, and B. Smith, son of an airman O.B., died over Germany on the same day as E. J. Saunders, his exact contemporary at school. Smeaton and Smith's parents gave respectively the lectern and Bible for the School Chapel, and Smeaton's headstone was paid for by the people of Castleford.

Honours were awarded to O.B.s during this period, for 'Valour and death go bound together'. D. E. Hawkins won the DFC, to which a bar was later added, when he sank a submarine. Continuing in the service after the war, he retired in 1974 as an Air Vice Marshal with the CB and CBE. Group Captain L. M. Iles was awarded the AFC and also appointed CBE for helping plan the attacks on German cities. The RAF constituted but a small proportion of His Majesty's forces, but throughout these middle war years they alone carried the war from England to Europe, and thus their losses were great.

Occasionally during this period there were raids on the French coast, usually carried out by a new group called the Commandos. These were volunteers from other regiments and units who underwent gruelling training in order to take the war to the enemy. When it became clear that the large docks at St Nazaire would have to be rendered inoperable so that the German battleship Tirpitz could not use the facilities, it was an obvious task for the new force. Equally, Lieutenant-Colonel A. C. Newman seemed the man to lead it.

Charles Newman had been at Bancroft's 1914–21 and joined

the Essex Regiment TA in 1923. A staunch O.B., a founding member of the Rugby Club, an enthusiast for boxing, he was, proverbially, a leader of men. Here is not the place for a detailed description of the assault, though the official announcement in the London Gazette awarding him the Victoria Cross (held up till 1945 in case the Germans shot him) explains what this man did. All that it omits is that Newman was approaching his fortieth birthday.

London Gazette, June 19th, 1945
LIEUT-COL AUGUSTUS CHARLES NEWMAN, The Essex Regiment (attached Commandos) (Salford, Bucks).

On the night of March 27–28, 1942, Lieut-Col Newman was in command of the military force detailed to land on enemy occupied territory and destroy the dock installations of the German-controlled naval base at St Nazaire.

This important base was known to be heavily defended and bomber support had to be abandoned owing to bad weather. The operation was therefore bound to be exceedingly hazardous, but Lieut-Col Newman, although empowered to call off the assault at any stage, was determined to carry to a successful conclusion the important task which had been assigned to him.

Coolly and calmly he stood on the bridge of the leading craft, as the small force steamed up the estuary of the River Loire, although the ships had been caught in the enemy searchlights and a murderous cross-fire opened from both banks, causing heavy casualties.

Although Lieut-Col Newman need not have landed himself, he was one of the first ashore and, during the next five hours of bitter fighting, he personally entered several houses and shot up the occupants and supervised the operations in the town, utterly regardless of his own safety, and he never wavered in his resolution to carry through the operation upon which so much depended.

An enemy gun position on the roof of a U-boat pen had been causing heavy casualties to the landing craft and Lieut-Col Newman directed the fire of a mortar against this position to such effect that the gun was silenced. Still fully exposed, he then brought machine-gun fire to bear on an armed trawler in the harbour, compelling it to withdraw and thus preventing many casualties in the main demolition area.

Under the brilliant leadership of this officer the troops fought magnificently and held vastly superior enemy forces at bay, until the demolition parties had successfully completed their work of destruction.

By this time, however, most of the landing craft had been sunk or set on fire and evacuation by sea was no longer possible. Although the main objective had been achieved, Lieut-Col Newman nevertheless was now determined to try to fight his way out into open country and so give all survivors a chance to escape.

The only way out of the harbour area lay across a narrow iron bridge covered by enemy machine-guns and although severely shaken by a German hand grenade, which had burst at his feet, Lieut-Col Newman personally led the charge which stormed the position and under this inspiring leadership the small force fought its way through the streets to a point near the open country, when, all ammunition expended, he and his men were finally overpowered by the enemy.

The outstanding gallantry and devotion to duty of this fearless officer, his brilliant leadership and initiative, were largely responsible for the success of this perilous operation which resulted in heavy damage to the important naval base at St Nazaire.

There were several other O.B. prisoners of the Germans and Japanese, and *The Bancroftian* gave addresses and instructions as to posting them letters and parcels: no mention of regiment, sender's name on reverse, no stamp needed and marked: 'Prisoners of War Post: Kriegsgefangenenpost'. Word occasionally came back: thanks for chocolate and cigarettes; news of meetings with O.B.s through the barbed wire. Parcels usually arrived, if rather late.

On the civilian and administrative front, O.B.s played a prominent part. Sir Reader Bullard, our man in Teheran, was host to Churchill at the summit there and was much involved in the diplomatic intrigue of that area. Sir Kenneth Peppiatt helped the economy to survive, Sir Henry Self collected knighthoods as in earlier days he had degrees, and headed the Air Ministry. Numerous O.B.s helped the war effort, including such scientists as F. E. Warner and the Townend brothers – both later made CBE in the Coronation honours list of 1953. By July 1943 there were 648 O.B.s in uniform, which had increased to 733 by the D-Day landings. In that final push for victory, for which so many soldiers had been preparing since Dunkirk, numerous Old Bancroftians participated, some making the ultimate sacrifice.

At School, little seemed to change. There were new staff, such as Mr Matraves, and others who did not stay long. The tragic events which led to Mr Wells' suicide have already been mentioned and Mr Peet found himself acting Head Master until a new man could be appointed. 174 applications were received and Mr Sydney Adams late of St John's College, Oxford, a housemaster at Sedbergh, was appointed in 1944. This was shortly before the attacks by V1s and V2s on southeast England. Again the boys returned to the shelters to sleep, and a lookout was kept on the school tower during the day, the watchers signalling the direction of the doodle-bugs to boys below, who relayed the word to the relevant part of the School. As luck would have it there was little damage at the School, though term ended early, in June 1944.

For the Governors, the approach of victory brought a new worry, the recommended reforms suggested by the Fleming Report on independent education, one of the many Royal Commissions of the Coalition Government deciding how the new world would be run. Sir Ernest Pooley sat on the Commission and produced a minority report. The 1944 Education Act established the principle of free education for all up to fifteen years of age, the last four years in one of three types of school: grammar, modern or technical. Those public schools completely outside the system were left alone, but schools such as Bancroft's which had happy relations with local authorities, and an endowment spent wholly on poor scholars, were in a more difficult situation. The Governors wished to maintain the status quo, as far as possible, insisting on the continuance of fee-paying pupils, and were prepared to take into account the abolition of the direct grant, as suggested by Fleming.

Throughout 1944, as the bloody rear-guard action of the Germans caused heavy casualties, Bancroft's began to return to normal. French's filled in the anti-landing trenches at West Grove for £176, new equipment was ordered, including a duplicating machine for £28 17s 0d, and some windows replaced with grants from the Board of Education of £900, and £367 12s 1d from the War Damages Commission. Masters' salaries rose by £58 each, and the maids were paid £69 a year, all found, the dailies receiving £2 12s 6d a week. Matron earned £200 and nurse £135, plus their keep. Rationing provided a tolerable level of sustenance and milk was provided for all pupils. The School simply waited for the final victory.

In France, Italy and the Far East, the might of the Allied forces gradually wore down and destroyed the enemy armies. Still the RAF was to the fore, covering our troops and bombing Germany; eight O.B.s won the DFC in the last year of the war and airmen still figured high on the roll of honour. In France, I. F. Peet, son of the master, and Kennedy, both won the MC for conspicuous bravery, the former in capturing a village, the latter in capturing, with the aid of an armoured car and eleven men, seventy Germans, killing forty more.

C. V. Simpson was appointed OBE, as were two O.B.s who later received knighthoods, A. Hudson-Davies and A. Mumford, all for war work. For helping to plan D-Day, R. G. Bennett was appointed CB and Colonel Blagden CBE. More importantly Mr Kentfield did sterling work in translating bulletins and orders for liberated Frenchmen. There were other liberations, those of O.B.s in POW camps and also of E. L. Baete, an officer of the Royal Belgian Guards who had been at Bancroft's while a refugee in the First World War – he had spent three years in a Gestapo concentration camp.

I. F. Van Ammel, a lieutenant in 'The Blues', was released from a camp in Italy, and several more O.B.s were freed as the German defence of their homeland collapsed, including Colonel Newman whose VC was announced. Eventually, after the dropping of the atomic bombs and the surrender of Japan, those O.B.s held in Burma were liberated – miraculously, none had died as a result of the Japanese methods of imprisonment. The war was over.

Bancroft's, tired and shabby, celebrated accordingly, with separate holidays for VE Day, VJ Day and Newman's VC. Vis. Day was held for the first time since 1939, Sir Ernest Pooley being Master of the Drapers' Company, and Mr Playne visited the School – one of his sons had been shot by the Italians while a prisoner of war and another awarded the DFC. The new Government decided to maintain the direct grant, based on a means test, which pleased most people, and a committee representing all parties prepared plans for the war memorial – they decided on the set of gates at the entrance to the Tower. With the return of Messrs Kentfield, Owens and Bradshaw, and despite stricter rationing, things could return to normal.

The cost in life was not as severe as in the Great War, though it took from the O.B.A. some of its most promising members – there is probably a correlation between keen rugby players and dashing pilots. The statistics show an impressive record of Bancroftian service: 828 O.B.s had served, of whom 71 were killed or missing, ten more had been prisoners of war and 63 had received awards. Some individuals have been mentioned, but many more are unsung in this book. To each of them the future generations must show the most profound gratitude.

The O.B.A. emergency committee prepared for fresh elections – Newman was the obvious choice for President – and the clubs began to re-form. And there was, of course, a dinner, a Victory Supper held at the School with 212 masters and O.B.s attending. Somehow, food and wines were produced, a bar set up in the boarders' day room, and dinner served in the dining hall. Newman proposed the toast to the School and received a thunderous ovation. There were many speeches, but it was an occasion to celebrate the fact that so many had survived, as had those things which had been fought for: freedom, democracy, the country – and the School.

The party did not disperse until long into the night, the President begging them not to awaken the sleeping boarders. No doubt the tranquil sight of the quadrangle lit only by the moonlight brought home to each and every O.B. the fact that peace really had returned, and all was well with the world.

NOTICE TO PARENTS.

DRAPERS' HALL,

LONDON, E.C.2.

July, 1941.

BANCROFT'S SCHOOL, WOODFORD.

REVISION OF CLOTHING LIST.

In view of the Government Scheme for the rationing of clothes, the Governors have approved the following arrangements in connection with the clothes required by boys attending the School:—

(*a*)   that generally, the requirements as scheduled be suspended until further order to meet the present emergency, except that the School Cap and Tie should be worn as at present.

(*b*)   that new boys be permitted to wear their present clothes on the understanding that parents will provide the School Uniform as soon as it becomes necessary to purchase new outfits.

(*c*)   that as a temporary expedient, the wearing of grey flannel trousers be permitted.

(*d*)   that all parents be requested to adhere, as far as possible, to the present Outfit and co-operate, in the best interests of the School and the boys, by arranging that all pupils be dressed in a quiet, tidy and suitable manner, pending the time when it will be possible to resume the School Uniform.

T. W. KIRK,

Clerk to the Governors.

Letter from Clerk concerning wartime uniform

183

BANCROFT'S SCHOOL.

GOVERNMENT MILK SCHEME.

Notice to Parents of Day Boys.

The Governors have been able to make arrangements to supply additional milk under the Government Scheme, and commencing the Spring Term, 1942, all day boys, whose parents so desire, can be provided with one-half of a pint of milk per day.

The charge will be 7s. 6d. per term, payable in advance, at the beginning of each term. This amount will be collected at the School and should NOT be included in the terminal charge for Tuition and Dinner Fees paid at Drapers' Hall.

Parents who desire their boys to have the daily milk ration should notify Mr. Belchamber at the School on or before the first day of term.

January, 1942.

Letter from Clerk concerning milk for all school children

184

BANCROFT'S SCHOOL

REPORT on _Thomson JA_ for the Term ended _1 Apr._ 194 3

Form _2_   Number of Boys in Form _30_   Average Age of Form _10.9_

Position in Form	Beginning of Term	1st Month	2nd Month	3rd Month	Final Order
	14	13	15		14

Subject.	Position in Subject.	Remarks.	Masters Initials.
DIVINITY	—	Quite war worse.	ALS.
ENGLISH GRAMMAR & LITERATURE	10	A very fair start	?v.
HISTORY	15	Quite good.	ACPS
GEOGRAPHY	2	Very good work	Rv.y.
FRENCH	22=	Will do better next term.	??
LATIN or GERMAN Division ... of ... Boys			
MATHEMATICS	11	Promising, needs steady work	Q?
CHEMISTRY)	—	Satisfactory.	?
PHYSICS	'		
ART	?	Is fair.	P?L
WOODWORK			

A very good first term ___ E.W. M...ley___ Form Master.

___F.F.Peet,___ House Master.

An encouraging start. ___T.G.Wells___ Head Master.

Report for pupil, 1943

185

The
Order of Service
On the Occasion of
The Dedication of the
Bancroft's School
War Memorial Gates

Saturday, March 10th, 1951

Service of dedication of War Memorial Gates

CHAPTER XIII

SYDNEY ADAMS
1944-1965

THE MIDDLE of war is no time to take over any enterprise, least of all a school deprived of its best young masters, but Mr Adams soon settled into the Head Master's house and office. Apart from the doodlebugs and the growing number of O.B. deaths, the War was proceeding towards ultimate victory in Europe without disrupting Bancroft's overmuch, and plans could be prepared for the future.

The circumstances of Mr Adams' appointment following Mr Wells' death made him unique amongst the school's recent Head Masters: his predecessors back to Symns, or even Hunt, were each chosen to perform a specific task, to lift the school into a new educational category, each building on his predecessor's success. Equally, Messrs Symns, Playne and Wells succeeded on the retirement of a Head Master and so were young, and fresh in their approach. Mr Adams succeeded a man under forty whose reforms were reaping great results, and consequently there was no need for him to make changes in the School. The Adams regime, with no real mandate, no target, simply continued the work of the previous headship, though in character and attitude Mr Adams was quite different from Mr Wells (They must have overlapped at St John's where they were both scholars, though no one seems to know if Mr Adams had ever met his predecessor). A tall, smiling figure, he brought a more relaxed and friendly atmosphere to the School. A relaxed regime occasionally led to administrative chaos, and Mr Adams would have been the first to admit that he was not always totally efficient in running the school. A firm leadership was provided, however, and the School grew quietly and unobtrusively during his reign, the administration overcoming or bypassing the growing difficulties which beset Britain in the 1950s.

The most important event of this period was the 1944 Education Act, taken through Parliament by Mr R. A. Butler. It raised the school-leaving age to fifteen and guaranteed for each child a free education 'appropriate to his age, aptitude and ability'. For the first time state schools were divided into two clear cut age categories: five to eleven at primary schools and eleven to fifteen or over at grammar, technical or secondary modern schools, entry being decided on an examination at eleven. Further education was expanded, the older universities enlarged, the university colleges given Royal Charters and technical colleges expanded, with more generous state scholarships. The Act was the result of various Royal Commissions from the peace years, and succeeded in bringing most voluntary-aided schools, the majority of them religious foundations, within the control of the new Ministry of Education, though allowing them a degree of independence on such matters as religious teaching. The old direct grant was abolished and Bancroft's and other such schools were given the option of becoming maintained grammar or completely independent schools. The public schools were the subject of a separate Commission which produced the Fleming Report on 'Public Schools and the Education System'.

While awaiting this latter Commission, on which Sir Ernest Pooley sat, the Governors followed the advice of the Public Schools Governing Bodies Association to hold fast and, as the Governors were not willing to surrender the right to charge fees, the School remained on the public school side of the great divide. Eventually, a new direct grant system was developed, by which parents paid fees on a sliding scale according to their income. Parents earning less than £390 a year plus £39 per child paid no fees, thereafter they paid £2 a year for each £26 earned. The fees at this time were £37.50 a year for day boys, with £6 for luncheon. Growing costs were to push up these fees several times before annual, or even termly, increases became a feature of the early 'seventies.

Bancroft's decided to take advantage of this scheme, despite fears of further government interference, so allowing the School to proceed as it had done during the inter-war years. The 1944 Act, however, had two important effects on the school. Firstly amidst local protests, the entry age was raised to eleven, under the Ministry's insistence. The second effect was that the growth of secondary education, coupled with a political philosophy strongly opposed to private schools (or private medicine, or ownership of the means of production) led to a growing difficulty in filling the LCC places at the school. The LCC failed to meet their quota in 1944 and in 1946 wrote to the Governors asking to

188

BANCROFT'S SCHOOL, WOODFORD.

NOTICE TO PARENTS OF DAY BOYS.

In reference to the notice dated the 7th January last, issued to parents of Day Boys, the Ministry of Education have, after protracted negotiations, now sanctioned the following revised charges for Tuition Fees, etc., to operate from the beginning of the Autumn Term, 1945 :—

Tuition Fee :—

INCREASED from £10 to £12 10s. 0d. per term subject to the following :—

Parents to pay fee on a sliding scale, in accordance with gross income based on following principle :—

Two parents with ONE child	Income up to £7 10s. 0d. per week (£390 per annum).	Nil.
An addition of 10s. per week (£26 per annum) to income.		Fee of £2 per annum.
With each further addition of a similar amount.		Fee increase of further £2 per annum.

For each additional child a further 15s. per week (£39 per annum) allowed.

For guidance, a detailed schedule is printed overleaf and a form of application is enclosed (Model form prepared by the Ministry of Education) which parents, eligible and wishing to avail themselves of the opportunity to apply for a remission or reduction in the Tuition Fee, are at liberty to complete.

The form should be signed by both parents, where practicable, and returned as early as possible and in any event not later than the 15th April next to :—

The Clerk to the Governors of
Bancroft's School,
Drapers' Hall,
London, E.C.2.

It will be a great convenience if parents who, for any reason, do not wish to make application for a remission or reduction in fees will please fill in the name of their son, mark the declaration " not required," sign and return the form as above.

Dinner fee :—

REDUCED from £3 to £2 per term.

As soon as the necessary adjustments can be made, an account covering the revised charges for the Autumn Term, 1945, and the Spring Term, 1946, less the amount already paid for the former term, will be forwarded and parents are asked to co-operate by giving their early attention to this matter.

Charge for Milk :—

REDUCED from 7s. 6d. to 4s. 0d. per term.

Following present practice, this matter will be dealt with at the School by Mr. Belchamber, and an account, duly adjusted, will be issued as soon as possible.

Books :—

Will be supplied free of charge.

T. W. KIRK,
Clerk to the Governors.

[P.T.O.

Letter from Clerk to Governors regarding new Direct Grant

increase the number of boys – at their own expense – though some would be sent to boarding school to 'help overcome their personal difficulties'. The governors rejected this, and Mr Adams united forces with the Head of Christ's Hospital to try to force the LCC to ensure that applicants, over which our Governors had no real control, were selected on the basis of educational merit alone. They were never successful in this, and the intellectual powerhouse of the boarder block waned.

In 1953, with the endowment income incapable of meeting the full boarding house costs, the Governors decided to lessen the LCC's influence by reducing free places to thirty at any one time, all for LCC boys. The Governors reserved the right to award free places to the sons of Drapers when the endowment allowed it, the scheme being agreed by the Ministry 'with regret' in 1954. Sadly, the architect of this scheme, Mr Sangster Simmonds, the only O.B. to be Chairman of the Governors, died suddenly the year before.

The school, then, entered the post-war world much as it had been in 1939, but with a friendlier face at the helm. As Mr Wells had appointed several young masters in the 1930s, the masters' common room seemed hardly to change during this period. Messrs Kentfield, Owens, and Bradshaw returned from active war service, while Messrs Semple and Beesley preferred to remain elsewhere as administrators. The latter, whose organisational skills were a byword for efficiency in pre-war days, became an educational administrator before retiring to run a Devonshire country inn. Still a regular attender of O.B. functions and the father of an Old Bancroftian, his energy and sense of fun belie his eighty-odd summers.

Of the senior members of the Common Room, Mr Peet retired in 1946 having seen in the new man, and Mr Wheeller and the Rev A. Stainsby left in 1949 and 1950 respectively. To 'Gaffer' Peet had fallen the task of administering the School during the 1943–4 interregnum. That he had performed the work well and conscientiously came as no surprise to the many Bancroftians who had been taught by him since 1919. A man of deeply held religious convictions, he always had his class under complete control and was seemingly popular with all boys. His syllabus never changed from year to year, nor did the regular tests, answered on small pieces of paper to encourage neatness and brevity. This allowed cheating, if one knew a boy in the year above. Mr Peet appears to have turned a blind eye to this – he was too shrewd not to have known what was happening – knowing that the cribber was learning the answers by heart and would have a perfect set of notes at the end of the year.

There can be no doubt that his methods worked. He used to recall in later years how a boy, F. E. King, in his first class asked for an explosion, with which Mr Peet gladly obliged. Professor King FRS, along with Sir Frederick Warner FRS, the Townend brothers, Curd, Cunningham and others presented their old master with a printed volume of essays to mark their respect, and there were other gifts and collections from boys and O.B.s.

At the beginning of his School career Mr Peet had ruled The Bryn for its last two years, and at the end he delayed retirement to act as Head Master and to give Mr Adams the benefit of his great breadth of experience. For the long period in between, his success must be judged by that of his former pupils, while his whole attitude and character may be summed up by Mr Monro, Chairman of Governors who appointed him acting Head Master: 'I found him a lovable person with a keen sense of humour but with a quiet firmness in a matter where firmness was required, that no specious arguments could break down'. He died in 1972.

Mr Wheeller replaced Mr Peet as second master, a position he held until 1949. Appointed at the same time as Mr Peet, he had been a great help to him during the interregnum, discussing problems and giving advice. A fine English master who retained his delightful West Country burr, he will be best remembered as the producer of the annual school play. Commencing in 1923 with *She Stoops to Conquer*, the play replaced the old Christmas concert. The stage was curtained off in old Great Hall, there being access to the neighbouring classroom, footlights were made from biscuit tins, costumes were made or hired and the plays were usually Shakespeare or an eighteenth century classic. The new Great Hall was an answer to his dreams and his boys came up to the mark.

The retirement of Mr Stainsby to a living in Lincolnshire, Witham on the Hill, removed an old fashioned God-fearing padre from the School. An active officer in the RNVR before the war, he had been called up in 1939 and saw some service before returning to the School. He was rumoured to have a gun in his desk, though his usual means of punishment was a hammer

191

borrowed from Mr Clark. A martinet in punctuality and for the carrying of dictionaries, his simple religious beliefs were readily imparted to his pupils. He maintained his links through his O.B. son and membership of the Old Boys' Lodge, of which he was a founder.

It takes a certain type of school to place a porter on a pedestal, and revere him and honour him. The position of George Haines, BEM, at Bancroft's was one of veneration, for he had been there since the School opened, having been taken on when the School moved to Tottenham in 1886. A short man with a moustache and spectacles – marvellously captured by R. H. Bradshaw's portrait – he donned a top hat and livery on state occasions, though he was more at home in an old serge jacket and cloth cap. He had asked to retire in 1932 and the Governors had offered him a pension, but he had changed his mind, and there was great celebration of his fifty years in 1936 when he was presented with a salver and a cheque on Vis. Day of that year. The diamond jubilee was also celebrated and congratulations were sent when he and Mrs Haines celebrated their diamond wedding anniversary, having been married at Hackney Church by Mr Symns in 1887.

Sadly, Mrs Haines, who had run the tuck shop since 1903, died before her husband received the following letter:

Ministry of Education
9th June 1947

Dear Mr Haines,

I am very glad to inform you that His Majesty the King is graciously pleased to award you the British Empire Medal (Civil Division) on the occasion of his Birthday. I have great pleasure in sending you my warm congratulations on this well earned recognition of your long and devoted services as Porter at Bancroft's School.

Yours sincerely,
John Maud

Her death, clearly, was a blow, and in 1949 he offered his resignation. He still attended Vis. Day and the O.B.A. Dinner wearing his medal and seemingly remembering everybody. The cheering on his last day went on for ever.

Apart from his memory and endurance, George's great

192

strength was that he was everybody's Dutch uncle, giving sweets 'on tick' to impecunious boarders, befriending very small and lonely boys, breaking up the occasional fights and never being able to disguise his generous heart behind the gruff manner in which he addressed young boys. He died in 1951, a little before his ninetieth birthday, the Governors standing to order in his memory at their next meeting, the only record of such a tribute reported in their minutes. The plaque on the lodge door, unveiled the following O.B.s Day, reads simply:

GEORGE
George William Haines BEM
School Porter
1886–1949

It is a record of service of which any institution can be proud, and George's memory is still held in high esteem by the many Old Boys who joined Bancroft's during these sixty-three years.

Such a break with the past is a suitable occasion to consider the great change in the School's environs since the move from Tottenham, for the development of Woodford and Chingford affected the School, providing it with many pupils. Woodford had been a village in 1889, though the area beyond the station, around West Grove, was built up, mainly with poorer types of artisans' dwellings. Much of the Monkhams Estate and Sunset Avenue dates from before the Great War, and during the inter-war period the Buxtons' Buckhurst Estate largely disappeared beneath bricks and mortar, and much of Loughton and Chingford was developed.

During the 1950s a larger proportion of day boys came from close to the School and far off Ilford still provided its fair share, though the number of Leytonites diminished. Many O.B.s moved into the new houses, commuting to the City, and second and third generation Bancroftians began to appear. This helped to encourage 'day bugs' to participate more in after-school activities, and the masters took advantage of this to organise more School societies.

Mr Jenkins founded the French Society; the new chaplain, the Rev A. A. E. Binns, started the Christian Union, and Mr Bradshaw ran the Sketch Club: he also won the Tomlinson Prize of the Royal Society of Picture Painters in 1955. The boys for their part ran the Aeromodelling Club and the Literary and Debating Society, both under Mr Kershaw, and the Natural History Society catered for the various needs of youthful curiosity. This was also the age of national service and few boys avoided serving their sovereign until its abolition in 1960 (Curiously no O.B. has risen to very high rank in the armed services with the very notable exception of the recent Chief of the Air Staff, Marshal of the Royal Air Force Sir Keith Williamson, whose time at the School was disrupted by wartime movement by his parents). The ATC continued after the War and the CCF soon developed into a basic section from which boys moved into the army or airforce sections. Apart from camps and field days, a dance was occasionally held and the annual inspection became one of the School's red letter days. Each year one or two boys opted for a regular commission, N. F. Hayward winning the Queen's Sword at Cranwell in 1961.

The 'extra-curricular' activity which came into prominence during this time was music. There was a School choir as well as a chapel choir, and the Combined Choir was formed during this time as a joint effort with Loughton County High School for Girls. The first concert at St Bartholomew the Great took place in 1947 and remained a regular feature of the School's calendar until the choir became a victim of co-education. That year a broadcast was also heard on the wireless at Children's Hour. The distaff side of the choir was under the guidance of Miss James of Loughton, a lady remembered with much affection by O.B.s of that period. The enthusiasm engendered by her and Mr Francombe continued after the singers had left School with the foundation of the Crofton Singers.

The importance of Mr Francombe during this period as the editor of *The Bancroftian* and the producer of concerts and plays cannot be overestimated. For several generations of boys he succeeded in making Shakespearean characters come alive, and can claim the credit for having spotted the talents of young Denis Quilley. On the musical side, too, his influence went beyond the choir. There was always a gramophone in his classroom where boys could play classical records in their leisure time (in mock rivalry Mr Jenkins allowed the Jazz Club to use his room). Despite lack of a professional music master, the continuous stream of gifted amateurs on the staff continued, Mr Francombe being joined during this period by Mr Wright, who regrettably

The Church of St. Bartholomew the Great,
West Smithfield, E.C.I.

CAROLS AND CHRISTMAS MUSIC

SIDONIE GOOSSENS
(HARP)

NICHOLAS CHOVEAUX
(ORGAN)

THE COMBINED CHOIRS
of
LOUGHTON COUNTY HIGH SCHOOL FOR GIRLS
and
BANCROFT'S SCHOOL FOR BOYS.

SUNDAY, DECEMBER 28th, 1947.
at 3 p.m.

Programme Two Shillings and Sixpence.

Combined Choirs Carol Service, 1947

195

soon moved on, Mr Lageard who was an Associate of the Royal College of Organists, and Mr Murray, a baritone of professional standing. The Head Master himself was very fond of music and encouraged individuals to develop their skills, to the extent of allowing one boy to dismantle the Chapel organ.

During this period the School produced R. H. C. Warren, Professor of Music at Bristol; R. Fisher and A. Thurlow, organists respectively at Chester and Chichester; C. C. Fry the conductor; and K. J. Bain, Head Master of the Purcell School.

THE BANCROFT'S PLAYERS

PRESENT

MACBETH

IN THE

GREAT HALL, BANCROFT'S SCHOOL

ON

SATURDAY, JULY 19TH AT 7.30P.M.

Row. A No. 9   GALLERY

Ticket for school play

The life of the boys at this time, especially the boarders, was much easier than at any previous time, though it was hardly soft. Mrs Pepper, who had a charming daughter, and her successor as matron, Mrs Young, improved both the quality and variety of the food, as rationing and shortages came to an end. Creature comforts were provided in day-rooms for both boarders and day boys, the latter also having their subterranean locker room, scene of the occasional fight or quiet smoke.

Of the staff who came and went during this period, the names of Kershaw and Lord are perhaps best remembered. Mr Kershaw was a first rate history master, who married in America

196

Date	Society	Function	Place	Time
Sat. 18th Jan.		**School Term begins**		
Thurs. 27 Feb.	Old Bancroftians Association	Annual General Meeting	Drapers' Hall, E.C.2.	5.30 for .6 p.m.
Sat. 8th Mar.	School 1st XV	v. Old Bancroftians 1st XV	School	2.30 p.m.
Fri. 14th Mar.	O.B. Football Club	End of Season Dance	Roebuck Hotel, Buckhurst Hill	8 p.m.—1 a.m.
Thurs. 27th May } Fri. 28th Mar. } Sat. 29th Mar. }	O.B. Dramatic Society	"Arms and the Man"	School Hall	7 p.m.
Sun. 30th Mar.	School Choir	Service of Music	School Chapel	6.30 p.m.
Thurs. 3rd Apr.		**School Term ends**		
Sat. 26th Apr.		**Summer Term begins**		
Sat. 3rd May	School	School Sports	School	2.30 p.m.
Sat. 24th May	School 1st XI	v. Chigwell School	School	2.30 p.m.
Mon 26th May	School 1st XI	v. London Hospital	School	2.30 p.m.
Sat. 7th June	School 1st XI	v. Haberdashers' Aske's S.	School	2.30 p.m.
Sat. 14th June	School	Visitation Day	School	
Sat. 14th June	School 1st XI	v. St. Alban's School	School	2.30 p.m.
Tues. 17th June	School 1st XI	v. Essex Club and Ground	School	11.30 a.m.
Sat. 28th June	School 1st XI	v. Queen Elizabeth's School	School	2.30 p.m.
Sat. 12th July	Old Bancroftians Association	Old Boys' Day }	School	11.30 a.m.
Sat. 12th July	O.B. Cricket XI	v. School 1st XI }		
Fri. 18th July	School	Swimming Sports	School	
Sun. 20th July	School Choir	Service of Music	School Chapel	6.30 p.m.
Thurs. 24th July		**School Term ends**		

Note.—Copy for *The Bancroftian* must reach the Editors as follows: for the March issue, by Monday, 10th March, 1947; for the July issue, by Monday, 23rd June, 1947.

Music Club Concerts are held in the School Library every Saturday at 8 p.m.

School and O.B.A. calendar, 1947

while on a teaching exchange and went to live in that country, dying aged 61. Mr Lord taught English and became involved with the first educational broadcasts, eventually becoming a full time producer for ITV, doubtless a more lucrative profession. He also emigrated across the Atlantic. A third master appointed at the end of the war was Mr Williamson. His trunk bore labels from all over the world and there was the sudden appearance of a clerical collar, but it was clear to his forms that he knew very little history. For reasons not stated he was banned from any school receiving government funds, so his trunks soon followed him from the School. With that exception, Mr Adams' appointments were usually successful, though the Common Room remained very static during this period. Amongst those whom he appointed still at the School are Mr Murray and Mr Giles, an Old Bancroftian who believes that schoolmastering does not end at four o'clock and has been involved in the CCF, school plays and, of course, the O.B.A. Both are now housemasters.

Academically, these were good though perhaps easy years. There were more places at the older universities, professions took more notice of the new GCE 'A' levels than they had of higher school certificates and more boys stayed on because of impending national service. Economically, also, it was easier for boys to go up to university. This is not to deride the School, for scholarship meant a good deal to Mr Adams, and he was proud that he and several of his colleagues had been scholars at their colleges.

197

Indeed, he was forever impressing on parents the importance of good 'A' level results, and the staff was increased to cope with and strengthen the sixth form, the School growing to 440 boys during this period, space being found for the extra classrooms, and the abolition of Forms I and II in effect enlarging each remaining year still further.

The standard form was still for most O.B.s to go straight to the City, where they seemed to prosper and rise to positions of prominence, but each year eight or so places were gained at the older universities, and a larger number went to London and the 'up and coming' places such as Manchester and Bristol. In 1958 there were eight places at Oxford alone, and the following year five Oxford and Cambridge awards were won. It is invidious to single out names but amongst those who left the school for Cambridge in the 'fifties are James Nursaw who later took the Blackstone Prize and Harroworth Scholarship at the Middle Temple and is a legal adviser at the Home Office; Fred Emery, of *The Times*; Geoffrey Smeed who sang his way to Gonville & Caius and is now a solicitor; Ian Jeffery who was President of the Cambridge Athletics Club and is now a director of a major Lloyds broking house; and J. D. Hoskin who won a hockey blue in 1961 and '62.

To Oxford went Tom Auber, solicitor and industrious O.B.; Michael Hill, lately a QC and Treasury Counsel; and Richard Shaw, son of an O.B. and partner in an eponymous firm of maritime solicitors. Also at Oxford in the immediate post-war period were D. Hawkes, who was Professor of Chinese during this period, and Alan Palmer who quit pedagogy to produce books which combine erudition and entertainment, and who has helped greatly with this less worthy tome.

There were many others, men whose age is now bringing them to the fore of their chosen careers and of whom the School should be justly proud, just as one hopes that they take pride in Bancroft's. The growing list of obituaries of old boys in *The Bancroftian* during this period tolled the years since the Association was founded. Percy Loft, surveyor to the Governors, died in 1951, as did James Thorpe, artist and cricketer who had done so much to found the Association and who left to the Drapers' Company on trust his extensive cricket library. Brigadier French died the year he became Junior Warden of the Drapers' Company, leaving money to the Mission and his library to the

School, and Goddard, President in the bicentenary year, another Draper described in his obituary as being 'by temperament shy, ultra-conservative . . . [who] had difficulty in adjusting to social and other changes'. The tragic loss of Sangster Simmonds will be referred to below.

O.B.s continued to gain distinction. In Coronation year, P. M. J. Mantle became CMG, while the two Townend brothers each were appointed CBE, surely a unique occurrence. Wilfred Sheldon, paediatrician to the Queen, and E. W. Light, Head of Protocol at the Foreign Office, received the accolade of KCVO, an order of chivalry reserved for personal service to Her Majesty, H. L. Saunders and W. G. Hynard had been knighted a few years earlier; the latter was one of the last Canadian knights.

Old Boys were well represented on the Board of Governors at this time. In 1943 the Court of Assistants appointed Sir Graham Cunningham as one of their five nominees, Sangster Simmonds being, of course, a member of the Court and sitting on the Board as a Draper rather than as an O.B., and T. H. Knight became an Essex County Council nominee in 1946.

It was a proud day for the O.B.A. when Sangster Simmonds became Master of the Drapers' Company in 1950, an office he held for two years, and the Association made him President for a second time. He also became Chairman of Governors when Mr Monro kindly stood down for him. His early death in 1953 was a great loss to the School, the Association and the Company, he being the one man who was truly a part of all three. A Drapers' scholar at Bancroft's, he had pursued a medical career, being elected FRCS, and having a thriving practice in Harley Street where many O.B.s were cordially received in his rooms. His natural charm and clear abilities made him an obvious choice for high office in the Drapers' Company, and the various O.B. societies such as the Exhibition and Loan Fund and the Mission received his time and financial assistance, while he took seriously his position as President of the Dramatic Society, entertaining the members each year at his country home.

On becoming Chairman of Governors he forced on an unwilling Ministry the necessary changes to stop the loss of £1,400 a year on the boarding scholarship account, and prepared the way for other changes brought about by the Company's generosity. After his death, the O.B.A. erected a memorial in the School Chapel, and Mr Monro resumed the

Chairmanship until 1954 when Col Mason, a geography don at Oxford, took over until 1959. Mr Monro's death in 1968 was a loss mourned by the Association, he having been a keen surrogate O.B., a fine club cricketer and always a witty speaker at dinners.

Another change at Drapers' Hall was the retirement of Mr Kirk as Clerk to the Governors in 1951 and his replacement by Mr A. A. O'Neill. Mr Kirk's devotion to Bancroft's was apparent, and he himself drew attention to the fact that so much of his time was spent on Bancroft's business to the detriment of the Company's many other trusts and affairs. He and Mr Monro did much to cement relations between the Company and the Association in the years immediately before the war, and their attendance at the Annual Dinner was a welcome innovation. Mr Kirk always made a point of spending a few moments with any parents who called at Drapers' Hall to pay fees and he guided the Governors well during his thirty years as Clerk. Fortunately, his successor, Alan O'Neill, proved an equally good friend of Bancroft's and is a local Essex man.

The administration of the School at this time seems remarkably amateurish from the viewpoint of the age of computers. Most of the paperwork was done at Drapers' Hall by the Clerk, Mr Adams being assisted latterly by R. S. M. West in all school work, and formerly with a secretary. The Governors had complete control over the administration and oversaw the finances, though after Mr Kirk's retirement there was an assistant clerk at the school. In an age of growing inflation the system proved inadequate in balancing the books or, it seems, in seeing where the problem lay.

At a time when domestic servants were disappearing from the Monkhams Estate, the School still maintained a large staff. In 1956 there was a matron, nurse, cook, sewing maid, seven resident maids and sixteen other women. The school field and West Grove were tended by four groundsmen under the charge of R. S. M. West, who also oversaw the engineer. The position of 'boots' was not replaced after the war. The wages of these employees were now linked to local labour exchange rates which doubled their pre-war figure. Masters' salaries had also edged up. The top Burnham scale London salary in 1939 had been £500. There had been wartime bonuses to help meet high income tax and in 1946 the top salary was £603, rising to £686 the following year. These increases were followed by others bringing the staff bill to £32,000 in 1963.

The poor Head Master had lost the generous salary of his predecessors, when it was twice that of the senior master, and his was now also linked to the Burnham scale, plus certain allowances. He had his house, too, which by that time had become an old-fashioned residence impossible to run without servants which the new man could not afford. Several times he offered his house for other uses – as a boarding house, as flats for young masters – and eventually a new kitchen was built on to the old servery next to the dining room, and central heating installed, the basement being closed off from the main part of the house.

The fees naturally rose to meet these increases, though the endowment income did not. By increasing the number of paying places to seventy in 1954, the projected income increase by 1960 was £5,100 a year, which covered the boarding house costs. The problem with fees was that they had to be agreed by the Ministry of Education who sought some justification for the rise. As the Company's books were audited once a year and trust and Company accounts balanced, the figures and corresponding rises were always out of date. This resulted in an ever-growing deficit estimated at £2,500 a year in 1948 – the year when the Labour Government talked of seizing all school endowments.

To add to the debts of simply running the School were the costs of basic repairs and decorations of a sixty year old building. Nothing had been done since before the War, and repairs were estimated at £3,000 in 1946, a sum loaned by the Drapers' Company. The Head Master also wished to extend the Dining Hall towards the Great Hall to seat all the school diners, and to build a new swimming pool. Neither plan was realised, though the Junior Day Room was used for luncheon. In 1954 the school account was overdrawn by £25,000 and the Drapers' Company covenanted £3,000 for seven years to pay off this debt and to help pay for some repairs and improvements, including new WCs by the swappers. With the extra income from boarding places the debt was cleared by 1961.

The only building during Mr Adams' time came at the very end of his reign when the Drapers' Company covenanted £100,000 to build a new boarder block and day boy locker rooms, as well as creating two flats for masters in the former maids' quarters.

The standard of life for boarders improved greatly after the War, although rationing kept the food at a poor level until the 1950s, when the dreaded Thursday Welsh Rabbit disappeared. Having been at Sedbergh as a house master, Mr Adams was keen that boys should have some privacy and better creature comforts. A proper high tea was instituted and improvements made to the sleeping accommodation. The new block, begun in 1964 to commemorate the Drapers' Company sexcentenary, provided better day rooms on the ground and first floor and sixth form studies on the top floor. This was, of course, a forerunner of the major building works of the last twenty years. He was greatly aided by the matron, Mrs Pepper and her successor, Mrs Young, in instigating these improvements.

As Mr Adams approached his retirement, so a number of colleagues also prepared to quit the school, having reached their threescore years. It was a particularly happy common room at that time: small, intimate, and full of characters who all got on very well together. Mr Schaerli, the tall athletic linguist had retired in 1955 having been at the school since 1920. A keen soccer player in his younger days, he had also played fives and had boxed. A man with a keen sense of humour, he delighted on occasion to 'forget' his mastery of the English tongue in order gently to mock a colleague with some solecism. Perhaps his methods were old fashioned but they achieved good results. At the end of term he acted as book broker in the days when boys bought their own books, and kept a different type of book on sports day, this occasion invariably leaving him out of pocket, much to his own amusement. More importantly he started the school tours abroad in the 'thirties, and the visit of boys from Germany in 1957, reciprocated the following year, was his idea. A congratulatory message was sent him by the O.B.A. on his ninetieth birthday in 1985, shortly before his death. He married the sister of the five Cohen brothers, all O.B.s.

The mass exodus from the School between 1964 and 1970 robbed Bancroft's of eight masters who had served 292 years between them. Of the four who left in 1964 or 1965, Mr Belchamber had come in 1927, Mr Jenkins in 1929, Mr Houston in 1930 and Mr Emtage in 1933. To these must be added a fifth, Mr Matraves who came during the War and retired in 1965.

Mr Ifor Jenkins, being a Welshman, was devoted to rugby and music as well as being a gifted linguist who took several parties abroad. Intellectually he came second only to Snape on the pre-war staff, and he devoted all his energies to Bancroft's, ever defending it or anything connected with the school. He was a great character, defender of the under-dog, and a declared bon viveur.

During the War when Mr Wells laid down that boys playing at Riggs Retreat – always the less skilled teams – must run up to the School when the siren sounded, Mr Jenkins stated that if any boy made it in time, he wanted to know, as he was clearly first XV potential. Fond of an occasional drink with a cousin in the City, he sometimes fell asleep on the last train, ending up at Epping or Chingford. One evening his wife Nellie, a great favourite still with O.B.s, found a note which she read as: 'have taken much'. Not thinking how the message had been delivered, she arranged for cars to meet the last trains, all to no avail. In the meanwhile her husband arrived home in a healthy state, and eventually the message, from a musical master more accustomed, perhaps, to writing Greek, was translated as 'have taken music'. An Honorary Member of the Old Bancroftians' Association until his death in 1979 when his widow was elected an Associate Member, his memory is held in high esteem by countless O.B.s.

Mr J. B. de C. Emtage was a very different sort of person. From a distinguished Caribbean family, he played cricket for the West Indies and was a member of the MCC. A keen mathematician, he regarded the cricket square as more important than trigonometry, and did sterling work with the cricket XI, creating a team which, for the size of School, performed well each season. Always a keen writer, his book *Foolscap and Bells* is an amusing whodunnit with thinly veiled reference to some of his colleagues and a fairly bitter judgement of Mr Adams. He still lives in Loughton but does not attend O.B. functions.

Mr Arthur Belchamber arrived at Bancroft's the same day as Mr Francombe, and the latter maintains that his colleague was too good a soul for the rough and tumble of life there, especially in Mr Playne's later days. A deeply conscientious and religious man, he studiously learned the rules of rugby football when the School changed the shape of its ball, and persevered with the teaching of mathematics even though in the grips of a fatal disease which killed him within a year of leaving school, after thirty-seven years of devoted service.

The following year, along with Mr Adams' retirement, Messrs

Matraves and Houston left the school. 'House' to the post-war boarders who came under his wing, had been Mr Playne's last appointment in 1930. Of radical politics, an internationalist to use an old pre-war term, Mr Houston was driven on by a strong sense of duty, no doubt inherited from his clerical father, and always expected even more from himself than from others.

He took over the boarding house when Mr Adams became Head Master and always strove to improve the standards of the boys' lives. More importantly, he stood up for the boarders at a time when they were subject to much criticism. Not that he ever gave any indication to the boys that he was on their side; he seldom smiled and was a strong disciplinarian. By those senior boys who got to know him well, he is remembered as a lover of good music, and the grower of roses above the old air raid shelters.

Mr Matraves bowed out at Easter 1965, having been a bastion of the physics department for over twenty years. The great joke remembered is of him explaining Newton's law that 'every action has an equal and opposite reaction' while leaning on the tap on his demonstration table, the tap bending under his weight. He was always delighted when his pessimistic reports proved wrong.

The retirement of Sydney Adams, at a time when a change of Government was threatening the very existence of Bancroft's, was very much a watershed. Looking back one can express amusement at the fears created by inflation at 3% and examining the amount of oil used when it cost 9d a gallon. The politicians of the time referred to this period as either one of Tory misrule, or alternatively as a period when some had never had it so good. Perhaps both are true and apply to Bancroft's as well as to other features of English society. A belief that the old pre-war world could be restored allowed the victors to fall behind in industrial and technological advancement. Similarly, Bancroft's failed to take advantage of the headstart it had on the expanding county high schools, which were allowed to catch up in both standard and attainment, until cut down in the name of educational equality and progress in the 'sixties and 'seventies.

One has the impression that the Adams regime happily muddled through the minor vicissitudes which occasionally arose without attempting to take measures to prevent future occurrences. When the Head Master, a gifted mathematician, made a complete mess of the sports account, there were no retributions; the Governors merely called in Mr Price from Price Waterhouse to sort things out, and then started all over again. These were the last days of the gifted amateur.

The great strength of Mr Adams was his spirit of laisser faire. Not that he was a soft master: he could be angry when some action hurt a colleague or brought the school into disrepute, but he was wise in realising that certain boys could not be pushed into orthodox paths. One of his pupils, C. C. Fry, a gifted musician, was given encouragement to pursue music and, with his great charm, broke all sorts of rules in that pursuit and is now a celebrated conductor. One of Mr Adams' first actions was to make light of two boys caught pilfering in South Woodford on the grounds that they were indulging in high spirits rather than a malevolent theft, and the Governors backed him. One has no doubts as to what Mr Wells' attitude would have been.

It was this pragmatic approach that made his time at Bancroft's such a success and few O.B.s look back to that period without a deep affection for Mr Adams. His love of the School was never in doubt, nor was his grasp of what was happening in every corner of the quad and beyond. As with any good captain, he knew how to delegate without losing control. He undoubtedly had presence – no one questioned that he was in the company of the Head Master – and yet it was tempered with a genuine humility based on a deep belief in fundamental Christian values. Few will forget his sermons in Chapel, or his prayers when remembering a deceased colleague or pupil.

Taking over Bancroft's at the time that he did, he had the great strength to kindle both the School's own spirit and character and the great work of his predecessor. It was probably alien to his innate conservatism to change the set pattern, he merely tempered the Wells regime with his own good natured ways, reaping academic successes beyond Mr Playne's wildest dreams and achieving it all with a happy school, no doubt an epitaph with which Mr Adams would have been pleased to concur.

BANCROFT'S SCHOOL.

Class Lists, Dec. 1948

The Holidays will end on FRIDAY, JANUARY 15th, 1949 The names of Boarders will be called over at six o'clock, when every boy must be present unless his friends have previously sent to the Head Master a Medical Certificate explaining the reason of his absence.

DAY BOYS will return the following morning, SATURDAY, JANUARY 16th, at the usual time.

The Services in the School Chapel on Sundays are:

8.0 a.m.	Holy Communion.
10.30 a.m.	Matins and Sermon.
6.15 p.m.	Evensong.

Day Boys are most welcome at all these services.

List of Staff, 1948

Christmas card, 1951

HONTO GOD ONLY BE HONOUR AND GLORY

The Governors and Headmaster

of

Bancroft's School, Woodford,

request the pleasure of the Company of

- -

on Visitation Day

Saturday, the 18th July, 1953, at 1.45 p.m.

Invitation to Visitation Day, 1953

207

BANCROFT'S SCHOOL.

REGULATIONS FOR RELIGIOUS INSTRUCTION.

The following regulations are made by the Governing Body of the above-named School in accordance with the Regulations of the Ministry of Education for Direct Grant Grammar Schools.

(1) Religious instruction distinctive of the Church of England will be given to pupils about to be confirmed, whose parents or guardians have, in the manner specified in these regulations, requested that such instruction shall be provided for them.

(2) Any request for such instruction by the parent or guardian of a pupil must be made in writing to the HEAD MASTER before the first day of the term in which it is desired that the instruction should begin.

(3) No catechism or formulary distinctive of any particular religious denomination shall be taught in the School to any pupil whose parent or guardian has not made such a request.

(4) A copy of these regulations shall be given by the Head Master to the parent or guardian of each pupil now in the School, and of each pupil hereafter admitted.

(5) The Head Master shall keep a record of all requests made in accordance with these regulations.

By order of the Governors,

A. A. O'NEILL,

Clerk.

Letter from Clerk regarding religious education

Mr Geoffrey Watts, Clerk to the Governors since 1973

Mr Ian Richardson, Head Master 1965–85

Uniform *c*.1865

School Uniforms: Mstr Chisholm, Christ's Hospital, 1985. Bancroft's uniform would have been similar in the eighteenth Century

The Author, 1975

L. and K. Clark. *c.*1914

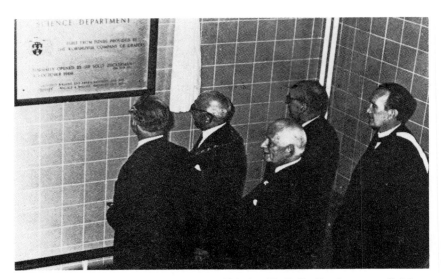

The opening of the Science Block, 1970, by Sir Solly Zuckerman, O.M.

C.C.F. Corps of Drums, 1969

BANCROFT'S SCHOOL.

Class Lists, Winter and Spring, 1966/7

The Housemasters are—

Boarders	...	...	...	...	P. J. C. MURRAY, M.A.
East House	...	...	...	...	E. A. OWENS, M.A.
West House	...	...	...	...	R. H. BRADSHAW, A.T.D.
North House	...	...	...	...	E. L. H. KENTFIELD, M.A.

Parents may consult the Housemasters with regard
to the work and progress of the boys.

SCHOOL TERMS 1966/7

Winter: Saturday, 17th September,* to Wednesday, 14th December. Half Term 29th October, to 1st November.

Spring: Saturday, 7th January,* to Thursday, 23rd March. Half Term 17th to 20th February.

Summer: Wednesday, 19th April,* to Wednesday, 12th July. Half Term 26th May, to 30th May.

The Winter Term 1967 will begin on Wednesday, 6th September.*

*Boarders return on previous evening.

List of staff, 1966

CHAPTER XIV

IAN MACDONALD RICHARDSON
1965-1977

IT WAS to be Mr Richardson's fate that his appointment coincided with the return of a Labour Government determined to alter the independent sector of education, and from the beginning he and the Governors knew that Bancroft's would have to fight for survival.

A son of the manse and educated at Merchant Taylors', Crosby, Mr Richardson held an RNVR commission at the end of the war and then went as a classical scholar to Emmanuel College, Cambridge. Teaching posts followed at Llandovery College and Woolverstone Hall, Suffolk, and he then became Head Master of The Grange School, Santiago, Chile in 1959. With his wife and four children in residence the Head Master's house was fuller than it had been since Mr Playne's time, though the basement floor was unused by the family, and the days of servants were confined to the past. Mr Richardson was not the man to decline a challenge, though the great pressure of the headmastership was to result in a serious heart attack as the office became less that of scholar–administrator and more that of a business executive of a concern with an annual one million pound turnover.

To problems with Government departments can be added both the evil of inflation, which saw everything, from the price of beer to school fees, rise in cost at a hitherto unknown rate, and the great change in attitude of the young to authority and the ways of their forefathers. Undoubtedly Mr Richardson's reign was more difficult, and saw greater change than that of any predecessor, and throughout it he remained calm and urbane, taking each challenge as it came and never losing his sense of humour.

An important change which affected the School was the creation of the Greater London Council in 1965, which merged the old London County Council with new suburban authorities. For the first time in nearly eighty years Bancroft's was again within the administrative boundaries of the capital city.

Bancroftians – and staff – have always been of a variety of political shades, as one would expect from such a school, and Bancroft's and all bodies associated with it should remain above political discussion, and this book should follow that example. One cannot, however, escape from the fact that one of the two major political parties destroyed the direct grant system and would like to see Bancroft's and schools like it change completely their character and lose their independence. For that reason this chapter will of necessity have to dwell on political decisions and make unfavourable comments on the policy of Labour government at both national and local level, the author's motives being pro-Bancroft's rather than based on political bias.

A Government takes a while to puts its programme into operation and no changes were made to the status of direct grant schools while the Public Schools Commission was preparing its reports, though the grant itself was cut. What was of immediate effect was the attitude of the new borough councils. With Redbridge, in which the School is situated – though only just – the Governors had, and continue to have, most felicitous relations, but then Redbridge was to become one of the 'rebel' councils determined to keep some selective schools. Essex County Council, who continued to be on friendly terms, surrendered one of its two places on the Board of Governors to Redbridge, a position held for a number of years by Cllr A. J. Escott, an Old Boy. With other councils, such as Havering and Waltham Forest, relations were severed. With the Inner London Education Authority, successor to the LCC, a more farcical situation arose, doubtless much to the embarrassment of Mrs Holman, their appointed Governor, who had always conscientiously filled that important office.

The School had long since surrendered its right to examine boys, relying on the LCC to put forward good candidates and, as has been shown, their choice included many very distinguished Bancroftians. Their previous unhelpful stance now turned to positive hostility when they refused to circulate details of the School's scholarships to their primary schools, and failed to fill up their quota of places. The School was obliged, of course, as a direct grant school, to maintain a quarter of its places for local education authority boys and, by its charitable deed, to give thirty places to LCC educated boys, and ILEA's attitude threatened both these obligations. The Governors therefore

211

decided to translate 'LCC' into 'GLC' and it was agreed that the Head Master and Clerk would fill those places not taken up by ILEA with boys from such councils as Barnet, Hillingdon and Croydon who were more appreciative that the sons of their ratepayers should receive Mr Bancroft's legacy.

At Bancroft's itself, Mr Richardson had inherited a happy School and a contented if ageing MCR. Academically, however, recent results had been disappointing, and in a cogent report he suggested that the old streaming system was not having its desired effect and recommended its abolition. He also sought an increase in staff, which was agreed, and pressed for a larger intake of boys, which caused further problems.

The finances of the School had never been in a healthy condition and were intended only to balance each year. Governors were reluctant to put up fees and consequently, when the account went into deficit, it was difficult to rectify the situation. The answer was, of course, to increase the number of fee payers, but this needed the sanction of the Department of Education, who paid the per caput direct grant. They opposed any increase as they intended that the School would soon be integrated within the state system.

They were also most reluctant to allow an increase in the fees, at £30 a term in 1965, despite a rising rate of inflation. By 1968 the situation had become critical, a substantial salary increase by the Burnham Committee not being met by an increase in the direct grant, and the Governors reluctantly turned to Redbridge to talk of a possible integration of Bancroft's with their school system.

As has been said, Redbridge had always been most sympathetic to Bancroft's and they fully appreciated the situation. They declined to consider taking on the School, but thought they would need to increase their number of places to thirty a year. A special sub-committee – the first of several during this period – was formed by the Governors to consider the School's future. It included R. V. Wingham, who had succeeded Sir Graham Cunningham as the O.B. on the board. Himself a boarder under Playne, perhaps a good training for his prolonged stay as a guest of the Japanese Emperor for much of the War, he has served the O.B.A. in a number of capacities, most especially as Secretary 1955–64 and as President in 1966, and was an obvious candidate to follow Cunningham as the representative O.B. on the Board of

Governors; a choice that has proved most successful as he has been a most conscientious and useful Governor.

The committee's report, presented in July 1969 and based on the assumption that Bancroft's would continue to operate as an independent school, recommended an expansion to 600 pupils from the current 440, space for new classes to be made by reducing the boarding house to thirty boys. The intake in September 1968 had been of ninety boys to make up for a fall in the total at School owing to alterations in the form structure. The Department of Education were most reluctant, however, for that number to become the regular intake of the School, though they eventually relented, while awaiting the results of the Newsom Report on direct grant schools. They refused, however, to allow the fees – £50 a term in 1968 – to be increased by enough to pay off the £17,500 overdraft, which the Drapers' Company underwrote. As the rate of inflation became worse, the obligation to justify an increase of fees to the Department of Education to meet increase in expenditure meant that the School was always in deficit. The feeling soon grew that the usefulness of the direct grant might have been outweighed by the advantages of full independence – the right to expand, to charge a more realistic fee, and to alter the syllabus.

When the Public Schools' Commission issued its report in 1970 it inevitably recommended the abolition of the direct grant, and the Governors, after much thought and discussion, formally appealed to the Drapers' Company to support full independence, irrespective of the forthcoming election result. The Company gave its support, and so began a decade of building and conversion of Blomfield's school.

The spate of retirements, such a feature of Mr Adams' last few years, continued. Mr Francombe retired in 1966 and Messrs Owens' and Clark's retirement in 1969, and Mr Kentfield's a year later, cut the last links with the pre-war era, for, although Mr Bradshaw was appointed in 1939, war service delayed the practical beginning of his long years of service.

Don Francombe, the doyen of the MCR, 'untidy arbiter of elegance, master of the dead tag and the living repartee, connoisseur of music and good conversation' had been appointed by Mr Playne in 1927 when straight down from Magdalene College, Cambridge, in theory to teach Latin, but in practice to teach several subjects to his form in the early years. A man who

213

made friends irrespective of age, he added a civilizing quality to the boarding house of those days, and the contemporary sixth form provided many life-long friends, including Sir Frederick Warner, D. E. Coult and L. S. Buss. As with most of his colleagues then, he was not a nine-to-four master, but became involved in numerous activities, including the choir – he is a fine organist and singer, and formed the Combined Choir with Loughton Girls School – the Arts Club, the Library, and school plays. He is especially remembered, however, as editor of *The Bancroftian* for over thirty years, and the joint editor with Coult of the 1937 book to which this one owes so much. A self-deprecating man who prefers to see the better side of everyone's character, his affection for Bancroft's, Bancroftians and all to do with them has never diminished, and Old Boys continue to make the pilgrimage to South Harting in Sussex where he and his wife Wynne have made their retirement home. The year following his retirement, the O.B.A. made him their President – he had been an honorary member since 1958 – the first assistant master, to be so honoured since the Rev W. C. Winterton in 1913. A fitting tribute is the way that O.B.s surround him at functions which he still regularly attends. Any school owes much to the devotion of the staff, and no-one exemplifies the good master more than Mr Francombe.

At the end of Summer term 1969 three more masters left, after a combined total of 94 years' service to the School. Mr K. G. Clark, an Old Boy, had completed forty years of teaching woodwork, firstly at the back of the swappers, then in a wooden hut known, inevitably, as 'Clark's College' and finally in the new 1937 workshop. A skilled and meticulous craftsman who conveyed the love of his craft to his pupils, he was always willing to help those boys who showed a keenness for his subject and resignedly accepted the 'below the salt' station of the woodwork master. He had manufactured and sold gramophones with his brother, L. H. Clark, before joining the staff. Unfortunately his retirement was blighted when he contracted Parkinson's Disease, a curse which he never allowed to depress him. He died in 1979.

Mr E. A. Owens had arrived at Bancroft's in January, 1933. A keen rugby player at Pembroke College, Oxford, and for the London Welsh, he turned the relatively young Rugby Club into a first rate school side, combining good training skills with an uncanny ability to spot good young players. Although able to avoid national service, he joined the RAF in 1941 and only

214

returned to the School in 1946. Like so many of his vintage he taught a variety of subjects and was especially popular and effective with younger boys. He held old-fashioned notions about education, believing that examination results were not the be-all and end-all of a school's job, but rather that it should turn out civilized, well-mannered human beings, proud of their school and its history and traditions, and working to put more into the community than they necessarily took out. As house master of East House from 1964–9, he greatly improved its sporting reputation and its cohesion, previously lacking as most of the boys lived in far-off Ilford. The boys will always remember him with affection, his ancient gown sleeves tied into knots which made a most effective weapon. He retired with his wife to the West Country, where he still plays a skilful round of golf.

The third of the trio, J. R. Clayton, joined the School in 1951 following a career in the army and colonial service, and soon became one of the School's characters. As he stood in the old, cold chemistry laboratory, a hole would be seen at each elbow, going through his lab. coat, overcoat, jacket and jumper to his (home-made) shirt, except on high days such as Visitation Day when his immaculate self-cut suits put others to shame. The vast bunches of keys he always carried gave rise to the nickname 'Clanger' which extended to his home-made cars, the 'clanger mobiles', for which, it was said, he found it increasingly difficult to find an insurer. The story of the balloon which rose from the front of the School and landed in the middle of the High Road is part of Bancroft's lore of the 1950s, as was his skill in repairing organs, which he taught himself to play.

It was significant that he retired before the new laboratories were opened, because he despised the new methods: when asked his opinion of the Nuffield syllabus he replied, 'I was studying chemistry while Nuffield was still making bicycles in Oxford High Street'. A character, he was popular with the boys, and, by tradition, he was presented with a cigar by the boys on his luncheon table at Christmas. In retirement he took to making clavichords, and died in 1983. If any criticism can be made of Bancroft's and other schools of today, it is that they do not have room for such characters.

The following year, Mr E. L. H. Kenfield left his room in the east cloister which he had occupied since 1932. Small in stature, he possessed a speed and agility seen to good advantage in hockey, a game which he introduced to Bancroft's in 1939, having played it at St Edmund Hall, Oxford. A linguist, he became head of the modern languages department teaching mainly German, but also French and Russian, and his extra-mural activities included command of the CCF in the 1950s, he having served in the RAF for most of the War, and creating the new North House in 1964. He became second master in 1966, when he proved an efficient administrator in the last days before that office became a more demanding occupation in its own right. On Vis. Day, which he organised with the flair of an Earl Marshal, he was in complete command of the situation, able to handle and smooth over the inevitable crises of that day. To mark his retirement, the Governors gave a luncheon for him and his predecessor Mr Francombe at Drapers' Hall, and presented each with a piece of silver. His departure was the end of an era in the School's history and, though a naturally conservative man, he doubtless approved of the new buildings which were being planned. He died in 1984.

When it became clear that full independence was a feasibility, Mr Richardson was able with confidence to place plans before the Governors for dramatic alterations to the buildings. The new Science block, erected on a loan – later converted to an outright gift – from the Drapers' Company in 1968–9, and opened by Sir Solly Zuckerman, OM, chief scientific adviser to Her Majesty's Government, was the first and most necessary improvement, the first new classrooms since the War. Designed partly by the School surveyor, R. V. Lone, and built by the Wallace family firm, it was very much an Old Bancroftian creation, and was a vast improvement on the great laboratories of the 1910 building. The science staff was increased and laboratory technicians employed to assist them as the School entered the technological age. Mr Franklin and Miss Stokes moved into the first floor physics laboratories., Messrs Copsey and Jeffery into the chemistry department above, while Mr Denyer, gentlest and kindest of men but the butt of too many ebullient pupils, transferred his biology classroom from the School's original laboratory on the library staircase to the 1910 building.

By 1970, pressure having been relieved by Mr Heath's new Conservative administration, the expansion to a three-form ninety boy intake was agreed with the Department of Education; Mr O'Neill, Clerk to the Governors, expressing mock surprise at the sympathy of hitherto awkward bureaucrats. An informal visit from Her Majesty's Inspectors of Schools occurred, and they pressed for an improvement in the gymnasium and library. Similarly, if the School were to expand, new classrooms would be needed. As no definite plans had been made for the boarding house as yet, the dormitories could not be divided up.

The Head Master's plan was for a development in three parts. Firstly, a cafeteria system should be introduced in Dining Hall, thus reducing serving staff and allowing the old Day Room to be partitioned into an enlarged MCR and staff office. Secondly, the Blue Room and library would be merged into one larger library, the music department moving to the 1964 boarder block which would also house lockers. The area under the library would provide four new classrooms, the day boys doing without day rooms. Also, the sea scout store, in what had once been part of the open assy in the west wing, was turned into a classroom. By far the most ambitious – and costly – scheme was the building of an entirely new gym complex. On the bottom of his report the Head Master sketched what was to become the new gymnasium, bath and swappers. At the same time, it was discovered that the Great Hall roof was in danger of collapse, and the opportunity was taken to remove the raked floor, thus allowing more uses for the Hall. The Drapers' Company gave £15,000 for this, but the Governors decided for the first time to launch an appeal amongst Old Boys, friends and parents, the target being £120,000.

The appeal did not prove a total success, raising some £112,000 and that slowly. The professional fund raisers – who received 15% of takings – blamed the failure on 'the deeply entrenched resistance of locally based Old Boys' but the answer probably lay in the uncertainty about the School's future at the time, for the 1981 appeal raised a larger sum with little difficulty; no doubt the Governors learned from past mistakes. The Drapers' Company granted £7,000 a year for seven years, and guaranteed an overdraft of £100,000, for, as much of the appeal came in seven-year covenants, the building had initially to be financed by a bank loan, an expensive business in the 1970s, as the effects of inflation both reduced the true value of the appeal and caused high interest payments. By the time the Lord Mayor of London, Sir Edward de Courcey Howard, Bt, laid the foundation stone in 1972, the scheme was in financial difficulties and the Drapers' Company, as Trustees, decided to take advantage of the great property boom and sell the Holborn property which was producing a low rent on a long lease. The original property of Francis Bancroft, added to in 1737 and 1938, its sale produced sufficient capital to complete the buildings and increase the Trust income by £10,000 a year, £8,000 of which was, by agreement with the Charity Commissioners, reinvested for sixty years to compensate for the loss of capital and eventual income caused by the sale.

All in all 1972 was a bad year. The Head Master suffered a serious heart attack which debilitated him for six months, the Second Master, Mr Millett, taking over for the time being. A tragedy occurred when a pupil of the School, M. J. Lambert, was blinded by an explosion of chemicals off the School premises. A particularly bright boy, he overcome the great disability and pursued his love of geology.

The year was filled with deaths: Mr Peet, Colonel Charles Newman, VC, and McMinn, senior Old Boy and an elder figure of the Association from its foundation. Along with J. H. Thorpe, his life-long friend, he did more than anybody else to found the Association, and was its first O.B. President in 1911, having previously organised the Annual Dinner, football and cricket XIs and countless other activities. A bachelor schoolmaster at Strand School, later renamed King's College School, he devoted himself to the School of his education, the one where he taught and to the Presbyterian Church in Croydon where his family worshipped. Aged 96, blind and frail, he kept in touch with the Association and the School to the last, and was pleased at the prospect of a museum of Bancroftiana being formed at the School, for he had kept all his old papers and memorabilia, and collected those of others as well, and his last thoughts before death were for the School and the Association. He had outlived all his contemporaries, and many of their children, but his funeral was attended by many O.B.s and also ex-pupils, one in his eighties. As Gooding wrote in his *Bancroftian* obituary, 'Farewell, leader of the Clan: fare well the Clan'.

Another O.B. death was that of C. E. ('Peter') Wiles, CBE, who had served many years in the Middle East. President when the Drapers' Company celebrated the sexcentenary of its first charter, he had arranged the presentation of silver, and bequeathed £1,000 each to the Chapel and Old Bancroftians' Lodge of which he had been Master.

218

Two other institutions changed their character in that year: the Rugby Club opened its doors to outsiders as full members in an effort to increase – or maintain – the number of sides, and *The Bancroftian* of McMinn and Francombe, which had travelled the world and appeared in Great War trenches, disappeared to be replaced by a larger magazine, more suited to the pupils than the Old Boys and seeming to the latter to contain more satire than record. Inevitably, within ten years a vast majority of O.B.s ceased to take it and so this strong link between Bancroftians aged eleven to ninety was broken. It is, perhaps, a pity that a separate pupils magazine was not encouraged, leaving *The Bancroftian* as a record of School and Old Boy events and characters, for the magazine has proved a great help in writing this book, and one wonders what source the next writer in 2037 will use for his research.

Not all was despair in 1972: J. Margolis won £1,000 for the School and £250 for himself in *The Spectator* essay prize, with a brilliant satire of *1984* geared towards multi-racial Britain. Margolis is now a successful journalist. More importantly, a new scheme was agreed by the Charity Commissioners. Finally sealed on 1st June 1973, it gave the Governors the power to abolish the boarding house, go co-educational and open a prep school department at its convenience. The ILEA representative was removed and replaced by a second Redbridge nominee, giving them two places, Essex one, the Drapers' Company five plus the Master ex-officio during his year, with the power to co-opt two others. The endowment, reinvested and earning £27,500 a year, was to be spent either on boarding or day boy scholarships and, for the first time since 1737, the boys of London were not given priority in the charity of Francis Bancroft.

It was clear that the School would need the space taken up by the boarders. Plans were made at one time to buy an hotel in Mornington Road to house sixty boys and several members of staff, and the Drapers' Company agreed to finance the project, but in the end it was considered an impractical scheme and the death knell sounded for the boarding house, which finally closed in 1981.

The co-educational clause was written in with no intention of immediate effect: indeed, while the direct grant was still being paid, the clause's implementation was not permitted by the Department of Education except for six or so girls a year in the sixth form. The first two girls arrived in September 1973 and now the majority of schools of Bancroft's sort have girls in their sixth form, and a growing number are following the trend by going fully co-educational, but that will be discussed below. The important thing was that the Governors had full scope to go independent if and when a change of Government caused the destruction of the direct grant, and to change the school in any way to facilitate that change and to maintain the new school.

Changes on the domestic and administrative fronts also occurred during this period. In 1972 the matron, Mrs Young, along with Nurses Megson and Foster retired after many years' service. They were three charming ladies, always kind to day boys and especially helpful to boarders, and their parting, with a dinner and many gifts, marked the end of the office of matron, Mrs Young being the twelfth since Miss Chamberlain's appointment in 1802. With the active support of Mr Adams, she had greatly improved the food for boarders, with cooked breakfasts and teas. Herself the product of a girls' public school, she really looked like a school matron. Her help and kindness was always of the hearty, practical type, and no slackers ever got past her. The present catering ladies are charming and young and do an efficient and more complicated job, but the aura of the office is not there, which is a pity.

The new caterer was an interesting Canadian called Mrs Kohlasch. Quality and quantity of food increased and cricket match teas were worthy of Drapers' Hall itself, but the cost was great and, as she refused to curtail expenditure, she left, to be replaced by the Midland Catering Company, who agreed to do all the lunches and boarders' food for £33,000 a year.

Several dinners were held at the School: the Lodge began meeting at the School in the Summer of 1961 and ate in the Dining Hall, and the O.B.A.'s Annual Dinner moved to the School in 1974, and has remained, being more popular than ever, and a number of other dinners and dances are held at school. The author can attest both to the helpful attitude of the staff and high quality of the food.

An added delight when attending dinners at the School is the chance to renew the acquaintance of old friends on the kitchen staff. As always, it is invidious to mention individuals, but Mrs Kay Barnes and Mrs Peggy Good have been at the School since the 'sixties. As one approaches middle age in a world obsessed

220

with dieting, nutritional values and *nouvelle cuisine* restaurants, it is comforting to meet ladies who still subscribe to the theory that boys need 'feeding up'. It is the devotion of such staff which helps any community to flourish, and Bancroft's is fortunate in being able to hold their loyalty.

In 1973 the Clerk to the Governors, Alan O'Neill, succeeded as Clerk to the Company, a great loss to the School, softened by the pleasure at his promotion and by the sterling qualities of his successor, Mr Geoffrey Watts, who has been associated with the administration of the School since 1954. Both were local men having attended Sir George Monoux School at Walthamstow (Monoux was a Draper). A great friend and, as he would put it, servant of the school, Mr O'Neill was instrumental in improving so many facets of the School and is one of that handful of Drapers whom the Association has elected an honorary member, and he is always an honoured guest at any O.B. occasion.

To complement the Clerks the Governors elected four dedicated Chairmen during this period. Mr Cyrus Boddington, Master of Drapers' Company during their sexcentenary in 1964, became Chairman in 1958, an office he held until his death in 1974. A man of great charm, he performed the duties of his office with an unforgettable style, seen at its best on Visitation Day. He presided at the appointment of Ian Richardson and guided the Governors through the difficult days of the first Wilson administration.

He was followed by Mr Edward Playne and then by Sir Arthur Drew. Mr Playne is one of the very few people actually to have been born at the School, in the Head Master's house in 1907. An architect by profession, he had a distinguished war service in the RAF, and Bancroft's appears amongst his very earliest memories. His devotion to the School is in its way as great as that of his father. Childhood memories include French's wagons carrying dirt along the unmetalled Epping Road, a Zeppelin falling in flames during the Great War, and playing bicycle polo on the assy with various friends, including the late Richard Crossman, MP, whose father, Judge Crossman, lived nearby.

His appointment as Chairman was welcomed by all associated with the School, especially those O.B.s who revered the memory of his father. Regrettably his tenure was brief and he was succeeded by Sir Arthur Drew, a distinguished retired civil

221

servant much involved in museum administration, being a trustee of five major London museums. He also chaired the highly successful 1981 Bancroft's appeal. His successor, Dr W. B. G. Simmonds, will be mentioned below. One of the great advantages of the School's continuing link with the Drapers' Company is that such urbane and charming men fill this important, though often overlooked, office.

With the growing bureaucracy necessary in running the School, it was decided to up-grade the office of bursar and relieve Drapers' Hall of some of the burden, allowing the Company's staff to concentrate on administering their substantial charities and philanthropies. A new bursar, Mr Graham Hale, was appointed and the classrooms on the ground floor facing the High Road converted into offices for the second master, the bursar and his staff, and other clerical help. People moan at the spread of bureaucracy – there are now four office helpers under the bursar – but the scheme seems to have worked as, for the first time, the school had its own accountant and by 1975 Mr Hale had balanced the books, aided by a substantial loan from the Company, again later converted into a gift, of £100,000 over five years, which paid off the overdraft and the building account deficit caused by the fearful rate of inflation.

By this stage School expenditure was £300,000 a year and the staff had just been awarded a 30% increase. Fees were increasing each term, by £28 to £120 a term in September 1974, from which date fees were paid direct to the school. There were 589 boys and eight girls in the School. The gym was opened by Mr Colin Cowdrey, CBE, the cricketer, and the new pavilion at West Grove was in operation by 1974, when it was formally opened by the rugby player Tony Bucknell – an event remembered, perhaps more for the political events of the day, as a 'hung' Parliament became inevitable as the last results were announced that afternoon of the previous day's general election.

The financial and constitutional changes of the 1960s and '70s easily dominate this period but there was a School functioning during the period as well. The staff was young: in 1970 only Mr Bradshaw went back to the war and Messrs Denyer and Lageard prior to 1960. Schoolmasters have changed in character since the days of Peet and Francombe, and there is a theory that the great growth of further education in the early 1960s attracted the best teachers who would otherwise have become schoolmasters. The older type of schoolmaster, from a similar type of school and Oxford or Cambridge, all pipe smoke and tweed jacket, trying and almost succeeding to make the MCR a cross between a senior common room and the back smoking room of a St James' club, is a creature of the past.

The great regret is that so many good masters have come and moved on. In this category one thinks of Mr N. H. Crickmay, a master who did much to help senior boys by introducing brief tutorial-type sessions for his 'A' level history set; Mr A. G. Milligan, a gifted linguist and philatelist; Mr R. H. Curtis, still retaining the cynicism and sense of mischief of a Trinity undergraduate, fitting in stimulating English classes between playing cricket, producing plays, and using his fine baritone voice; Mr R. P. H. Mermagen, a gifted historian who brought his subject alive for the most bored of indifferent pupils; and Mr C. G. Clark, a character worthy of any school. A mathematician, though his degree was in history, his bachelor life style involved travelling to and from school by 'cab and going to bed and rising at very strange times. His addiction to cigarettes gave him the nickname 'Fag' and none will forget the end of term quizzes for 'valuable prizes' – sherbet fountains produced from his great suitcase which he carried everywhere – the boys gave him a new one when he left.

Finally, none will forget the Chaplain, the Rev M. J. Rippengal. A kindly, no-nonsense type of Christian, a Persian and Hebrew scholar, he took his ragging very well, for the boys were most unkind to him. A man who spoke his mind, he made his disapproval quite clear one morning in Chapel, when two boarders read out a 'modern, left wing' passage. He did great work for charity, organised sponsored walks and began the social service tradition in the local community which has formed an important part of Bancroft's extra-mural life ever since. He was a good man who deserved better treatment. He died in 1985. There have been many more, and one hopes that Bancroft's was a pleasure for them and that, like their pupils, they gained something from being within its red-brick walls.

The revolt of youth during the sixties affected Bancroft's as it did most other schools, and the combination of bright pupils encouraged to speak their minds, with a traditional liberal attitude – though not all boys appreciated this at the time – allowed the School to evolve during the period and to channel such energies into debate and argument rather than to materialise as a full-scale rebellion. Between 1965 and '73, the School cap, in existence in one form or another since 1738, disappeared completely, mostly unlamented, and the dark grey suit replaced the blazer and flannels of the late 'fifties, and looked less incongruous than the black jacket and sponge bag trousers. By the early 'seventies, furthermore, the ultimate in liberality, coloured shirts, were introduced, though only for monitors and prefects. Hair grew longer, which the authorities wisely accepted, and the more sinister aspects of the age, such as drugs, were largely avoided at the School, for Bancroftians at that stage were profoundly conservative creatures. The few radicals tended towards the Liberal rather than the Labour Party; fortunately they tended to include bright and articulate boys, able to provide sound debaters: especially one thinks of D. P. Pannick who went on an early scholarship to Hertford College, Oxford, in 1974, took one of the top firsts in jurisprudence in 1977 and achieved the ultimate in Oxford's glittering prizes, a Fellowship of All Souls.

The Literary and Debating Society flourished throughout the period and motions both flippant and serious were debated. For sixth formers there were guest speakers on a variety of subjects dealing with specific careers and political and social subjects, and the sixth form studies courses, while not leading to any specific examination, broadened the minds and improved the lucidity of 'A' level candidates.

The tendency to stay on at sixteen was the product of an earlier generation, the development of Mr Richardson's era was the increasing number of boys who went on to university, and by 1977 the vast majority of 'A' level candidates went on to further education, not only to Oxford and Cambridge and London, but to both the 'redbrick' and the newer campus universities, and the solid grounding in both academic and other subjects served them well.

The GCE results of 1965 had given rise to some disquiet for the new Head Master and his first decision was to abolish streaming. By 1970 new boys were divided into four forms on a house basis. French was taught from the Thirds, Latin from the Remove and German or Greek were optional in the Lower Fourths. By the Upper Fourth, the pupils had chosen their 'O' level options, English and Mathematics being compulsory subjects. It was an

224

exceptional Bancroftian who failed to gain seven or more 'O' levels and the results were consistently better than those of neighbouring rivals, be they within or without the State System.

The acting side of the School expanded greatly during this period. The choice of Senior Play was catholic. There was the classical repertory *The Tempest* and *A Midsummer's Night Dream* and Ben Johnson's *Volpone* with excellent performances by Allan Bignell and Nigel Bowden, two very gifted actors who also performed Pinter's one act play *The Dumb Waiter* in 1968, the Common Room Players performing *The Dice* on the same evening. The previous year the Common Room had put on that hardy annual of an all-male society, Sherriff's *Journey's End*, produced by David Giles who played with relish Mason, the mess cook.

Masters appeared in the leading roles of two plays in the early seventies, Mr Crickmay playing Dr Faustus and Mr Curtis was Rattigan's *Ross*. *Royal Hunt of the Sun* was an ambitious production and *Oh! What a Lovely War!* was as pleasurable to watch as it was to perform.

From 1968 a junior play was performed, beginning with *Everyman* and including such Dickensian adaptations as *Oliver Twist* and *A Christmas Carol*. These plays helped to encourage the younger Thespians, as did the House Play Competition, started in 1972. The competition gave thé older boys the opportunity to direct and produce the play, and the four selections came from a wide variety of authors. All these acting activities helped to encourage pupils, especially day boys, to see the School as more than an 8.45 am to 3.20 pm place of drudgery, and the other school societies, usually with lunch time meetings, also helped to do this. The clubs specialised in such subjects as philately, numismacy, history, polyglotism, classical studies, music, Christianity, heraldry and computers, and at one stage the B.S. Tiddlywinks Club claimed to be national – or was it world – champions. All were under the presidency of the Head Master and were overseen by another member of staff, but the boys elected their own officers who arranged programmes and meetings. It was happily a far cry from the days of Mile End when boys were forbidden to speak to each other; and in university interviews, it was often these extra-curricular subjects which showed Bancroftians in such a good light, much to their benefit.

With the School making such progress, the Governors were most loath to see it change radically, far less for it to disappear completely. With hindsight, independence has proved a success, but at the time the future sometimes seemed gloomy. When the Drapers' Company lent £120,000 – later made into a gift – to allow a subsidised mortgage scheme for staff, they carefully created a special trust to protect it if the School and its endowment were taken by the State. (The School had suffered by being in such an expensive area, as staff could not afford houses. Since 1964 two houses had been bought, one in Woodford, a second in Buckhurst Hill, and several flats created in the old domestic block, and were rented to the staff at a reduced rent. The subsidised mortgage has proved very successful.) The new Government also talked of removing the charitable status of independent schools and of levying value added tax on fees, so the path to follow when the direct grant was withdrawn in September 1977 was by no means clear.

In a wonderfully succinct report in 1975 the Clerk to the Governors, Mr Geoffrey Watts, set out the options. They had not changed since 1966, namely the School could close – unthinkable; it could join the Redbridge system – which that authority rejected; or it could achieve full independence. The finances of the School, which were now showing a small surplus thanks to the hard work and diligence of the bursar, Mr Hale, showed a source of income as follows for 1974/5:

	£			
Endowment	27,500	with pupils:	272	LEA
Fees	312,945		133	fee payers
Direct Grant	60,727		164	partial
	———		18	free
	£401,172		24	foundationers

The loss of the direct grant, Mr Watts argued, would be more than compensated by the extra freedom given to the Governors. The fees would have to rise, perhaps to include a surplus to implement the endowment in providing scholarships – for Bancroft's without scholars would be unthinkable – and he cited that curious law of economics by which certain luxury goods rise in demand as prices increase, the experience at Howell's School in Denbigh.

226

The report also recommended the abolition of the boarding house: it was too expensive and took up too much space and all the endowment income; and the possible admission of girls at fourteen for 'O' levels, though not at eleven which would involve too many structural changes. It concluded by stating the obvious: the only way to test the scheme was by going independent.

Developments throughout 1976 led towards independence. Redbridge, under pressure to go fully comprehensive, said they would take thirty places the following year and the Secretary of State for Education allowed this, reluctantly, as long as there was no examination. Furthermore, the Charity Commissioners sealed a new agreement on 23rd December 1976. For the first time the School and West Grove became the property of the Governors rather than the Bancroft Trustees, and the endowment was reinvested, increasing the income by £9,000 a year. It otherwise gave the Governors full powers to run a boys'/mixed, boarding/day school as they saw fit.

It was at this stage that Redbridge announced that they would take no more places at the School. This was a blow to the Governors, though not entirely unexpected, leaving a gap to be filled by fee payers, and it also ended over eighty years of close co-operation with the local authority. The Governors decided that, if standards were to be maintained, girls would have to be admitted at eleven, as there had been only 120 male applicants for September 1977 entry. The die was cast: the boarding house would be abolished and Bancroft's would enter the 1977 school year as an independent school with a fully co-educational intake.

JUNE
14TH. 1971

Bray	L4A	Late to class	Mr. Milligan
Hurley	3A	Talking	Mr. Giles
Ferguson	5B	Failure to attend sports	~~Smith~~ of five (Gowan)
Nelson	L4C	Late side (4)	Mr. Baker
Miller	L4C	Horseback riding	Mr. Clarke

15TH

Jared	V4A	Not doing maths prep (5)	Mr. Clarke
Housman	V4A	(1) Not attending sports day (2) Furlong's report	Mackie
Hayes	V4B	Not reading notices	Mackie
Hurley	3A	Late side	Mr. Giles
Priddle	RC	Not reading notices	Mackie
Winfold	L4C	Late side (4)	Mr. Baker
Coxall	3A	No books	Mr. Milligan
Lewis	5A	Disobedience	Mackie
Cooper J	5A	"	"

16TH

Hall	2A	Talking	Mr. Delaney
Hurley	3A	No permission	Mrs. Baker
Tennison	L4C	Missing games	" "
Miller	L4C	Talking (4)	Mrs. OK Thompson
Shirai	3B	" " (4)	Mr. Thorley

17TH

Foster	L4A	Talking in assembly	Mackie
Moen	" "	" "	" "
Fanning W	L4A	No book	Mr. Kirstey
Hunsicar	V4B	Not doing prep	Mr. Housden

West House imposition Book, 1971

228

Bancroft's
School

Development Campaign

‡UNTO GOD ONLY BE HONOUR AND GLORY

Report on
Progress 1973

1973 Appeal leaflet

CHAPTER XV

IAN MACDONALD RICHARDSON
1977–1985

CONSIDERING the momentous impact of the dual alteration in the School's status the voices raised in anger were as few as they were muted; one O.B. with sons at the School and a prospective parent complained about girls in the third form, and there was grumbling from some sections of the O.B.A., but the change was accepted and even welcomed by those who saw it as a chance for Bancroft's to lead in the co-educational movement amongst boys' public schools. The O.B.A. had already welcomed the first girl sixth formers to its bosom, as it were, on leaving school, and now looked forward to the diversity of activities which a mixed Association would bring.

There were, perhaps, more sighs for the demise of the direct grant, although people knew that it was something beyond the control of the Governors. There were some who would have preferred Bancroft's becoming a part of the State system, to continue to provide a free education for local people, but again a majority of those connected with the School welcomed Bancroft's survival as a School free from the control or influence, however benign, of a local education authority, and able to give its pupils a sound grounding in the liberal arts and sciences, and to prepare them for life in the adult world. The support of the Drapers' Company for full independence had been sought and obtained well in advance, and now the Company agreed to enhance the endowment to provide scholarships and bursaries, as the School had to attract the very bright who would set a standard to which the less able could aspire, for every good boat needs a 'stroke'.

The endowment at this time produced £36,500 a year, invested largely in income shares in the Charities Official Investment Fund, along with the income from the Godliman Street and Cornhill properties, the latter having been exchanged in 1963 for the Poultry property, and £1.16 a year in fee farm rents from Manor Farm, Knottingley, near Pontefract in Yorkshire. This, with a £100 from Apley Grange, Wragby in Lincolnshire was all that remained of the extensive farm rent charges bought by the Trustees in the 1740s, and paying, of course, the same income as at their date of creation hundreds of years before.

The greater part of the endowment income was still being spent on the boarders whose house was quietly being run down. For the future, however, the Governors decided to offer six full scholarships to cover all fees, granted irrespective of parental income, one of the awards being for excellence in music. In addition, bursaries would be offered to bright pupils, the size of the award depending on parental circumstance. To assist in financing the scheme and to create about ten awards a year the Drapers' Company covenanted each year a sum to meet three such bursaries. The rest of the School's income would have to come from fees, the first time ever that a majority of the income was dependent on parental contributions.

The School naturally trod warily during these first years, anxious to maintain standards as well as increase its fee income. Under the old direct grant system there were doubtless some pupils receiving free places whose parents could have afforded fees, and it was now the task of the Governors to persuade them to pay for their younger children. They were to find that those parents who were opposed to comprehensive schooling were happy to pay a sizeable part of their post-tax income to give their children a traditional type of schooling. One problem which the School had with prospective parents was the habit of entering their sons for Chigwell or Forest as well as Bancroft's, thus causing difficulties in allotting places. Relations between the three schools had always been good, and contact at Chairman of Governors level had been made at the time when the very future of independent schools had been threatened. A joint entrance examination with the two other schools was suggested, making the parents opt for one of the three at an early stage, but this proved impracticable. Parents also had to pay one third of a term's fees in advance on entering their children, refundable if the child was not accepted.

The School was almost twice as large as it had been in 1964 and had undergone an enormous change. To help run it efficiently the house structure was reorganised. School House had included day boys since 1972 and in future would include all pupils living within a two mile radius of the school, the other houses retaining their geographical boundaries. The four house-

231

masters were each to have an assistant, the house tutor groups continuing as before. This system has since been further modified. To assist in the overall administration of the School a senior mistress was appointed alongside the Second Master.

Mr R. F. Millett came to Bancroft's in 1970 from John Lyon School, Harrow, to replace Mr Kentfield as Second Master. He taught Mr Kentfield's language subjects, completely overhauling the department, and was also a skilful administrator, making his presence felt in the School and acting as Head during Mr Richardson's illness in 1972 and sabbatical in 1980. As the administration became more complicated, so more duties fell on his shoulders and he has borne these duties with fortitude and without losing his sense of humour.

Mrs Jean Giles joined the staff in 1969, the first full time lady member of staff since Miss Clarke in 1918. The daughter of a distinguished writer of language text books, the late Mr W. F. H. Whitmarsh, she married Mr D. H. Giles, the O.B. English master, and lived with him in a flat at the School. Their two sons duly entered the School, and, with her willingness to help in various extra-curricular activities, Mrs Giles soon became a prominent member of the MCR and the School community. She was an obvious candidate for the new post of Senior Mistress, an office she has filled with dignity and grace.

The advent of girls caused a change in various school prizes and the creation of new ones. F. Winmill gave an annual prize for domestic science and various new sporting cups were given. Most of the old prizes were endowments for boys at Bancroft's, and those had to be changed, where possible the heirs of the original donor being consulted. The only endowment preserved for boys was Dr E. G. Housden's very generous gift of several years earlier. The original intention, to educate a widow's son, was maintained, the Governors increasing its value to meet the full fees of the recipient. Since then Dr Housden has agreed that a widow's son need only be given preference over a like daughter.

The Company came to the School's aid over the Stern Cup, given by Sir Albert Stern to be awarded annually to the best cadet. Its insurance value was £3,000, though the inscription reduced its sale value to about £600. The Company, of which Sir Albert had been Master in 1946, bought it from the School for

£1,500, the income therefrom being given as travel bursaries. Thus, in both major and minor ways Bancroft's was ready for co-education; it had to be seen what support from the neighbourhood would be received.

In the first year the novelty of the scheme meant that about one-third of the successful applicants were female, a proportion which soon increased to a half. Now, ten years after the first third form entry of girls, the School is fully integrated and the scheme has been adjudged a great success. That the School has changed cannot be denied, and the changes are most obvious in sport and the CCF, while the musical life of the School has gained enormously from the presence of girls.

Under Mr Adams the whole School had games on Tuesday and Thursday afternoons, placing great strain on the fields and changing rooms. Apart from Mr D. R. Main there had been no fully qualified sports master since Major Murray's retirement, and Mr Richardson resolved to improve the situation by rationalising sports afternoons and modernising facilities. Riggs Retreat was abandoned, the whole School had sports on Wednesday plus one other day per week, and a PE master was appointed, Mr R. B. Baker. In his twenty years at the School he has presided over a great improvement and expansion of facilities, with a change towards individual rather than team sports, without sacrificing the School's reputation in rugby and cricket.

The tradition of masters being involved in coaching team sports continued. Mr Bradshaw was involved with the rugby XV and chaired the School's Games Committee up to his retirement, Mr R. H. Curtis was succeeded by Mr J. G. Bromfield in charge of cricket, and numerous other members of staff helped out. Mr R. Kisby was appointed as second PE master in 1970, bringing skills to the gymnasium and wit to the MCR, especially at staff end of term revues. He was succeeded by Mr M. R. Burke, and in 1977 Mrs S. E. Taplin became the first female PE teacher.

The 1972 gymnasium complex and new West Grove swappers have been mentioned. The advent of girls caused certain changes, with seven tennis courts and an all-weather hockey pitch being laid at West Grove. A fully integrated sixth form was not reached until 1984 so the girls have not had time to prove themselves, yet a team reached the final of the Aberdare Cup for tennis in 1984 and 1985 and girls have played at county level in both hockey and tennis.

For the boys, the major achievement of this time was in 1973 when the U13 XV won the Rosslyn Park Public Schools Sevens Competition. During this period, also, R. Booth and P. Barnes played for England U16 XV and others played for London counties. The teams Bancroft's met at rugby had not changed greatly in fifty years: Haberdashers' Aske's, Bishop's Stortford, Davenant, and the cricket fixtures still included Chigwell after almost a hundred years, Forest and other local and Livery company schools, though Grocers', Parmiter's and Owens were no longer met.

By 1981 pupils had far greater scope for playing such games as tennis and squash, with two further courts built in that year adjacent to the 1973 gymnasium – harking back perhaps to the old fives courts – and other options included basketball, badminton, gymnastics and orienteering. Major Murray would have approved.

The CCF had, in the days of national service, enjoyed great popularity, but the abolition of the latter, coupled with a change in attitude in the 'sixties, led to a sharp decline in recruits, eventually losing its Friday afternoon period in 1971. Those who did join, however, – about one quarter of the school at that period – tended to be very keen, and most years saw boys heading for Sandhurst or Cranwell. The two principal masters involved were Mr P. J. C. Murray and Mr D. H. Giles, aided at various times by Messrs R. H. Curtis, R. B. Baker, J. G. Bromfield and N. H. Crickmay. The annual inspection and march past, led by the corps of drums, was a regular feature of the School's calendar, and camp, occasionally abroad, was very popular with the boys.

The advent of girls was no great shock to the CCF, as two world wars had accustomed us to the idea of women in uniform. They soon formed an important and useful part of the Cadet force. The sea scouts had a rougher journey. Always, it seems, it was maintained by the enthusiasm of one master, Mr I. K. Drake, a great scout outside school, was at the helm until 1970 when Mr D. Copsey and Mr E. J. Richardson steered it through difficult times. For a few months in 1983 it failed to function but was rescued by Mrs Kyrou and several O.B.s. An O.B. sailing club has been in existence since 1980, based on Burnham, and includes several former Sea Scouts.

The report of Mr G. C. Watts in 1975 had pointed out the

234

inadequacy of the existing school buildings for the education of young ladies, lacking both lavatories and facilities for domestic sciences. The School also needed new classrooms if it was to expand to 725 pupils. The boarding house was due to close in 1981 allowing the remaining boarding space and the extensive domestic offices to be used for classrooms and studying areas. For this, more money would be required and so a second appeal was launched amongst Old Bancroftians, parents and friends of the School.

The aim of the appeal was threefold: to develop computer sciences in the School with the School's own computers, to lay an all-weather hockey pitch and build more swappers and squash courts; and to develop the old service block into study areas and domestic science rooms. Learning from the 1973 appeal, the new appeal chairman, Sir Arthur Drew, Chairman of Governors and a distinguished retired civil servant, approached various prominent O.B.s for initial support before circulating the whole O.B. membership. The early results were very promising and within two years the target of £300,000 was reached, the surplus being placed in a newly-formed scholarship endowment fund.

By 1983 the last vestiges of the boarding school had disappeared. The 1941 bathrooms were partly converted into the domestic science rooms where both boys and girls learnt the basics of culinary arts and, in the numerous small rooms in the matron's block of the same vintage, sixth form studies were created. Also, a small Bancroftiana museum was created, filled with the papers and photographs of McMinn and Gooding and numerous other donors. It includes a wealth of team photographs and other memorabilia dating back to the earliest Woodford days and beyond. Originally under the charge of J. S. R. Mead, it is now under the control of K. J. Campbell who shows much energy and enthusiasm in cataloguing and extending its contents.

The Head Master's office was expanded during this time, acknowledging the need for space to receive parents and to hold meetings, and the MCR swallowed up the remaining boarder day room – it also acquired a bar. The size of the staff naturally expanded during this time, and more female staff were employed. The trend for some to move on after a short while continued, though the contraction of the education system nationally and the advantages of teaching at Bancroft's encouraged many to stay, with large numbers of applicants for any vacancy.

There were two retirements during this period, Mr C. M. Denyer and Mr R. H. Bradshaw. Mr Denyer was the kindliest of men, a fact which, added to a slight stutter, made him the butt of much schoolboy ragging. Originally a farmer, he entered Bancroft's in 1956 to teach biology. His retirement in 1976 took away a loyal and truly gentle man.

Mr Bradshaw's retirement in 1978 was an even greater wrench with the past, since he was the only remaining master who remembered the MCR of Mr Wells. One of three brothers at Bancroft's, Mr Bradshaw took the Essex County Arts Scholarship and studied at Hornsey College before returning to Bancroft's in 1939, just in time to be called up for war service which was spent in Intelligence. His works as an artist remain in the School with the portraits of George and Colonel Newman, but it is for such activities as organising school tours and his successful housemastership of West House that he will be equally remembered. Between 1953 and 1972 he organised nineteen school tours, some to the usual tourist countries of France, Italy and Germany, but also to less popular places such as the Netherlands, Denmark and behind the Iron Curtain to Russia, Czechoslovakia and Romania. Those who enjoyed the tours did not appreciate at the time the great work necessary to make them a success and the pressures of responsibility while acting *in loco parentis* to thirty adolescents abroad.

As housemaster of West, his old house, he was very much the conscientious head, taking very seriously the duties of office, such as vetting UCCA forms and administering punishment where deserved. Like his fellow O.B. master, Mr Clark, he resigned himself stoically to the 'below the salt' status of his subject, though several of his pupils went on to distinguished careers, especially in architecture – one thinks of John Dalton, Robert McGuire, head of Architecture at Oxford Polytechnic, and John Young – and his pupils, reduced to the very keen boys by the lower fourth, much appreciated his guidance and help.

On the sports field he continued to play for the Old Boys until 1964 and chaired the School Games Committee and was President of the MCR. It was therefore clear to all O.B.s, pupils and staff that Bancroft's was losing in him a loyal son and a very civilized human being. In retirement he still attends O.B. functions when not visiting one of his daughters whom he has contrived to place in Switzerland, much to his advantage at holiday times.

Academically, the early Richardson era was noted for the great improvement in GCE results, and the trend continued after 1977. It was not unknown for the more gifted pupils to obtain ten or eleven 'O' levels, the average being about seven, with most pupils going on to the three 'A' levels and further education. A tendency for some girls to leave at sixteen was compensated by a continuing sixth form entry. Most importantly, the girls and Bancroft's each adapted to the other's wiles and the co-educational scheme has proved a great success.

Perhaps the most notable achievement of this period was the growth in music, greatly helped by both the annual musical scholarship and the advent of girls. In 1968 Mr Richardson appointed the first full-time music master, Mr Bosanquet, who was succeeded by Mr C. M. Dolan a year later. Under Mr Dolan the department expanded and flourished. A second master, Mr Connelly, joined him in 1971, to be replaced by Mr Rossiter in 1980. He, in turn, was replaced by Mrs K. Edmondson in 1985. Apart from Vis. Day the School orchestra and choir performed two major concerts a year, one in the School and the other at Drapers' Hall. The School orchestra reached such a high standard that it felt itself capable of performing such works at Brahms' *Academic Festival Overture* and Handel's *Messiah*. Equally, the various virtuosi performed singly or in small groups and reached a very high standard, performing well in competitions. They were taught by the full-time staff and some nine part-time specialists. Music, like art and PE, tended to be pushed aside by a majority of pupils as public examinations approached, leaving only the very keen to pursue such studies, resulting in some notable successes by musicians from the School; much to Mr Dolan's delight, there was in 1985 an O.B. organ scholar at Balliol and another at Durham University; whether they will follow him to become ARCO remains to be seen.

The music at the School has always depended on gifted amateurs on the staff: Messrs James Hall, Walker, Francombe and Lageard being obvious examples from the past. In Mr Richardson's time Mr P. J. C. Murray was a baritone of professional standard and Mr J. Pearce's fine tenor voice was heard on the wireless. A younger master, Mr J. Dunston, continued the strong choral tradition of the School by forming a choral society called the Bancroft's Singers. Originally for male voices only, the choir produced two records and performed at

237

concerts both at home and abroad.

The strength of the music department housed in the 1964 boarder block, renamed the Adams Building after Mr Sydney Adams, was shown to good effect when a performance of Handel's *Messiah* was performed in honour of Mr Richardson's retirement. The two lady soloists were imported and regrettably Mr Murray was ill, but Mr Pearce sang the tenor role and Mr Dolan conducted an orchestra and choir of Bancroftians, O.B.s and friends of the School – it was a very professional performance, strongly supported by an audience of parents and O.B.s.

The Old Bancroftians Association weathered the storm of inflationary years which saw its subscription rise from £1 to £4 a year, with extra for *The Bancroftian*. The Dramatic Society went from strength to strength performing in Great Hall and celebrating its diamond jubilee in 1984 with a performance of Gogol's *The Government Inspector*, as always under the direction of Alfred Greenaway.

The Rugby Club – now open to non O.B.s – and the Cricket Club jogged along, although the tendency for universities to draw Bancroftians away from Woodford made it difficult to field young sides. A general sports club was formed in 1985 by a group of female members to encourage use of the School's facilities, and the Golfing Society, sixty years old in 1984, held regular matches and played in tournaments.

The Old Bancroftians' Masonic Lodge celebrated its fiftieth birthday in 1986 and continued to attract members of all ages from the ranks of the O.B.A. Apart from the regular meetings at Great Queen Street, the members and their guests enjoyed the School meeting held on a Saturday in June when the School's caterer demonstrated her organizational and culinary skill. As has been mentioned, the O.B. Annual Dinner moved to the school in 1974 and has proved very successful. In 1983 the Association returned to Drapers' Hall for a dinner to which partners and other guests were welcome. It was a great success, and was repeated in 1985 when Mr and Mrs Richardson were the guests of honour. By allowing the School to do the catering the Drapers' Company made it possible for the tickets to be sold at a reasonable cost.

The 1970s saw the end of the Bancroft Mission. The decision of Newham Borough Council to open their own youth club, at the same time suggesting that there was no longer a place for public

238

school philanthropy in East London, tolled the knell of the club after sixty-five years. People were very sad and perhaps a little bitter, and the decision caused new problems. The club was owned by a trust, the young of West Ham being the beneficiaries. After much debate and discussion with the Charity Commissioners the latter allowed the income to be used to pay the fees for a Newham child to go to Bancroft's in the sixth form.

Amongst the O.B. achievements of this period, the election of Neil Macfarlane as Member of Parliament for Sutton in 1974 stands out. The grandson of an MP and always a strong debater at School, Macfarlane gained office on the return of the Conservative Government in 1979 as an under-secretary of state, first at the Department of Education and then as Minister of Sport, until 1985 when he returned to the back benches.

Also serving the Crown were S. P. Day, Her Britannic Majesty's Ambassador at Qatar, B. M. Day, an under-secretary at the MOD, Michael Hill, QC, senior Treasury Counsel and J. Nursaw, Principal Assistant Legal Adviser to the Home Secretary.

It is always difficult knowing whom to mention and whom to omit from passages such as this; as elsewhere, the author apologises for failing to mention numerous other O.B.s who have gained distinction in their chosen professions.

The list of deaths during this period included those who had gained distinction in public life as well as loyal servants of the O.B.A. Amongst the former was Mr A. J. Gardham, formerly senior surgeon at University College Hospital, London, and, in his spare time, secretary of the Devon and Somerset Stag hounds, and Sir Kenneth Peppiatt, sometime Chief Cashier of the Bank of England. Amongst the latter, space allows mention of 'Hoppy' Stride, footballer and scholar who bequeathed his library to the school; D. E. Coult, for long O.B. Editor of *The Bancroftian* and the 1937 book; Sydney Gooding, doyen of O.B.s and collector of O.B. memorabilia; and Frank Fry, bastion of the Lodge, the Mission, the Rugby Club and the Exhibition and Loan Fund. Lastly, the death of S. H. Webb in 1985 robbed the O.B.A. of its last tangible link with the School in the nineteenth century. The Association lamented their and many other deaths but, as a living and thriving organization it had to look to the future. It must be said, therefore, that during this period the O.B.A. reached its largest membership ever, of nearly 1,800 members, and its motto was, 'Onward and upward!'.

239

As the Richardson era drew to a close, so people associated with Bancroft's stopped, drew breath, and regarded the changes. Not since Symns had so much been achieved in one administration, often against opposition from the most powerful bodies in the land. The description of the School as Ian Richardson left it belongs to the final chapter of this book, but here is the place to recall the changes which occurred under his aegis and to try and assess the spirit of Bancroft's in 1985.

In 1965 Mr Richardson inherited an elderly MCR, a boarding house with, reputedly, the longest school dormitory in England, the mode of choosing its inmates having hardly changed in seventy years; a day boy contingent almost wholly financed by the State in one way or the other; and a school administration based on the skills of the gentleman amateur. It was a happy School, though with a certain amount of bullying, and an identity of its own. It was also living in the past, and was quite unprepared for the social and political upheavals of the mid 1960s. Mr Richardson had the foresight to know what could be done to save and enhance the school; at times he appears to have been almost alone in thinking that salvation was possible, though the two Clerks to the Governors, Alan O'Neill and Geoffrey Watts, shared his vision and the Governors themselves always gave full support. In the process the boarder disappeared, as did the direct grant and the other LEA places, though the School has welcomed assisted places pupils since 1981.

With full independence came co-education, the School expanding to 725 pupils, and to house them the Drapers' Company and two appeals provided new laboratories, a new gymnasium and swimming pool, a pavilion at West Grove and the creation of twenty new classrooms. The library was extended, more departmental libraries created and new studies provided for sixth formers. Without doubt Bancroft's in 1985 was a more relaxed place than it had ever been before and as happy as the School which Mr Richardson found in 1965. Most importantly, despite all the changes both within and without, it still knew its identity, and rejoiced in it, for like his predecessors, Mr Richardson preserved and harnessed that indefinable quality of spirit which Mr Bancroft's foundation has always had, turning the success of his period of office into a triumph.

The final year saw numerous tributes to both Richardsons, for Bridget's contribution to the life of the School had not gone

The new Pavilion, West Grove, opened 1974

The new Swimming Pool, opened 1973

Dining Hall, *c.* 1973

M. C. R. Hockey XI 1966
Back Row l to r: Messrs I. K. Drake, J. D. Bradford, G. N. E. Lageard, D.
H. Giles, and P. J. C. Murray.
Front Row l to r: Messrs D. N. Aldridge, P. G. Joignant, A. N. Long, E. A.
Owens, E. L. H. Kentfield, and S. P. Cadman.

Dr Peter Southern, Head Master since 1985

Dr Walter Simmonds, Chairman of Governors since 1981

The School from the front, *c.*1982

The School from the rear.

unmarked. The performance of *Messiah* has already been referred to, there was also a dinner at Drapers' Hall given by the O.B.A., with nearly two hundred people present, who gave Mr and Mrs Richardson a standing ovation. During the same period the Drapers' Company made Mr Richardson free of the Company by Presentation, an honour reserved for those who have given service to the Company or one of its principal trusts. Finally, on Visitation Day and O.B.'s Day, the Governors and O.B.s respectively showed their thanks and appreciation. There were speeches, presentations and much much cheering and applause. To paraphrase King George the Fifth, people really did like him for himself.

It is too soon to attempt to analyse the success of Mr Richardson. When these last chapters are re-written in fifty years' time a true comparison between him and his predecessors will prove possible, showing the relative success of their aspirations for Bancroft's. It will be a close run race, but Ian Richardson may well win it.

BANCROFT'S SCHOOL

Name .... Form ....

| Mon. | Tues. | Wed. | Thurs. | Fri. | Sat. |

Offence ....

Set by ....

Adequate	siege	definite	beautiful	weird

Emperor	grammar	all right	immediately	seize

Imposition sheets ('sides')

UNTO GOD ONLY BE HONOUR AND GLORY

Bancroft's School

BOARDERS REUNION DINNER

22 MAY 1981
7.30 pm

Final boarding house dinner, 1981

THE LOYAL TOAST
M.A.J. Smith
Head of Boarding House

***

Apologies on behalf of
Absent friends
given by
J.G. Bromfield Esq, B.A.
Boarding House Master

***

TOAST TO BANCROFT'S SCHOOL
Proposed by
R.V. Wingham Esq (1925-1931)
School Governor

***

Floreat Bancroftia
Floreant Discipuli
Vivat Et Memoria
Fundatoris Nostri
Nobis in Aeternum
Magni Sint Honores
Floreat Bancroftia
Floreant Rectores
***

REPLY BY
I.M. Richardson Esq. J.P., M.A.
Head Master and
President Old Bancroftians Association

Final boarding house dinner, 1981

243

ANTIQUES & COLLECTORS FAIR

in
The Great Hall
Bancroft's School
Woodford Green

Sat. 6th Feb. 1982

ᴄᴏᴄᴏᴄᴏᴄᴏᴄᴏᴄᴏᴄᴏᴄᴏᴄᴏ

50 Stands

ᴄᴏᴄᴏᴄᴏᴄᴏᴄᴏᴄᴏᴄᴏᴄᴏᴄᴏ

Brass	Porcelain
Copper	Glass
Pewter	Jewellery
Silver	Bric-a-brac

Postcards

10am — 5pm
Admission 15p
Refreshments all day

All profits to the School's Appeal Fund

Antique Fair, 1982

OLD BANCROFTIANS'  **ASSOCIATION**

The President

requests the pleasure of your company at

The Annual Dinner

to be held

at Bancrofts School

on Friday, 31st October, 1986

6.45 for 7.30 p.m.
Black Tie

Invitation to O.B.A. Annual Dinner, 1986

OLD BANCROFTIANS'  **ASSOCIATION**

The President

requests the pleasure of your company at

A Dinner

to mark the retirement of the Head Master

Mr Ian Richardson, J.P.

at Drapers' Hall

on Wednesday, 15th May, 1985

7.00 for 7.30 p.m.   Black Tie
Carriages 10.30 p.m.

Invitation to testimonial dinner for Mr Ian Richardson, 1985

245

CHAPTER XVI

PETER CAMPBELL DAVID SOUTHERN
Appointed 1985

THERE WERE 66 applicants who sought Mr Richardson's office, of whom some 30 were of sufficient calibre to warrant serious consideration. A sub-committee of the Governors vetted these, to produce a short list which was considered by the whole Board. The man finally chosen was Dr Peter Southern, Head of the History department at Westminster School. The son of a distinguished Oxford historian who was sometime President of St John's College, Dr Southern is the first historian and holder of a doctorate to be Head Master: in height he reaches the requisite two yards of his five predecessors.

Educated at Magdalen College School and at Merton College, Oxford, Dr Southern then studied for his doctorate at Edinburgh where he also met his wife Dinah and together they settled down at Dulwich, prior to the move to Westminster. Fortuitously, the family have lived at Woodford for some years and have now moved into the Head Master's residence with their two sons and a golden-haired retriever.

Clearly, it is too early to judge the effects of Dr Southern on Bancroft's, and any changes which he may envisage will be for the next school historian to consider. This chapter, therefore, must describe a School that, to a degree, remains Mr Richardson's creation. This is not to suggest that the new Head Master is not impressing his personality on Bancroft's and its constituent parts; his views on some subjects have been stated with a refreshing forcefulness and, as an example, he has taken the organisation of the 1987 festivities very much in hand. There can be no doubt that he will expend similar energy and enthusiasm on promoting whatever changes prove necessary for Bancroft's to develop and flourish.

The body which ultimately controls the School's destiny is the Board of Governors, consisting of the Master of the Drapers' Company during his year of office and five other nominees of the Company, two nominees of Redbridge Borough Council and one of Essex County Council, and two co-opted members. The

Drapers' Company nominees include Mr D. H. Tindall, a retired publisher, Mr P. D. J. Hippisley-Cox, a Parliamentary Agent and solicitor, Mr A. A. O'Neill, the Company's former Clerk (who now sits on a body which, fifty years ago, declined to give him a scholarship to Bancroft's), and R. V. Wingham, an Old Bancroftian. They represent a wide spectrum of experience and are greatly assisted by the local authority nominees, Messrs B. W. Tarring and R. I. Barden from Redbridge and Mr S. G. Barnett, CBE, DL, from Essex, and by the two co-opted members, Dr Jean Chalk, the wife of a member of the Court of Assistants, and a distinguished physician in her own right, and Dr K. B. Pretty, Senior Tutor of New Hall, Cambridge.

The Clerk to this body, as mentioned above, is Mr G. C. Watts and the Bursar, Mr G. Hale, also attends meetings as do the Head Master and the Clerk to the Company, Mr R. G. C. Strick, the latter bringing to the School's counsels the great breadth of knowledge and wisdom gained in administering the Company's complicated affairs.

The task of presiding over this body is no sinecure, and Bancroft's has been fortunate in the series of Drapers who have held this office; and of the eight chairmen since 1920, none has performed his duties more conscientiously than the present incumbent, Dr W. B. G. Simmonds. As the nephew of Sangster Simmonds his credit would automatically stand high with the Bancroft's community, and his own conduct and actions have increased the esteem in which he is held. There is hardly a School or O.B. function which he fails to attend, and he is often accompanied by his charming wife. His great kindness shown to Old Bancroftians at Drapers' Hall is as gracious as it is heartfelt.

The School itself has fully adjusted to its co-educational state: indeed, it seems difficult to think of it as having been anything else. In Mrs Jean Giles the fairer sex has an erudite champion who has ensured that the progression towards a fully integrated school has been smoothly achieved. The number of difficulties has been remarkably small and the teething problems of selection and discipline were overcome within two or three years. Bancroft's is proud that its girls do not follow the national trend and avoid the mathematical side of the curriculum, and that they regard themselves as Bancroftians first and girls second. Equally, the boys' natural good manners and consideration have allowed the influx of girls to seem perfectly natural, and in 1986 two boys won the Home Economics Prize, while all four heads of house were girls, situations readily accepted by all involved with the School as a sign of the success of co-education.

The changes to the structure of the School reflect both the transition from a partly boarding school of 440 boys to a co-educational day school of 700 pupils, and also the growing need for the School to justify its existence to fee-paying parents by providing a curriculum based on old standards yet containing all the elements necessary for the modern world. As will be seen below, each department has risen to the challenge of combining these two facets.

The house structure remains the same, the catchment areas of North, East and West Houses being geographical segments from the School, and School House taking pupils from the area to the south of the School. The growing importance of the housemaster has meant that it is now impossible to hold that office with a departmental headship, and consequently Messrs Giles, Murray and Franklin remain as housemasters of West, School and East Houses but have quit being head of English, Classics and Physics respectively. Mr Murray, in his twenty-seventh year at the School, is the longest serving member of staff and now heads a somewhat different House from the School House he controlled twenty years ago. Mr Giles heads the house which he entered as a pupil in 1945 and in 1987 celebrates his silver jubilee on the staff. Mr B. J. Franklin entered Bancroft's MCR in 1967 to teach Physics in the 1910 laboratories and succeeded Mr G. N. E. Lageard as head of East House in 1974. As with most masters of his generation Mr Franklin has involved himself in extra-curricular activities which have included taking school parties abroad and supervising the electronics and loudspeakers on Visitation Day and for school plays. His keen sense of humour has always readily imparted itself to pupils with whom he has always had the most felicitous relations.

The retirement of Mr R. L. Bowley in December 1985 produced a vacancy in the headship of the history department as well as the housemastership of North. Mr Bowley replaced Mr Mermagen as Head of History in 1980 and, with the assistance of Mr N. H. Crickmay and later staff, established the department as one of the most successful in the School. Himself a published author, Mr Bowley has been involved in the preparation of this book. To his pupils, especially those whom he groomed for 'S' level and Oxford and Cambridge entry, he transmitted both his enthusiasm for and deep knowledge of his subject, and also gave a hint of the great insight which he had for events in the past. As House Master of North he continued the work of Messrs Kentfield and Drake in establishing a new house fully capable of competing against the other houses in the various school competitions. He has retired to the West Country where his family has long had connections.

His place as housemaster has been filled by J. G. Bromfield who has been a history master since 1973. A keen all-rounder, involved in Cricket and the CCF, he recently married a member of staff, Miss Mary Moylan.

Each housemaster is assisted by a deputy and the School forms continue to be organised as tutor groups on a house basis. The role of housemaster has clearly become more demanding than in former times, each house consisting of almost two hundred pupils and staff, and some of the growing weight of bureaucracy has fallen on the housemasters' shoulders. Equally, it is deemed necessary to give far greater guidance to pupils, not only on academic matters and university entrance, but also on matters which fall under the heading of 'pastoral care'. The geographical nature of the houses has always made team loyalty easy to engender, and arranging the forms on a house basis further encouraged that tendency. Equally an expansion of inter-house competitions beyond the sports field – the drama competition, for example – has involved such pupils who do not excel at games. Social occasions such as the House Chapel services have also enhanced house unity and enabled staff to meet parents on a less formal basis. All a long way from the creation of East and West Houses by Mr Playne before World War One.

Most pupils enter Bancroft's at the age of eleven following an entrance examination, on the strength of which scholarships and bursaries are awarded by the Governors along lines described in the preceding chapter. There are also ten Assisted Places given each year to eleven year olds, with a further five for sixth-form entry, these being financed by the Department of Education, based on a parental means test. The naming of school forms, so baffling to outsiders, is a relic of the days when entry at nine was common. Consequently, pupils at eleven are put in the Third form, e.g. 3 East whence they progress in yearly stages to the Remove, the Lower Fourth, the Upper Fourth and the Fifth form, when 'O' levels are taken. The Lower and Upper Sixth take the pupils to eighteen and 'A' levels. From 1988 the GCSE will replace the GCE 'O' level.

The masters of eighteenth-century Bancroft's Hospital found it expedient to appoint senior boys as monitors to assist them in teaching the younger boys and maintaining discipline. The role of monitor gradually grew in stature and, under Mr Playne, he was appointed on a house basis and was supported by a number of house prefects, the latter enjoying certain powers only over boys in their own house. Today, the office of prefect has been declared redundant and Bancroft's has resorted to a dependence on monitors selected from the sixth form on ability and suitability, with two also being appointed head and deputy head of each house.

The role of monitor is no easy sinecure, convenient for UCCA forms and mentioning at interview. It involves maintaining discipline, supervising activities, guiding visitors on tours of the School and assisting with the administration of many evening functions. Each successive Head Master has relied on his monitors to support him and the load which falls on their collective shoulders is great. We live in an increasingly bureaucratic age and the willing assistance given by senior pupils to assist in administering the School enables the machinery of government to continue to function.

This chapter cannot be described as 'historical' in any accepted meaning of the word, as it tries to explain how the School functions in this Year of Grace One Thousand Nine Hundred and Eighty-Seven. Equally, such is the tide of progress that any attempt to describe contemporary Bancroft's becomes out-of-date before it reaches the press. It is essential, however, to conclude this story by describing some of the workings of the School at the time of its two hundred and fiftieth birthday, and it is hoped that the innate ability of the Bancroft's community to preserve what is good from its past will, to a degree, hold back the ever-rolling stream of time and not make this chapter completely old hat by the time it is first read.

It is hoped that the last chapters of this book give some idea of the development of education in England since the 1944 Education Act, with emphasis, of course, on how it has affected Bancroft's. During the last twenty years a quiet revolution has changed the teaching of most subjects which have had to adapt to the use of modern technology. Easier accessibility to television and 'visual aids' has affected the teaching of History and Classics as much as Physics and Mathematics, and some current educational thought emphasises that all subjects should be 'relevant' to a contemporary society. Bancroft's and schools of its sort have rejected the more extreme elements of such educational thought and it is probably the case that the growth in demand for independent school places has been caused by a similar rejection by parents who are willing to make great sacrifices to provide their children with a 'traditional' education.

The School remains an Anglican foundation with a clergyman in charge of the Chapel and the Religious Education department. Until Christmas 1986 this office was held by the Rev Arthur Ellery, assisted by Miss Halton. As a growing minority of pupils come from 'non-Anglican' backgrounds the syllabus has been extended to emphasise the importance of moral values, and sex education is handled by this department in the Removes.

Allied to the development of religious education is a new subject called Integrated Humanities, a compulsory subject leading to a GCE 'O' Level examination, shortly to be replaced by the new GCSE. This subject, a progression of the old general studies course, treats such topics as law, consumer affairs, education, leisure and conservation. Apart from awakening the interest of pupils in such matters, the course hopes to encourage them to learn to find and evaluate information from a variety of sources. Visits are made to various institutions and a variety of people visit the School to give talks on their specialist subjects.

The Chapel ceased to hold regular Sunday services in 1981 when the boarding house closed, though the Woodford Ecumenical Church have been given permission to hold services on Sundays there. On weekdays the lower, upper and middle schools hold services on Tuesday, Wednesday and Thursday mornings respectively, with a house service on Friday. On the major feast days of All Saints, Ash Wednesday and Ascension Day communion is celebrated, and a confirmation service is held each year by the Bishop of Barking. There is also a family chapel service for each house on a Sunday, and the Armistice Day Service is still held: the services on O.B.s' Day and at the School Masonic Lodge meeting ensure that the Chapel is not a neglected part of the School.

It was once said that the backbone of the Public School system was the three Cs: Christianity, Cricket and Classics. The third of the three is still an important part of Bancroft's syllabus, Latin being compulsory for all in the Remove and Lower Fourth with a large number taking 'O' Level. The course today is a mixture of traditional linguistic work combined with a study of Roman life, using archaeological and other evidence. A number of pupils study Greek, and also Greek literature in translation, while at 'A' Level Classical Civilization has proved a popular course, combining ancient history with a study of classical art and literature.

The study of modern literature and of the English language remains a corner-stone of the English syllabus. For long maintained by Mr and Mrs Giles, this department is now under Mr T. R. C. Jones. All pupils take 'O' Level in English Language and English Literature and the latter is one of the most popular 'A' Level options. Wherever possible visits are arranged to local theatres and the department has enjoyed great success in the public examinations.

The History and Geography departments also remain stalwarts of the syllabus. The former is under a new departmental head, Mr C. Taylor and, being the Head Master's own discipline, benefits from his keen interest and intellectual gifts. The Geography department is headed by Mr J. D. Pearce, a gifted tenor, who has been at the School seventeen years, ably assisted by Mr C. S. O'Connor Thompson who joined Bancroft's in 1970. The latter also specialises in teaching Geology. These two departments have taken full advantage of field trips and visits to museums.

The move away from a classroom-bound existence has affected the Modern Languages department, where each pupil has been encouraged to stay with a family in France or Germany, the English family then reciprocating the hospitality. More importantly, under its present head, Mr J. Dunston, the department has become more orientated towards the importance of foreign languages in the world of commerce, especially for senior pupils.

A recent innovation (in 1976) – also, one presumes, to prepare Bancroftians for the business community – is the teaching of Economics at 'A' Level. Mr C. H. Pearson is the sole purveyor of this subject and has quickly established a thriving and popular department. The highspot of the academic year is said to be a

252

study weekend at York University, an interesting eye-opener for sixth-formers preparing for university entrance.

The scientific side of Bancroft's has always been strong and the teaching of Mr Peet and others in the old 1910 laboratories has produced three Fellows of the Royal Society and numerous other successful chemists, doctors and other scientists. The Physics department is now under Mr Krzyz, Mr Franklin concentrating his energies as Head of East House, and Mr Copsey heads the Chemistry department, having been at Bancroft's since 1966. The new laboratories built in 1970 enabled the necessary expansion of departments. The Nuffield system of teaching, with greater emphasis on practical work, replaced the out-dated former courses and laboratory technicians were appointed to assist the teaching staff. Again, more use was made of visits to outside establishments including Porton Down and Calder Hall, and pupils have enjoyed lectures and courses at The City University, Queen Mary College and the Royal Society.

Biology, now under the supervision of Mr J. Wilson, has expanded also, with three members of staff. The proximity of Epping Forest has provided a useful place for field exercises – older generations of Bancroftians will concur in this, but may be thinking of different forms of practical biology lessons – and an encouraging number of Bancroftians progress to medical school where the groundwork learned at Bancroft's proves beneficial. Recently, M. Ferrari, T. Lovell and N. Holland were awarded prizes at their respective hospitals.

The importance of computers has been recognised and Mr A. V. G. Hagedorn, a member of the staff since 1968, has ceased to be head of Mathematics in order to concentrate on organising the Computer department, in addition to acting as Director of Curriculum Studies. His successor as head of Mathematics is Mr T. Smith who has continued the change in direction of the syllabus towards 'modern' mathematics, with its emphasis on matrices, vectors and calculus, without forgetting the importance of a sound grounding in traditional arithmetic. As with all departments, successes have been achieved academically, with a number of pupils going to Cambridge to continue their studies.

The above is only a brief outline of the work performed in the various departments, and does not do justice to any of them. What is so impressive is the enthusiasm and drive of the

253

department heads which inevitably affects both their junior staff and the pupils who seem to respond accordingly.

The advent of girls in 1977 also brought a new subject, Home Economics, housed in the refurbished 1940 boarders' bathroom. It is a compulsory subject for boys and girls and some take an 'O' Level. Under Miss Wallace the pupils are taught not only the rudiments of practical cookery, but also such things as nutrition and the development of food.

Another subject which has greatly changed is woodwork, which has now developed into a design technology course. As part of the 1987 celebrations the Drapers' Company has granted £75,000 to the School which will be spent in building rooms in the space under the 1970 Science block. These rooms will be called a Technology Unit, and will allow the design technology department to expand into metalwork and enable the department to teach the new GCSE course. Mr Mitchell's department has travelled a long way since the days of 'Jix' Chapman.

The new rooms will also allow the chemistry, physics and computer departments to develop skills in control technology and investigations into metals and micro-electronics, as well as giving pupils the chance to explore the wonders of technology in extra-curricular studies.

The art department, under Mrs Oelmann, will also benefit from the new facilities, enabling pupils to use their skills in a practical way, whilst still allowing those who follow the dictum of 'art for art's sake' to develop those talents in drawing and painting wherewith God has blessed them.

The excellent work of Mr Dolan in the Music Department has already been described, as has that of Mr Baker on the sports side of the School. It is a great credit to all those in charge of Bancroft's that they have achieved the balance between developing old disciplines yet retaining their many beneficial features.

Outside the curriculum it has been appreciated that changes were necessary. The old way in which Bancroftians drifted into a City position through the influence of an O.B. or family friend does perhaps still exist, and the School's pupils undoubtedly have a head start at interviews, both academically and in presenting themselves. The expansion of the Careers department, however, to guide pupils towards a suitable university course and/or profession, has resulted in a special room being allotted for this purpose, under the charge of Mr O'Connor Thompson and Mrs Hutchinson.

Both parents and O.B.s help to give advice on the various professions, and visits are arranged through the Independent Schools' Careers Organisation, successor to the Public Schools' Appointments Bureau. University entrance is also most carefully considered and pupils applying to Oxford or Cambridge are pointed in the direction of the most suitable colleges. Bancroftians are not pampered, and the whole system still tries to produce well-balanced individuals capable of standing on their own two feet. It is, however, necessary to give sixth formers some guidance at such a crucial stage in their lives.

Mr Symns' philosophy when Head Master has already been quoted, that the fostering of good character is as important as securing academic attainment, and, whilst the necessity of examination success has to be to the fore in any headmaster's scheme of things, Mr Symns' successors – each of them a proven scholar – has accepted that broad philosophy. Perhaps, in reality, they have had no choice, for the peculiarly powerful corporate feeling which pervades Bancroft's and any Bancroftian gathering is too strong to challenge.

Dr Southern has said that one of the most striking things about any Old Bancroftian gathering is how O.B.s of all ages readily mix with each other, united by a peculiar freemasonry which few other schools instil. It is hard to explain either the spirit in general or the character of a 'typical' Bancroftian which it presumably has created, or at least moulded, but each is readily identifiable for those who know the species.

Undoubtedly the advent of girls changed some things greatly, but others not at all, and it is now difficult to think of Bancroft's other than as a co-educational school. Perhaps the girls have made it a more civilized place, though that tendency was already present from the 'sixties onwards. On the whole, they have blended into the system, making what some saw as a traumatic change now seem a very natural progression.

School societies abound more than ever, though the demise of the boarder has meant that they tend to be held during the luncheon break rather than in the evening. A list would be repetitive of earlier parts of the book, but, suffice to say, the new school societies such as the junior mathematics and the biology clubs have an obvious academic bent, a comment on both the

255

intellectual calibre of pupils and the enthusiasm engendered by the staff.

The plans for 1987 have been fermenting for some while and include a service at St Helen's, Bishopsgate, on March 18th, one day before the 259th anniversary of Francis Bancroft's death, followed by a reception at Drapers' Hall; an Old Bancroftians' Association Ball at the Hall on June 12th which, excepting Company functions, will be the first such use of the Hall since the O.B.A. Ball in 1964; a similar event principally for parents and sixth-formers at the School in July; and a special Visitation Day when it is hoped that the Master of the Drapers' Company will officially open the building work made possible by the Company's gift of £75,000. All things considered, it promises to be some year, a tribute both to the School and to the way in which the School Governors, the Staff, the O.B.A. and the parents have co-ordinated their efforts.

This story now approaches its end, for the book must have a cut off point, in practice late 1986; the School itself, of course, continues. The 1937 book ended on a note of optimism overshadowed by the growing threat from Europe. That challenge was met and overcome. Today, the threat to schools such as Bancroft's comes from nearer home and, one hopes, it too will be overcome, giving the School a very promising future.

Bancroft's story is similar to that of many old schools. It has been a fruitful life, conceived by a beneficent founder, nurtured by conscientious trustees, loyally served by gifted staff and honoured and cherished by generations of Bancroftians. No doubt it has its faults, and it is regretted that a sizeable parental income is still necessary to enable most pupils to attend, but that, of course, is a matter not within the control of the Governors.

The 100 pupils who enter Bancroft's each year receive advantages quite literally incomprehensible to the dozen or so boys who annually joined Bancroft's Hospital in the eighteenth century. What they have in common is the singular experience of having enjoyed Mr Bancroft's charity and being allowed to bask in the pleasure of being part of an unique school. One can but entertain conjecture as to what Francis Bancroft would think and whether he realised that his foundation would still be in existence two hundred and sixty years after his death. One sincerely hopes that the development of the School and the great success of its pupils are in accordance with his expectations.

The Founder's Will decreed that the pupils should be taught loyalty to their Sovereign and the ability to read, write and cast accounts. The loyalty of Bancroftians has been put to the test twice this century, and they have come through with great credit. Similarly, most seem to be able to read and write, though this is questioned by various O.B.A. officers who try to obtain information from the Association's members. In the field of casting accounts, the current pupils of the School are taught the ways of computers and the hidden mysteries of software, VDUs and input programmes, worlds away from the quill pen and ledger book of George the Second's reign.

It is hoped that the atmosphere of the School where these mysteries are unravelled will impress on the pupils' minds the importance of tempering progress with conservation, of not perpetrating change for change's sake but of preserving what is good and valuable from the past. Achieving such a balance is the aim of the new Head Master and his Staff, supported by all those who have the best interests of Bancroft's at heart. If they succeed – and the signs are propitious – the future for Bancroft's looks very promising; one suspects Francis Bancroft would approve.

Floreat Bancroftia!

Old Bancroftians' Association

UNTO GOD ONLY BE HONOUR AND GLORY

BANCROFT'S SCHOOL

1737–1987

The Chairman and Committee
request the pleasure of your company

at

A SUMMER BALL

to be held at

DRAPERS' HALL

on

Friday, 12th June, 1987

White or Black tie   **8pm — 2am**

250th Anniversary Ball

258

Will of Francis Bancroft, 1728

THE LAST WILL

OF

MR. FRANCIS BANCROFT.

———————

I, FRANCIS BANCROFT, Citizen and Draper of London, considering the uncertainty of human life, do make my last Will and Testament, in manner and form following :

First, I recommend my soul to God my Creator, hoping through his mercy, and the merits of Jesus Christ my blessed Saviour and Redeemer, to receive pardon for all my sins, and life everlasting.

My body I desire may be embalmed within six days after my death, and my entrails to be put in a leaden box, and included in my coffin, or placed in my vault next the same, as shall be most convenient; and that my coffin be made of oak, lined with lead; and that the top or lid thereof be hung with strong hinges, neither to be nailed, screwed, locked down, nor fastened any other way, but to open freely, and without trouble, like to the top of a trunk. Directi for em- balming the boc &c.

The place and manner of Interment.

And I desire to be buried in a vault which I have made and purchased for that purpose under my tomb in the parish church of St. Helen's, London, within ten days after my decease, between the hours of nine and ten o'clock at night. And I do direct, that the

Expense of the funeral.

whole expenses of my funeral, over and above what I have hereafter given for mourning and rings, shall not exceed the sum of two hundred pounds, which I leave to the care and management of my executors hereinafter named. And as to such worldly estate, as God in his mercy has been pleased to bestow upon me, subject to, and charged with, the payment of my debts, funeral charges, and legacies, hereby given, I give, devise, settle, and dispose thereof as follows :

Legacies and annuities.

Imprimis, I give my silver basin to the said church of St. Helen's, there to be used at the communion service, or otherwise in the service of that church ; and for no other use or purpose whatsoever.

Item, I give to my cousin, William Turner, Junior, a ring of twenty shillings value, and my diamond table ring, and ten pounds for mourning ; and I give to my cousin Martha Turner, a ring of twenty shillings value, and my rose-diamond ring : I give to my cousin, Nathanael Cole, the sum of one hundred pounds: I give to my cousin, Thomas Catmore, son of Captain Thomas Catmore, the sum of five hundred pounds, in case he shall attain his age of twenty-one years, and serve out the term of his apprenticeship; and not otherwise :—likewise I give him my large trunk, marked *T. B.*, full of linen; and the bedding and furniture of my chamber; and all my pieces of tapestry; together with my books and pictures; but not to have them removed till a month after my death, and then to be delivered to him : I give to my cousins John and Anne Wallis, a ring of twenty shillings value to each of them; and to their children John, Robert, Thomas, Rebecca, and Martha, five pounds per annum each, during their natural lives respectively, to be paid half-yearly by even portions : I give to Mr. Francis Howard, Toyman, in St. Paul's Church-yard, and his wife, ten pounds a-piece for mourning; and five pounds per annum to the said Francis, during his life, to be paid half-yearly by equal portions : I give to Sarah Marsh, in Coleman-street, and her daughter, Sarah Shaw, seven pounds ten shillings each, for mourning; and ten pounds per annum each, during life, to be paid half-yearly by equal portions : and to the said Sarah Shaw, my silk-damask night-gown : I give to Mr. Robert Dobson, Woodmonger, and to Mr. Henry Hadley, Distiller, ten pounds each, for mourning; and to my cousin Eade, and his wife; Thomas Essington, and his wife; Thomas Norton, and his wife; Robert Dobson, Corn Factor, and his wife; Mr. Henry Bedell, Scrivener; Mary Bales, William Phillips, Distiller, and Phillis Deane; and to each and every of them; a ring of twenty shillings value: I give to my tenants James Stokes and wife; William Mollose and his wife; Edward Earling, and his wife; and to each and every of them; a ring of ten shillings value: I give to Mr. Mark Bates, in St. Paul's Church-yard, Toyman, the sum of forty pounds: I give to Mr. John Turner, of Drapers' Hall, London, twenty pounds: I release and forgive unto Nathanael Frank the ten pounds due to me, by note under his hand, and all interest in respect thereof; and do order the same note to be delivered up by my executors: I give to William Burges, Wire-drawer, all my wearing apparel, both linen and woollen, except what is in the trunk aforesaid, together with my hats, wigs, and shoes.

Devise of Freehold, Leasehold and Copyhold Estates to the Drapers' Company.

Item, I give and devise to the Master and Wardens, and Brethren and Sisters of the Guild or Fraternity of the blessed Mary, the Virgin, of the mystery of Drapers, London, and to their successors and assigns for ever, all my messuages, lands, tenements, and hereditaments, as well freehold and leasehold as copyhold, situate and being in the several parishes of Woodham-Ferris, Clement's Green, Dunmore, and Prittlewell, in the county of Essex; and in the several parishes of Chiswick, St. Giles's in the Fields, and St. Margaret's, Westminster, in the county of Middlesex; and in the parishes of Raydon, Layham, and Hadley, or elsewhere, in the county of Suffolk; and in the parish of St. Gregory, in London; and all other messuages, lands, tenements, and hereditaments, whatsoever and wheresoever, whether freehold, leasehold, or copyhold, whereof, and wherein I am seised or possessed, or any other person or persons in trust for me, or to my use; such of the premises as are copyhold, having been by me already surrendered to the use of my Will.

And also all my goods, chattels, ready money, plate, bills, bonds, mortgages, South Sea stock, Annuity stock, Orphans' stock, East India bonds, South Sea bonds, and all other my personal estate whatsoever, not herein otherwise disposed of, subject unto, and charged with, the payment of my debts, legacies, and funeral expenses. All the said estate, real and personal, amounting together, as I compute the same, to the value of twenty-eight thousand pounds, more or less; To have

Residue of personal Estate to the Drapers' Company.

The value of the real and personal estates computed.

and to hold all and singular the premises before mentioned, unto the said Master and Wardens, and Brethren and Sisters, of the said Guild or Fraternity aforesaid, their successors and assigns for ever ; so subject nevertheless, and charged, as aforesaid, upon the Trusts of the estates declared. several trusts, and to and for the several intents and purposes hereinafter mentioned and expressed; and to and for no other use, intent or purpose whatsoever ; that is to say, upon trust, That the said Master and Wardens, and Brethren and Sisters of the said Guild or Fraternity, and their successors, do and Money to be expended in ground and buildings for an hospital. shall, out of my personal estate, lay out and expend the sum of four or five thousand pounds, or thereabouts, more or less, as in their discretion they shall see most fitting, in the purchasing of a convenient piece of ground of inheritance, within the weekly bills of mortality of London, where they shall judge most advisable ; and for the building thereon alms-houses for twenty-four old men, with a convenient chapel, and school-room for one hundred poor boys; and two dwelling-houses for two masters ; and such other out-building, walling, and accommodations, as shall be adjudged necessary and commodious for the purposes aforesaid.

Twenty-four old men to be placed therein. And my desire is, that the said twenty-four old men shall be members of the Drapers'

Company, of good life and conversation ; and shall, from time to time, be chosen and admitted by the Master and Wardens of the said Company for the time being, or the major part of them, in case so many deserving and real poor objects of that Company can be found ; and for want thereof, then such other poor old men to be taken from any place, as the said Master and Wardens shall best approve of.

And I do direct the said two masters shall, from time to time be chosen and approved by the Court of Assistants of the said Company ; and that, before they shall be admitted, they do give bond, with two sufficient sureties, in the penalty of one hundred pounds, or more, to be obedient and conformable to the orders of the said Company ; and quietly to leave and depart from the said school and habitation, upon three months' notice, in case of dislike or misbehaviour, upon order made for that purpose by the said Court of Assistants ; and that a new master be afterwards by them chosen in his stead.

The two masters to be chosen by the Court of Assistants and to give bond.

Condition of the masters' bonds.

And I do further direct and appoint, that the said one hundred boys shall be chosen and placed into the said school by the order and authority of the said Master and Wardens ; subject nevertheless to such Orders

One hundred boys to be placed in the school.

and Rules as the said Court of Assistants, or Committee thereof shall, from time to time, make for the good regulations and government of the said school ; and for breach thereof, or other reasonable cause, that such boys shall be displaced and expelled by the same authority, and other boys chosen in their stead ; and that no children shall be capable of being chosen under the age of seven years, nor above ten years, at their Election ; nor be continued in the said school after the age of fifteen years.

None to be admitted under seven, nor above ten years of age ; nor to be continued after fifteen years old.

And I do recommend to the said Company those excellent rules prescribed for the government of charity schools in Great Britain and Ireland, in a book printed by John Downing, for Jonathan Bowyer, in Ludgate Street, in the year one thousand seven hundred and ten, if the Company shall approve the same.

Recommends the printed rules for government of charity schools.

And my will and mind is, that the said number of one hundred boys shall be constantly kept up, in case so many poor children shall be produced and tendered for the choice and approbation of the said Company at their Wardens' Court ; and that they shall be taught to read, write, and cast accounts, and well instructed in the principles of the Christian religion, according to the doctrine of the

The number of one hundred boys to be kept up.

To be taught to read, write and cast accounts, &c.

Church of England, as by law established;
and I do appoint, the said masters shall read
prayers in the chapel every morning and
evening alternately; and that the said old
men, unless hindered by sickness, or other
reasonable cause, together with the boys,
shall constantly attend the said service.

Masters
to read
prayers in
the chapel
alternately
to the old
men and
boys.

And upon further trust, and my will and
mind further is, that the said twenty-four old
men, by and out of the rents and produce of
my said trust-estate hereby devised, shall have
eight pounds per annum a-piece duly paid
them towards their support and maintenance,
by four even quarterly payments; and six
sacks, or half a chaldron of coals, each yearly;
and a bays gown every third year.

And that the said two masters shall have
thirty pounds a-piece salary, to be paid quarterly, as aforesaid; and that twenty pounds
a-year be allowed to buy coals and candles
for the use of the said school and masters, as
the said Court of Assistants shall direct and
appoint; together with a sufficient allowance
for books, pens, paper, or other necessaries,
for the said school; and that the said boys
shall be clothed yearly with blue coats, caps,
stockings, shoes, and linen, like to other
charity-children; which I leave to the discretion and direction of the said Court of Assist-

Salary to
the two
masters
and allow-
ance for
coals and
candles.
Also for
books and
necessa-
ries for the
said school

ants, or care of the said Master and Wardens, for the time being : and I do desire the said Master and Wardens, and such others of the said Court of Assistants as are usually appointed for their visitations, will be pleased *Yearly visitation directed.* once a year, or oftener if occasion requiring, to visit the said school and alms-houses ; to cause the said children to be publicly examined and catechised; and to inquire into the state, condition, and behaviour of the said poor men ; as well as to take, view, and give orders for the needful repairs of the said school and alms-houses ; and that a sum not exceed-*Visitation dinner.* ing five pounds be expended in a dinner on that day for the said Committee ; and the two masters invited to partake thereof.

Two sermons annually. Also I desire and appoint two sermons to be preached on a Sunday in the forenoon yearly for ever, in commemoration of these *One in April at St. Helen's.* my charities ; the one in April, in the parish church of St. Helen's aforesaid, by the minister of that parish ; and the other in October, *The other in October at St. Michael's or elsewhere.* in the parish church of St. Michael's, Cornhill, or elsewhere, as the said Master and Wardens for the time being shall direct and *Masters, old men, and boys to be present, and the boys catechised* appoint : and that the said masters and children, and old men be then and there present, and the children publicly examined and catechised ; and that public notice thereof be given in the respective churches the preceding Sundays immediately after morning and evening prayer : and the ministers shall have twenty shillings each for preaching the said sermons ; and the readers ten shillings each for examining and catechising the said children ; and the clerks and sextons two shillings and six-pence each respectively.

Allowance to the minister, reader, &c. for this service.

And my will and mind further is, that when any of the said children shall be fifteen years old, they shall leave the said school, and be paid two pounds ten shillings to buy them clothes to fit them for service, or four pounds to place them apprentice to honest handicraft trades, as the said Master and Wardens shall think most proper ; and that the said Master and Wardens and Court of Assistants shall have full power, from time to time, to displace and put out the said masters, or children, or old men, or any or either of them, and place in others in their stead, at their wills and pleasure, in case they shall conceive sufficient cause for their so doing.

Children to leave the school at fifteen, and allowance for placing them out.

Power of displacing masters, old men, or boys.

And whereas I have been at considerable expense in purchasing a piece of ground, making a vault, and erecting a tomb, in the church of St. Helen's aforesaid ; I do hereby give and appoint the sum of two pounds per annum for ever, and more, whensoever needful, for the cleansing, taking care of, preserv-

Allowance for repair of the vault and tomb at St. Helens.

ing, and repairing my said vault and tomb as aforesaid; it being my intention and express desire, to have the same kept up in good order and repair for ever, whether the church be standing or not; and to that end, I hereby subject and charge all my said estate in London and Middlesex with the payment and support thereof, before any of the charities hereinbefore mentioned.

Directions for keeping the vault and tomb in repair; and charge on his estate for that purpose.

Item, I give to the said Fraternity of Drapers the sum of thirty-five pounds, to buy six or more silver plates, to be by them used, and kept in remembrance of me; and to the Master and Wardens and Clerk, that shall be in such office or station at the time of my decease, to each of them a ring of twenty shillings in value, whom I desire to be present at my funeral, and hold up my pall; and to the Clerk of the Company for the time being, for his care and trouble in receiving my rents, keeping my accounts, and looking after my charities, I give him the sum of twenty pounds per annum; and to his man for the time thirty shillings per annum.

Six silver plates to the Drapers' Company.

Rings to the Master Wardens, and Clerk.

Twenty pounds per annum to the Clerk for trouble; to the clerk's servant £1 10s. per annum

Item, I do direct and appoint, that the said Fraternity shall, out of the rents and produce of my said trust-estate, pay and allow to my executors, all such costs and charges and expenses as they shall be put unto on account

Expenses in executing the trust to be allowed.

of their executorship; and likewise shall
thereout be allowed, and retain to themselves
all such sum and sums of money, costs,
charges, and disbursements, as they shall at
any time hereafter be put unto, or reasonably Also for
expend, in and about the proving of my Will proving
the Will in
in perpetuam rei memoriam, in the Court of Chancery.
Chancery, or otherwise; and for all repairs, And for
views, journeys, charges in law or equity, repairs,
views,
visitations or other expenses and outgoings law-
charges,
whatsoever, on account of this my trust: &c.
hereby willing and desiring them, after my
said school and the alms-houses are built and After
building
finished, as aforesaid, to dispose of the residue the Hos-
of my personal estate in the purchasing of pital, the
residue
lands, or estate of inheritance, in fee-simple, of the personal es-
to be settled and assured as counsel shall tate to be
laid out in
advise, unto and upon the said Company, lands.
and their successors for ever, to answer the
several charitable ends and purposes aforesaid; and, in the mean time, until such And in the
mean
purchase or purchases may be had, to place time to be
placed at
out or continue the same at interest, or in interest,
or in the
any of the public funds or stocks, or other- funds.
wise, for the improvement thereof, as in their
discretion they shall see fit; or to assign and
transfer the same, as occasion may require.
But my will is, that neither they, nor any of Not to be
answer-
them, shall be answerable in any-wise, for able for
losses by
any loss that shall or may happen by reason any purchase or
of any purchase, or defect in any security defect in
security.

to be by them made or taken in pursuance hereof.

The overplus of the estate (if any) to go for improving this charity. And in case, at any time hereafter, there shall appear any considerable overplus of any estate beyond what is hereinbefore by me given and provided for, I then leave it to the Master and Wardens and Assistants of the said Company, for the time being, to apply and dispose of the same, for improving of this my charity, as they shall think fit.

To make a proportionable reduction of this Charity in case of deficiency in the estate; and the Company not to be prejudiced by this trust. And in case my said estate shall prove deficient to answer the purposes aforesaid, then I likewise leave it to the said Company to make a proportionable reduction of this my charity, in such method and manner as to them shall appear most reasonable; it being my express desire and meaning, that neither the said Company, nor their estate, shall in anywise be lessened, prejudiced, or impaired by reason of their acceptance of this trust.

The executors to make over the stocks to the Company. And I do hereby direct and appoint my executors to assign, make over, and transfer all and singular my several stocks herein before mentioned, and all other stocks whatsoever, which I have, or am entitled unto, in any of the puplic companies, or otherwise, unto the said Master and Wardens, and

Brethren and Sisters of the Fraternity aforesaid; and shall likewise assign and deliver And to
over unto them all mortgages and other assign and
deliver
securities whatsoever; and all other my per- over to
them the
sonal estate, before mentioned to be by me rest of the
personal
given and devised unto them, to the end that estate.
the same may be applied by them to the
several trusts, and for the several charitable purposes, hereinbefore directed and
appointed.

And lastly, I do nominate and appoint Executors
appointed.
my worthy friends, Samuel Webb, and John
Gould, of Hackney, Esquires; Nicholas
Cripps, of the county of Kent, Gent.; Thomas Barnard, of London, Gent.; and James
Jackson, of Woodford, in Essex, Gent.;
being all of them Citizens and Drapers of
London, aforesaid, executors of this my last
Will and Testament: and I give unto each A legacy
of £20 to
of them twenty pounds a-piece for their care each of
them.
and trouble in the execution thereof.

And I do hereby revoke and make void, Revoca-
tion of
all former or other Wills by me at any time former
Wills.
heretofore made; and do declare this present
writing, contained on six sheets of paper,
to be my true and only Will. In witness
whereof, I, the said Francis Bancroft, the
testator, to all and every of the said six
sheets my hand and seal have subscribed

B

and set, this eighteenth day of March in the year of our Lord one thousand seven hundred and twenty-seven, and in the first year of the reign of our Sovereign Lord King George the Second.

F. BANCROFT.

Signed, sealed, published, and declared by the said Francis Bancroft, the testator, to be his last Will and Testament, in the presence of us, who subscribed our names as witnesses thereunto, in the presence of him, the said testator, this 18th day of March, 1727.

George Waite, Lecturer of St. Mary, Islington.
John Bateman, of Islington.
William Unwin, Clerk to Mr. Turner, of Drapers' Hall.

Licence in Mortmain, 1731

TO THE KING'S MOST EXCELLENT MAJESTY.

May it please
Your Majesty.

In humble obedience to Your Majesty's Commands signified to me by the Right Honourable the Lord Harrington one of your Majesty's Principal Secretarys of State referring to me the annexed Petition of the Master and Wardens and Brethren and Sisters of the Guild or Fraternity of the Blessed Mary the Virgin of the Mistery of Drapers of the City of London, and directing me to consider thereof and report my Opinion what may be fitly done therein, I have considered of the said Petition which sets forth That Francis Bancroft Esqr. deceased Member of the said Company having an Estate in Land and old Houses of about four Hundred pounds p Annum, and in Government and other Security and ready money twenty one Thousand pounds and upwards, by his last Will bearing date the 18th of March 1727, duly executed and proved in the Prerogative Court of Canterbury, (after his Debts paid and some pecuniary Legacys therein given) Gave and Devised to the Petitioners and their Successors and Assigns for ever, All the Residue of His said Estate UPON TRUST that they expend four or five thousand pounds in the purchasing a piece of Ground of Inheritance within the Bills of Mortality of London for Building Alms-houses for twenty four old Men with a Chappel and Schoolroom for one hundred Boys, and two Dwelling-houses for two Masters. And devised eight Pounds per annum to be paid to each of the said old Men, and that they shall have Gowns and half a Chaldron of Coals each : And to the two Masters thirty Pounds p. annum each and twenty pounds p annum for Coals and Candles, with a Sufficient allowance for Books, Penns, Paper &c. for the School, and that the Boys shall be yearly clothed and taught to read, write and cash Account and instructed in the Principles of the Christian Religion according to the Doctrine of the Church of England, and appointed two Sermons to be preached yearly, and the Children to be publickly examined and Catechized for which he allowed three Pounds p. Annum and upwards to the Ministers &c. and five Pounds for a Dinner for a Committee of the Company on that Occasion.

That the Boys shall leave the School when Fifteen Years old and thereupon be paid two pounds ten shillings each to buy Clothes to fit them for Service, or four Pounds to place them Apprentice to handicraft Trades, and appointed two Pounds p. annum or more for taking care of and repairing his Vault and Tomb, and gave to the Clerk of the Company and his Man twenty one Pounds ten shillings p. annum, and made divers other necessary Provisions to be paid out of his Estate for the support maintenance and carrying on those Trusts.

And when the said School and Almshouses &c. are built and finished That the Residue of his personal Estate be laid out in purchasing Lands or Estate of Inheritance in Fee simple to be Settled upon the Petitioners and their successors for ever to answer the several Charitable Ends and Purposes aforesaid, And in the meantime to place out and continue the same at Interest in any of the publick Funds or otherwise as the Petitioners should see fit to whom he left the Disposition Regulation and Government of his said Charitys with Power for the Petitioners to improve his said Charitys in case his Estate should encrease, or to reduce the same in case his Estate should prove deficient.

That the Petitioners have Exemplified his said Will in Chancery in perpetuam Roi memoriam, paid the Testator's Debts, Funeral Expenses and pecuniary Legacys and now compute they have remaining in Stocks and Securities about twenty three thousand Pounds.

The Petitioners therefore most humbly beseeched Your Most Sacred Majesty to grant them Licence to purchase Lands or Estate of Inheritance in Mortmain not exceeding one Thousand Pounds p. annum to Support and maintain the several Charitable Ends and Purposes aforesaid.

AND I humbly certifie Your Majesty that the Probate of the Will of the said Francis Bancroft hath been laid before me, by which it appears that the Testator hath given his real and personal Estate after the payment of his Debts, Funeral Charges and Legacys to the Petitioners and their Successors for the Charitable Uses and Purposes mentioned in the Petition.

AND John Turner of Drapers Hall London Gentleman Clerk to the said Company of Drapers by his Affidavit hereunto annexed hath Sworn that to the best of his knowledge and belief, after Debts, Legacys and Funeral Expenses paid, there is now remaining in Stocks and Securitys of the personal Estate of the said Francis Bancroft, given by his said Will for the Charitable Uses therein mentioned, the Sum of twenty three thousand Pounds or thereabouts.

By a Statute made in the Seventh Year of the Reign of his late Majesty King William the third, Your Majesty hath an undoubted Power of granting such Licence as is desired by the Petition.

And as the Charitys intended by the Testator are to be perpetual and can not be effectually Secured, but by investing his personal Estate in the Purchase of Lands of Inheritance, I see no Objection to Your Majesty's granting to the Petitioners a Licence to purchase Freehold Lands or Tenements in Mortmain, with the Testator's personal Estate, for the Purposes mentioned in his Will, so as such Lands or Tenements do not exceed One thousand Pounds p. annum if Your Majesty shall think fit to grant the same.

All which is most humbly submitted
to Your Majesty's Royal Wisdom.

4th June 1731.

C. Talbot.

276

GEORGE THE SECOND BY THE GRACE OF GOD of Great Britain France and Ireland King Defender of the Faith &c. TO ALL to whom these presents shall come Greeting WHEREAS the Master and Wardens and Brethren and Sisters of the Guild or Fraternity of the Blessed Mary the Virgin of the Mystery of Drapers of the City of London have by their Petition humbly represented unto us that Francis Bancroft Esquire deceased member of the said Company having an Estate in land and old houses of about Four Hundred Pounds per annum and in Government and other securities and ready money Twenty One Thousand Pounds and upwards by his last Will bearing date the Eighteenth day of March 1727 duly executed and proved in the Prerogative Court of Canterbury (after his debts paid and some pecuniary legacies therein given) gave and devised to the Petitioners and their successors and assigns for ever all the residue of his said Estate upon trust that they should expend Four or Five Thousand Pounds in the purchasing a piece of ground of inheritance within the Bills of Mortality of London for building Almshouses for twenty four old men with a Chapel and School Room for one hundred boys and two dwellinghouses for two masters and devised £8 per annum to be paid to each of the said old men And that they should have Gowns and half a chaldron of coals each And to the two masters £30 per annum for coals and candles with a sufficient allowance for books pens paper &c. for the School And that the boys should be yearly clothed and taught to read and write and cast account and instructed in the principles of the Christian Religion according to the doctrine of the Church of England And appointed two sermons to be preached yearly and the children to be publicly examined and catechised for which he allowed Three Pounds per annum and upwards to the Ministers &c. and £5 for a dinner for a Committee of the Company on that occasion that the boys should leave the School when fifteen years old and thereupon be paid £2.10.0. each to buy cloths to fit them for service or £4. to place them apprenticed to handicraft trades And appointed £2. per annum or more for taking care of and repairing his vault and tomb And gave to the Clerk of the Company and his man £21.10.0. per annum And made divers other necessary provisions to be paid out of his Estate for the support maintenance and carrying on these Trusts And when the said School and Almshouses &c. are built and finished that the residue of his personal Estate be laid out in purchasing lands or estate of Inheritance in fee simple to be settled upon the Petitioners and their successors for ever to answer the several charitable ends and purposes aforesaid And in the meantime to place out and continue the same at interest in any of the public funds as the Petitioners should see fit to whom he left the disposition regulation and government of his said charities with power for the Petitioners to improve his said charities in case his Estate should increase or to reduce the same in case his estate should prove deficient as by the above recited Will of the said Francis Bancroft relation being thereunto had (amongst other things therein contained) may more fully appear That the Petitioners have exemplified the said Will in Chancery in perpetuam rei memoriam paid the Testator's debts funeral expenses and pecuniary legacies and now compute they have remaining in stocks and securities about Twenty Three Thousand Pounds And the Petitioners having therefore humbly prayed us to grant Our Licence to them and their successors to purchase lands or estate of

277

Inheritance in Mortmain not exceeding One thousand Pounds per annum to support and maintain the several charitable ends and purposes aforesaid We being willing to give all due encouragement to such charitable gifts and legacies have thought fit to condescend to their request   Know Ye therefore that We of Our especial grace certain knowledge and mere motion Have given and granted and by these presents for Us Our heirs and successors DO give and grant unto the said Master and Wardens and brethren and sisters of the Guild or Fraternity of the Blessed Mary the Virgin of the Mystery of Drapers of the City of London and their successors Our especial licence full power and lawful and absolute authority with the said Testators personal estate and effects to purchase acquire take and hold in Mortmain to them and their successors for ever from any person or persons bodies politic or corporate their heirs and successors respectively any freehold lands or tenements within that part of Our Kingdom of Great Britain called England or Our Dominion of Wales not exceeding in the whole the clear yearly value of One Thousand Pounds

above all charges and reprizes And It is Our Will and pleasure that all the clear rents issues and profits of the said freehold lands or tenements so to be purchased shall according to the true intent and meaning of the said recited Will of the said Francis Bancroft be applied from time to time by the said Master and Wardens and brethren and sisters of the Guild or Fraternity of the Blessed Mary the Virgin of the Mystery of Drapers of the City of London and their successors to the several charitable uses intents and purposes in the said recited Will of the said Francis Bancroft and hereinbefore specified and to no other use intent or purpose whatsoever AND FURTHER Our Will and pleasure is and We do by these presents for us our heirs and successors grant ordain declare and appoint that it shall and may be lawful to and for any person or persons bodies politic or corporate their heirs and successors respectively to grant alien and dispose of in Mortmain to the said Master and Wardens and brethren and sisters of the Guild or Fraternity of the Blessed Mary the Virgin of the Mystery of Drapers of the City of London and their successors for ever any freehold lands or tenements within that part of our Kingdom of Great Britain called England or our Dominion of Wales not exceeding in the whole the clear yearly value of One Thousand Pounds above mentioned above all charges and reprizes to the end the same may be by them held and the   (illegible owing to decay of parchment)
applied to the said several charitable uses intents and purposes in and by the above recited Will of the said Francis Bancroft mentioned and
AND LASTLY we do hereby   (illegible owing to decay of parchment)
and successors declare and grant that these our Letters Patent or the inrollment thereof shall be in and by all things good firm valid sufficient and effectual in the Law according to the true intent and meaning thereof notwithstanding the not truly or fully reciting the said Will of the said Francis Bancroft or the not truly or rightly describing the several charitable uses intents and purposes therein mentioned or thereby directed or any other omission imperfection defect matter cause or thing whatsoever to the contrary thereof in any wise notwithstanding   IN WITNESS whereof We have caused these Our Letters to be made patent WITNESS Our Selfe at Westminster the First day of July in the Fifth Year of Our Reign
By Writ of Privy Seal

COCKS

278

SEAL.

RULES and ORDERS

Made and Ordained by

The Worshipful the Court of Assistants of

The Company of Drapers, *London* ;

Governors of the *Alms-Houses* and
School at *Mile-End*,

Founded by

Mr. FRANCIS BANCROFT, Deceased :

For the good Government of

The MASTERS, ALMS-MEN, and BOYS,
Admitted, and to be Admitted, and Placed
therein.

L O N D O N :

Printed in the Year M.DCC.XXXVIII.

RULES and ORDERS

Made and Ordained by

The Worshipful the Court of Assistants of the Company of DRAPERS, **London**;

GOVERNORS of the *Alms-Houses* and *School* at *Mile-End*, founded by Mr. FRANCIS BANCROFT, deceased; for the good Government of the *Masters*, *Alms-Men* and *Boys*, admitted, and to be admitted and placed therein.

I.

IT is ORDAINED and ORDERED, That the Two Masters shall read Prayers in the Chapel to the Alms-Men and Children every Morning and Evening alternately; and take Care that the said Alms-Men and Children do constantly and devoutly attend the said Service, unless hindred by Sickness or other just Cause.

II.

THAT they shall carefully Teach the Children to Read, Write, and cast Accounts; and Instruct them,

A 2

as

as well in the Principles of the Chriſtian Religion, according to the Doctrine of the Church of *England*, as in Loyalty to the KING : And that each Maſter ſhall take his Share of the Trouble, in teaching and inſtructing them according to the beſt of his Capacity.

III.

THAT the ſaid Maſters ſhall diligently attend the School on every Day, (except Sundays, Calendar Holidays, and the Times hereafter mentioned for Breaking up) from *Michaelmas Day* to *Lady Day*, from Eight of the Clock, till Eleven in the Morning; and from One of the Clock till Four in the Afternoon : And from *Lady Day* till *Michaelmas*, from Seven of the Clock till Eleven, in the Morning ; and from One of the Clock till Five, in the Afternoon ; (*Thurſday* from Three in the Afternoon, and *Saturday* Afternoons alſo excepted.)

IV.

THAT the Times for Breaking up ſhall be Three Weeks at *Chriſtmas*; a Fortnight at *Eaſter*, and a Fortnight at *Whitſuntide*.

V.

THAT each Maſter ſhall keep a Book, and ſet down therein ſuch Defaults and Offences as are worthy of his Notice ; which ſhall from time to time be committed, in breach of any of the Ordinances herein after contained, to be obſerved by the ſaid Alms-Men ; or which ſhall come to their Knowledge reſpectively ; and ſhall deliver a Copy thereof to the Clerk of the Company, on the firſt *Monday* in every Month: To the End the ſaid MASTER and WAR-

DENS

281

DENS may be Informed of the fame; and that due Punifhment may be inflicted on fuch as fhall prefume to offend.

VI.

THAT the faid Alms-Men fhall devoutly attend the Publick Worfhip of God in the Chapel, conftantly, every Morning and Evening, in their Gowns; and fhall take their Seats there, in order as they come.

VII.

THAT after the Bell hath Tolled the fpace of a Quarter of an Hour, the Perfon officiating as Clerk to the Chapel, fhall call over every Alms-Man's Name, and note down fuch as fhall be abfent without juft Caufe or Leave, in a Book to be kept by the Mafters for that Purpofe.

VIII.

THAT in cafe the MASTER and WARDENS for the Time being, fhall permit the Wives of any of the Alms-Men to refide with their Hufbands, fuch Wives fhall conftantly attend Divine Service in the Chapel every *Sunday*, Morning and Afternoon; unlefs hindred by Sicknefs, or other juft Caufe, to be allowed by one of the Mafters: and fhall take their Seats, in order as they come in, on the Forms in the Middle of the Chapel.

IX.

THAT one of the Alms-Men, to be appointed by the MASTER and WARDENS for the Time being, fhall officiate as Clerk, every Morning and Afternoon, in the Chapel; and fhall alfo Toll the Bell for the fpace of a Quarter of an Hour every

A 3

Morn-

Morning and Afternoon, before the Prayers ; and
shall Sweep and keep the Chapel and School in clean
and decent Order, and bring up Coals, and make the
Fires in the School, when necessary ; and shall also
Sweep and keep clean the Portico, Stone Steps,
Pavement, and Gravel Walk before the Chapel,
School, and Masters Houses : and shall be allowed
for his Pains and Diligence herein *Forty* Shillings a
Quarter, over and above what is allowed to each
Alms-Man by the Founder.

X.

THAT one other of the said Alms-Men, to be
appointed by the MASTER and WARDENS for
the Time being, shall keep the Keys of the Gates,
and shall every Night (from *Michaelmas Day* to *Lady
Day*, at half an Hour after Eight of the Clock ;
and from *Lady Day* to *Michaelmas Day*, at half an
Hour after Nine of the Clock) Toll the Bell fifty
Strokes : and then, so soon as the Clock shall
have struck the respective Hours of Nine in the
Winter, and Ten in the Summer, lock up the
Gates ; and then make due Enquiry at every Alms-
House, Whether any, and which of the Alms-Men
are absent , and enter the Names of such as be absent in a Book, to be kept by him for that Purpose.
And every Alms-Man who shall be shut out after
the Hours aforesaid, (except such as shall be absent
with Leave) shall, for every such Offence, forfeit
and pay *One Shilling*. And in case any of them
shall be found to have offended herein more than four
times within the space of one Year, He or They shall
not be received again into the said Alms-Houses, or

be

be entitled to the Penfion or Allowance of an Alms-Man ; unlefs afterwards reftored thereto by an Order of the Court of WARDENS, on good Affurance of Amendment for the future.

XI.

THAT the Alms-Man who fhall be appointed to keep the Gates, fhall Sweep, and keep clean the Pavement and Gravel Walks, from the South end of the Alms-Mens Houfes, on each fide, to the Gates leading into the High-way ; and alfo the Gravel Walks, throughout the whole Front of the Ground, as well without as within the Wall next to the faid High-way ; and fhall be allowed *Forty Shillings* a Quarter, over and above what is allowed to each Alms-Man by the Founder, as an Encouragement for his Care and Diligence, in all the Services herein before mentioned.

XII.

THAT either of the faid Mafters, when he fhall fee juft Caufe, may give Licence to any one or more of the Alms-Men, not exceeding two in Number at one time, to be abfent from his Habitation and Prayers, for the Space of one Day and Night, fo as he do not Licence any one Perfon to be abfent more than four times in one Year: And that the Perfons obtaining fuch Licence, from time to time give Notice thereof to the other Mafter, to the End he may note the fame.

XIII.

THAT any two or more of the WARDENS, from time to time, as they fhall fee Caufe, may give Licence under their Hands to any of the Alms-Men

A 4   to

to be abfent from their Habitations for any fpace of Time not exceeding 21 Days: And in cafe the COURT of ASSISTANTS, or the MASTER and WARDENS for the Time being, fhall think fit, for the better Support and Encouragement of any of the faid Alms-Men, to employ any of them in the Company's Service at their Hall, That the faid *Wardens,* or any two of them, may Licence fuch of them as fhall be fo employed, to be abfent from time to time, in the Day time only, as the Duty of fuch Service may require ; giving Notice thereof to the two *Mafters.*

XIV

THAT the faid Alms-Men, and their Wives (if permitted to refide with them) fhall behave with Submiffion and Refpect to the two Mafters, and in Brotherly Love and Friendfhip towards one another.

XV.

THAT none of the faid Alms-Men, or their Wives, fhall ufe any railing, bitter, or uncharitable Speeches to any other of the Alms-Men, or their Wives, under the Penalty of Sixpence for each Offence, to be paid by the Alms-Man offending, or whofe Wife fhall fo offend ; and that none of the faid Alms Men fhall prefume to ftrike any of their Brethren, or any of their Wives, under the Penalty of One Shilling for the firft Offence, Two Shillings and Sixpence for the fecond Offence, and for the third Offence, to be for ever expelled.

XVI.

THAT if any of the faid Alms-Men, or their Wives, fhall prefume to take the Name of God in
Vain,

Vain, or be Drunk, That every Alms-Man so offending, or whose Wife shall so offend, shall, for the first Offence, forfeit and pay Sixpence ; for the second Offence, One Shilling ; for the third Offence, Two Shillings ; for the fourth Offence, Five Shillings ; and for the fifth Offence, to be expelled.

XVII.

THAT if any of the said Alms-Men shall haunt or frequent any Alehouse or Publick House, and shall resort thereto, after Notice given him by either of the Masters to refrain therefrom, that the Person so resorting thereto, after such Notice given, as aforesaid, shall, for the first Offence, forfeit Sixpence ; for the second Offence, One Shilling ; and for the third Offence, Two Shillings.

XVIII.

THAT if any of them shall commit Adultery, or Fornication, or shall be guilty of Theft, or such like enormous Crime, He or They so offending shall be for ever expelled.

XIX.

THAT if the Wife of any of the said Alms-Men, who shall be permitted to reside with her Husband, shall prove with Child, she shall not be permitted to Lye-in in any of the said Alms-Houses, or in the Parish where the same are situated (unless the same Parish be the Place of his Settlement) by which any Charge may possibly accrue to the said Parish, but shall be removed by her Husband (so soon as it shall be discovered she is with Child) to the Place of his Settlement, there to remain until she shall be delivered, under the Penalty of his being
for

for ever expelled, in cafe of Breach or Difobedience of this Order.

XX.

THAT neither of the faid Alms-Men fhall prefume to take any Apprentice, or do any other Act by which any Charge may poffibly accrue to the Parifh where the faid Alms-Houfes are fituate, under Pain of Expulfion.

XXI.

THAT neither of the faid Alms-Men fhall prefume to marry during his continuance in the faid Alms-Houfes, without leave of the WARDENS for the Time being, under Pain of Expulfion.

XXII.

THAT if any of the faid Alms-Men, or their Wives, fhall prefume to beg, during the Time He or She fhall be harboured in the faid Alms-Houfes, He or She fo offending, fhall fuffer Expulfion for the fame.

XXIII.

THAT none of the faid Alms-Men, or their Wives, fhall fell any Chandlery Ware, Liquors, or Fruits, within the Ground belonging to the faid Alms-Houfes, or keep any Bulk, or Stall there, or any Publick Shop for expofing any thing to Sale, or fhall put up any Sign or Shew-board within the Premifes, under the Penalty of forfeiting Three Months Penfion for the firft Offence ; and under Pain of Expulfion for the fecond Offence.

XXIV.

THAT no Linnen fhall be laid upon, or dried in the Ground before the Alms-Houfes.

XXV.

XXV.

THAT the said Alms-Men, or their Wives, shall not keep any Swine, or Rabbits, or Poultry, within the Ground, under the Penalty of five Shillings for every such Offence.

XXVI.

THAT they shall not keep any Dog within the said Alms-Houses, or Ground, under the Penalty aforesaid.

XXVII.

THAT they shall not take in any Inmate, Servant, or other Person, to inhabit the said Alms-Houses, other than such as shall be allowed by the *Master* and *Wardens* for the Time being, in case of Sickness or Inability, under the Pain of Expulsion.

XXVIII.

THAT every Alms-Man shall daily before the Hour of Ten in the Morning Sweep and make clean the Pavement and Walk before his Dwelling ; and that no Ashes, Soil, Dust, or other Thing, shall be cast out, or laid in any part of the Ground belonging to the said Alms-Houses, other than the Places appointed for that Purpose.

XXIX.

THAT none of the said Alms-Men shall presume to take down, break, or deface any of the Brickwork, Tiling, Wainscot, or other Thing belonging to the said Hospital, under pretence of altering or amending the same, or otherwise, under the Penalty of *Forty Shillings*, over and above the Expence of restoring the same to the Condition it was in before such Alteration was made.

XXX.

XXX.

THAT the Alms-Men shall from time to time Repair the Glass Windows of their respective Houses at their own Charge, to the End they may be careful to prevent the same from being broke.

XXXI.

THAT upon the Death, Expulsion, or other Removal of any Alms-Man, all the Cupboards, Dressers, Shelves, Locks, Bolts, and such like Improvements, which he may have put up in his House, shall be left therein for the Benefit of the said House.

XXXII.

THAT the Ground on the East side of the said Alms-Houses, being appointed for the Burial of such of the said Alms-Men, or their Wives, who shall die in the said Alms-Houses, It is Ordered, That on the Death of any of the said Alms-Men, or their Wives, the Person to be appointed for doing the Duty of Clerk, or Sexton, shall dig the Grave ; and the Alms-Men, except such as shall be appointed for Bearers, shall follow the Corps in their Gowns, two by two, from the House of the Deceased, to the Place of Interrment : And after the proper Service is performed, shall return in the same Order to their respective Houses. And that four of the said Alms-Men, whom the Masters shall think most fit for that Service, shall officiate as Bearers at the said Burial ; and that the Minister officiating at every such Burial shall be allowed Two Shillings and Six-pence ; the Sexton or Grave digger, Two Shillings ; the four Bearers, One Shilling each ; One Shilling for the Searchers, and Sixpence for the Affidavit.

XXXIII.

XXXIII.

That all the Forfeitures and Payments to be incurred by Breach of any of these Ordinances, shall be deducted out of the Pensions of the respective Offenders, or whose Wives shall so offend as aforesaid, and be kept in a Box to be distributed and given by the Master and Wardens of the Company for the Time being, or the major Part of them, at their Visitation, amongst such others of the Poor Alms-Men, and in such Proportions, as the said Master and Wardens in their Discretion shall think most needy and deserving.

XXXIV.

That for the better Observation of the Ordinances aforesaid, and that no Person concerned may plead Ignorance thereof, It is Ordered, That the same shall be fairly Wrote or Printed, and kept in a Frame, and constantly hung up in the Chapel and School-Room, and shall be read by one of the Masters, on the first *Monday* in *March*, and the first *Monday* in *September* Yearly, and every Year in the said Chapel, immediately after the Morning-Service.

For

For the BOYS.

I. THAT they shall attend every *Sunday*, and other Days, in the Chapel (unless hindred by Sickness) at the Times appointed for the Masters to read Prayers there ; and shall behave themselves decently and reverently during the Service ; and such of them as shall be able to Read, shall bring with them their Bible and Common Prayer-Book, that they may the more readily and devoutly make their Responses, and attend to and understand the said Service.

II.

THAT they shall constantly come to School by the Times appointed for the School to begin, and not be absent therefrom (except in case of Sickness) on any Pretence whatsoever.

III.

THAT they shall come clean washed and combed, as well to the School as to the Chapel ; and shall be constantly habited in their Caps, Bands, and Clothes, as well when Abroad as at the Chapel and School ; to the End their Behaviour may be the better observed and known.

IV.

THAT they shall behave with Duty and Obedience to their Governors, and Masters set over them,

and

and with Meekneſs and Reſpect to all others; and
ſhall ſubmit to ſuch moderate Correction, from time
to time, from either of the Maſters, as he ſhall think
their Faults may deſerve.

V.

THAT they ſhall give good Example to each
other, and refrain from Vice ; and more particularly
from Stealing, Lying, Swearing, Curſing, Profanation of the Lord's Day, and other enormous Crimes,
under Pain that every one practiſing any ſuch Crimes
ſhall be expelled, and diſmiſſed from the School,
on Complaint made of ſuch Offence to the MAS-
TER and WARDENS.

VI.

THAT there ſhall be given and read to the Parents of each Child, at the Time of his being firſt admitted into the School, a printed Copy of the OR-
DERS appointed for that Purpoſe ; and that the ſame
ſhall be obſerved by the Parents or Friends of ſuch
Children ; or in caſe of their Neglect, after having
been admoniſhed thereof by the Maſters of the ſaid
School, or either of them ; that the Child whoſe
Parents or Friends ſhall be guilty of ſuch Neglect,
ſhall, on Complaint thereof made to the MASTER
and WARDENS, be forthwith diſmiſſed from, and
expelled the ſaid School.

VII.

THAT in all Caſes where any Boy ſhall be expelled, or diſmiſſed from the ſaid School for any
Miſbehaviour, or Neglect, or Diſlike to be conceived againſt him by the Court of *Wardens* for the
time being, or ſhall leave and depart from the ſaid
School

School without the Confent of the MASTER and
WARDENS of the Company, The Clothes of every
fuch Boy, which fhall have been given him by the
Founder's Allowance at the time of his Admiffion
to, or laft before his Expulfion, or Departure from
the faid School, fhall be forthwith returned back to
one of the Schoolmafters, to be difpofed of as the
MASTER and WARDENS of the Company for the
Time being fhall direct.

F I N I S.

Order and Regulations 1802

BANCROFT'S HOSPITAL.

—➤➤✿◀◀—

The Officers and Servants, with their Salaries, Duties, and Emoluments.

There are TWO SCHOOL-MASTERS and an USHER.

One master is called the HEAD MASTER; and the present one has an annual salary of two hundred and fifty pounds; which, with the use of a house and garden, free of rent, and free from all expense of repairs and taxes, and fifty-four sacks of coals, is in full of all emoluments whatever to him; but the above-mentioned salary is not to be considered as appertaining to the office of head master, as the Court have reserved to themselves the right, upon any future appointment, of fixing it at such sum as they shall deem fit and proper.

The other master is called the UNDER MASTER, and the present one has an annual salary of one hundred and eighty pounds; which, with the use of a house and garden, free of rent, and free from all expense of repairs and taxes, and fifty-four sacks of coals, is in full of all emoluments whatever to him—the same observation which is made upon the subject of the salary of the head master, also applies to that of the under master, as well as of the matron and servants of the establishment.

The USHER, who is appointed by the school committee, has a salary of fifty pounds per annum, which with board, lodging, and washing, is in full of all emoluments whatever to him.

There is also a FRENCH MASTER who has a salary of fifty pounds per annum, which is in full of all emoluments to him.

There is a CHAPLAIN, a clergyman of the Church of England, who has a salary of thirty-one pounds ten shillings per annum, which is in full of all emoluments whatever to him. For many years past the offices of Head Master and Chaplain have been united.

There is a MEDICAL ATTENDANT who has an annual salary of one hundred and five pounds, which is in full of all emoluments whatever to him; the drugs, &c , being provided by him.

There is a MATRON, who is a single woman, who has an annual salary of eighty-four pounds; which, together with board, washing, and lodging at the hospital, free of cost, is in full of all emoluments whatever to her.

There is a WOMAN COOK, a single woman without children; who has eighteen pounds per annum wages, which, together with board, washing and lodging at the hospital, free of cost, is in full of all emoluments whatever to her.

There is a NURSE, a single woman without children; who has sixteen pounds per annum wages, which, together with board, washing, and lodging, at the hospital, free of cost, is in full of all emoluments whatever to her.

There are four other WOMEN SERVANTS, all single women without children; each of them has wages, fixed from time to time by the school committee; which, together with board, washing, and lodging at the hospital, free of cost, is in full of all emoluments whatever to them.

The masters, officers, and servants are not permitted to take or accept any fee, perquisite, or gratuity whatsoever from any of the tradesmen employed, or from the friends of any of the boys, or any other person upon any occasion or pretence whatsoever.

The Duties of the Two Masters.

The head master has the management of, and is responsible for the general conduct of the whole establishment, and is to see that the other officers and servants perform the several duties allotted to them. The under master is in all things to be subordinate to the head master; and in the absence or sickness of the latter, the under master is to perform all his duties; and in the absence or sickness of the under master, the head master is to perform all his duties.

The duties and authorities of the two masters with respect to the alms-men are set out in the rules and orders for the government of the hospital.

The two masters (subject to the subordination of the under master to the head master) with the assistance of the usher, are to instruct, educate and govern the boys, pursuant to the directions contained in the founder's will; and to teach them to read, write, and cast accounts; and such other branches of a commercial education as shall from time to time be settled by the school committee; moreover, to educate them as well in the principles of the Christian Religion, according to the doctrines of the Church of England, as in loyalty to the Sovereign: and each master is to take his share of the duty according to the best of his ability. All corporal punishment to be inflicted on any of the boys is to be inflicted by the head master, and the under master is not to inflict corporal punishment on any boy, but is to report any boy who, in his opinion, shall deserve corporal punishment, to the head master, for him to inflict it; but this does not extend to delinquencies during the absence of the head master, which, in the opinion of the under master, shall require immediate punishment.

The usher is to assist in instructing the lower classes and to superintend the boys out of school hours, in the playground and boarding house, and also to play the harmonium, and to lead the singing in the chapel.

Prayers are to be read in the chapel excepting in holidays, by one of the masters every morning on a week day, throughout the year, at half-past eight o'clock; and every evening on a week day at half-past four; on Christmas-Day, Good-Friday, and on Sundays, the hours are left to the discretion of the head master.

The under master or usher is always to be present, with the matron, at each of the boys' meals of dinner and supper, and at their prayers.

Either the under master or usher is always to be within the hospital, excepting during the Christmas and summer holydays, when the usher may be absent, but one of the masters is always to be in residence; so that at all hours, as well out of school time as in school time, and in holiday time, one master or usher may always be responsible for the government of the alms-men and boys.

The duties of reading prayers in the chapel, and attendance for government of the hospital out of school times and during holidays, are to be performed by the two masters alternately day by day, or otherwise, as they shall agree upon, or the school committee shall direct.

Each master is to have a master-key of the boarding-house, and of the two dormitories, and of every other apartment therein; except the private apartments of the matron and servants, and except the pantries, store-room, cellar, and wardrobe, the keys of which are to be kept exclusively by the matron, but the masters are to have access thereto at reasonable times, at their pleasure, but in her presence.

The head master is to attend the school committee at the Hall, from time to time, to settle accounts, and other business of the hospital.

The head master, with the assistance of the under master, is to keep all the accounts at the hospital, and have disbursement of the petty expenses, and other sums payable which are not paid by the clerk of the Company, in usual course, or in pursuance of bills previously signed by the chairman of the school committee.

Both or either of the masters, as the school committee visiting the hospital shall at any time direct, is to assist them in taking and entering the minutes of their orders and proceedings at the hospital; and both the masters are to have access thereto at all times unless it shall be otherwise directed.

The two masters are freely to communicate with each other and act in concert in all matters relating to the hospital and school, subject, nevertheless, to the subordination of the under master to the head master, as herein mentioned; and in case of difference of opinion, the head master shall decide. And the head master, and in his absence the under master, is to report to the clerk of the Company, for the information of the court of assistants and committee, all vacancies in the school and almshouses immediately after they shall arise, with such special information connected therewith, as it may be thought desirable should accompany the same; and are also to report all misbehaviours, breaches of order and neglects of the officers, servants, alms-men, boys, and others, with all matters requiring the notice and attention of the court or committee.

THE DUTIES OF THE CHAPLAIN.

The chaplain is to read prayers and preach in the chapel of the hospital once every Sunday throughout the year, and also on Christmas-Day and Good Friday, at such hour as shall from time to time be settled.

THE DUTY OF THE MEDICAL ATTENDANT.

He is to attend at the hospital daily, as well on the alms-men as the boys and domestic servants, and is to enter minutes of such his attendance in the book which is kept at the hospital for that purpose; he is also to attend at Drapers' Hall, from time to time, to furnish information to either the court of assistants, master and wardens, school committee, or clerk of the company.

THE DUTIES OF THE MATRON.

The matron and usher are to have the chief control and management of the boys out of school hours, subject to such orders as may from time to time be issued by the masters, and such assistance as may be personally given by them. The matron is to receive by weight and measure, and examine the quality, keep under lock and key, and deliver out by weight and measure, all provisions and stores whatever, and keep regular accounts thereof. She is to attend at all the boys' meals with either the under master or usher and assist in the carving and distribution of the victuals. She is to have the charge of the furniture and boys' clothing, and is to see that the same is kept in proper repair, and mended and kept clean, and is to keep such articles as are not in actual use locked up. She is to attend the boys and see that each boy is twice every day properly washed and combed, and especially to superintend the washing and combing such of the little boys as cannot do those offices for themselves. She is to examine and take care of the state of the boys' health, under the direction of the medical attendant, and report to the head master, or in his absence, to the under master, such as are sick, and require con-

finement or medical assistance; and when sick, she is
to see that the boys are properly nursed and assist
therein, and take charge of the boys' persons in health
and in sickness. She is to superintend and direct all
the operations in the kitchen, and manage the whole
domestic economy of the boarding-house. She is to
superintend the performance of the duties of all the
women servants, who are subordinate to her.

The matron is daily to visit every room in the
boarding-house, and go through the dormitories every
night after the boys are in bed, to see that they are
properly lodged, and that no irregularities are committed therein.

The matron is to make up her account of petty
expenditure weekly to every Saturday night, and on
the Monday following to deliver it to the head master,
or in his absence, to the under master, to the end that
it may be regularly drawn out and entered by him.

The matron is subordinate to the masters, and
should report to the head master, or, in his absence,
to the under master, all irregularities and misconduct
whatever, or anything worthy of notice, either in the
boys, the servants, or relating to the building, furniture, clothes, stores, or otherwise; and she is also to
make like reports of the same things to the school
committee, or the clerk of the Company, at any visitation, as well as communicating the subject of them to
the masters; for which purpose she is to keep a journal

wherein to enter daily all occurrences requiring note, which journal is to be produced to the committee and the clerk of the Company, and be open to the inspection of the masters.

The Duties of the Women Servants.

All the women servants are immediately subordinate to the matron, and are to follow her directions in all things.

The cook is to perform all the cooking, light the kitchen and furnace fires, and clean and take care of the kitchen, back kitchen, sculleries, pantries, and cellar, and the cooking coppers, kitchen utensils, dishes, porringers, plates, and spoons.

The other servants are to clean and take care of all the other parts of the boarding-house, and light the other fires therein; and make all the beds, and do such other work as the matron shall direct.

They are to assist every evening in washing and combing the boys, and attend upon and nurse any of the boys who may be sick.

They are to mend all the house linen and boys' shirts and stockings.

The cook and the other women servants, with the assistance of such of the boys as may be appointed thereto, are to do all other domestic business not hereinbefore described, which is to be done in or about the boarding-house, the furniture and the boys' persons and clothes, under the superintendence and direction of the matron.

The Boys' Conduct.

The boys are to be admitted to the school by the master and wardens, at their courts at Drapers' Hall, subject to the regulations made by the court of assistants.

Every boy, previously to his being received into the school, is to bring a certificate from the church-wardens and overseers of the poor of the parish to which he belongs, acknowledging that he has a legal settlement in their parish, and undertaking to receive him on his being sent from the school at the expense of the parish, the signature of which certificate is to be verified by a declaration before a magistrate; and he is also to bring an authority in writing from his father, or nearest friend, consenting that he may be sent to his parish, or, in case of sickness or hurt, to any hospital for relief of sick persons. And every boy, previously to his admission, is to be examined by the medical attendant of the hospital, and to bring a certificate in writing from him as to the state of his health.

Forms to be observed in these documents are in the
appendix hereto, and are furnished to the friends of the
boys by the clerk of the Company. These papers
must be produced to the clerk of the Company, and
are afterwards regularly filed and preserved by the
head master, at the hospital. Nevertheless, the master
and wardens, on consideration of any particular circumstances, are at liberty to dispense with the production of the said documents, or any of them, and to
make a special order for any boy being received into
the school without them, on such conditions as they
shall see fit.

No boy can be received into the school until after
he shall have had the small-pox or cow-pox, and every
boy is to be vaccinated as soon as possible after his
admission, and whenever the medical attendant shall
consider it desirable, and no boy afflicted with rupture
will be admitted into the school.

No boy can be received into the school without an
order in writing for that purpose, signed by the clerk
of the Company, addressed to the head master, or in
his absence to the under master of the school ; and
which order is given by the clerk, on production of
the documents above mentioned, or on an order being
made by the master and wardens for any boy being
received into the school without them.

The order for the admission of any boy will become
void, unless the documents above mentioned shall be

produced within four weeks from the date thereof, and unless the boy be admitted on the same day on which the medical certificate is dated ; and it also will become void, if within four weeks he shall not become entitled to be received into the school, unless the master and wardens shall by a subsequent order allow further time for either of those purposes.

Eight boys, whose discretion and good behaviour entitle them to confidence, are appointed by the head master from time to time and are called monitors, and are removable at the pleasure of the head master. Such monitors act as assistants to the masters, and superintend and are responsible for the conduct of the other boys, and report all misbehaviour to the masters ; the monitor appointed for that purpose by the master rings a bell for the boys' rising in the morning, and by way of notice of school times, meal times, and bed time, and on any other occasion when it is necessary to convene the boys ; and they wear some badge or token, to denote their authority and responsibility. The appointment to the office of monitor is considered as a reward for good behaviour, and such boys as conduct themselves well therein, are presented by name to the governors at their annual visitations, for their notice.

The head master appoints by rotation or otherwise, as he may deem most advisable, such of the boys as it is found convenient to employ in assisting the servants in any domestic business ; and no boy not so appointed is on any account to be employed therein, nor is any boy to be employed in any such business, in any other manner, or at any other time than shall be fixed by the general rules of the school, or than the head master, or, in his absence, the under master shall direct.

The boys are lodged in separate beds, and are quartered in the dormitories, at the discretion of the head master, three monitors being quartered in each of the larger dormitories, and two in the smaller, and no boy, after bed-time, and before the hour of rising, is allowed to be absent from or leave his dormitory on any occasion without the previous permission of a monitor.

The boys, on the ringing of a bell in each dormitory, rise at six o'clock in the morning from Lady-Day to Michaelmas, and at half-past six o'clock in the morning from Michaelmas to Lady-Day; and they then immediately wash their faces and hands and smooth their hair with a comb, after which they remain in the dining hall, or school room, until it is time to proceed to their breakfast, at eight o'clock, and at half-past eight they attend in the chapel.

The school duties commence at seven o'clock in the morning from Lady-Day to Michaelmas, and at nine o'clock in the morning from Michaelmas to Lady-Day, and continue from nine o'clock till noon throughout the year. When the boys come out of school at noon they proceed to do such domestic duties as may have been assigned to them.

The boys dine at half-past twelve o'clock every day, when a bell is rung to summon them for that purpose.

School recommences at two o'clock in the afternoon, and continues till four p. m. in winter and half-past four in summer—the afternoon of every Wednesday and Saturday, which are half-holidays, excepted.

The boys sup at six o'clock every evening.

Grace is said before and after breakfast, dinner, and supper each day, by one of the monitors, or other boy appointed by the master or under master.

At half-past seven o'clock in the evening, from Lady-Day to Michaelmas, and at half-past six o'clock in the evening from Michaelmas to Lady-Day, the boys assemble in divisions and clean their shoes and brush their clothes; and the boys are then stripped to the waist and thoroughly washed with soap and their heads and hair washed and thoroughly combed and brushed; and as they are finished, they retire into the dining-hall. And at nine o'clock in the evening from Lady-Day to Michaelmas, and at eight o'clock in the evening from Michaelmas to Lady-Day, the boys go to bed, having previously united in a decent orderly manner in the dining-hall in a short evening prayer, said by one of the monitors, or other boy appointed by the master, with the exception of Sunday, on which day the house prayers are always read by the senior monitor.

The boys are constantly habited in the school dress, as well when absent on leave as when at school, to the end that their behaviour may be the better observed and known.

A distinct play ground is allotted for the boys, and therein there is a covered shed for them to play in, in wet weather; and such shed is paved with flag stones, and the boys are prohibited from ever remaining or playing in the front court.

The boys are not permitted to go into their dormitories in the day-time, so that they may be fresh for their sleeping in, and the windows thereof are to be kept open all day, when the weather permits.

Out of school-time, the boys are in the play-ground before mentioned, or in the school room.

If any boy is discovered wilfully injuring the clothes or books provided at the expense of the institution, the parents or friends of such boy shall be deemed responsible for the value of the same.

The boys are to behave with duty and obedience to their masters, and with meekness and respect to all; they are to set a good example to each other, and refrain from vice, and more especially from stealing, lying, swearing, profanation of the Lord's-Day, and other vicious courses; and if a boy shall be found guilty of any such he is to be reported to the school committee, and punished in such way as they may see fit.

There are no calendar holidays, and the only holidays are as follows, viz., from the day before Christmas-Day to the 8th of January, from the Thursday before Easter to the Monday-fortnight following, and from the last Thursday in July till the Tuesday four weeks following; and the following days only are whole holidays, viz., the 18th of March, in commemoration of Mr. BANCROFT, the founder, St. George's-Day, Whit-Monday, and Whit-Tuesday, the Sovereign's birth-day, and Lord Mayor's-day, and on the Monday after the last Sundays in April and October, on which latter days the boys who have been catechised, if their conduct shall have been satisfactory to their masters, are permitted to visit their friends, from the hours of 9 a. m. to 7 p. m., or, with the special permission of the head master, to leave the church with their parents or friends and return to the school by 7 p. m. on the following day.

The house is kept open for the boys board, as well during the holidays as at other times, it being optional with the friends of the boys whether they have them home or leave them at the hospital during the vacations.

At all times previous to the boys' going to chapel, they are to assemble under the shed or in the school, and go from thence in a sober orderly manner, two by two, and return in the like order, and leave their books in the school.

Whenever the boys assemble for school or chapel, they meet five minutes before the time when school or chapel shall begin; and one of the monitors appointed for that purpose calls over the names of the boys and notes down such boys as are absent, and delivers the list of the absent boys to the master present, who deals with them for such neglect according to their respective deserts.

No boy is permitted to leave the hospital-ground, either during holidays or at any other time, upon any occasion, without the special leave of one of the masters of the school, nor to sleep from the hospital without leave in writing from the master, wardens, school committee or one of them, or from the clerk of the Company, or from the head master of the school, to be granted only for some very special reason to be assigned; and no leave of absence shall be given for more than one night, but a member of the school committee shall have power to extend the leave for a longer period, subject to the approval of the head master. All leaves to sleep out are to be registered in an absence book, with the special reason for leave having been given. Such book to be submitted for the inspection of the school committee at all their meetings, and on any leave of absence being granted, the masters are to be informed where and to whom, and for what, the boy applying for leave wishes to go;

and if leave be given, the master is to give the boy an absence badge, with some number or other distinguishing mark, to be carried about such boy. Any boy being out of the hospital-ground without such absence badge, or in case of any deceit touching the same, or his absence, or in case any boy having leave of absence, does not return within the time limited, he is deemed guilty of misbehaviour, and punished accordingly by the master, or expelled or otherwise punished at the discretion of the school committee or court of assistants, if they shall see fit to interfere therein.

The first Wednesday and Saturday in every month, from half-past one till half-past four, are appropriated for the admission of the friends of the boys, who at such times are allowed free access to them, and they may also visit them between the hours of one and two daily, in the playground, excepting on Sundays.

The friends of every boy who shall be expelled or dismissed the school, or shall depart therefrom without the consent of the proper authorities, shall return his clothes to the matron.

The Boys' Clothing.

Each boy has annually two suits of clothes—jacket, waistcoat, and trousers.

Two shirts.

Three pairs of socks.

Two pairs of shoes.

One cap and two ribbons to put round the neck.

Night shirts.

The boys have clean shirts every Sunday and every Thursday, and clean socks once a week.

Each boy's hair is cut by a person employed for that purpose once every month.

The boys have clean sheets once a month.

Boys and Servants' Diet.

Each boy has for breakfast, four days in the week, bread and butter with milk and water, in equal quantities of each ; and on the intermediate mornings with half a pint of cocoa.

The boys have each day for dinner fifty pounds of either roasted or boiled meat, with potatoes and occasionally greens, and a quantity of bread, averaging two ounces for each boy.

The meat is contracted for, and is to be of the best quality—the best ox beef and the best wether mutton.—The beef is either rounds or buttocks for boiling, in pieces, as nearly as possible, of twenty-five pounds each, and without bone, and the upper part of the thick flank called the veiny piece, in pieces of ten pounds each for roasting; and the mutton is the leg of about ten pounds each, with the shanks cut off, to the upper joints.

The boys on three evenings have bread and cheese for supper, about six ounces of the former, and an ounce and a half of the latter for each boy; and on three evenings bread and butter, with milk and water, and once in the week bread and treacle, with milk and water.

The boys' beverage is water.

The weekly diet provided for the servants is as follows:

Ten and a half quartern loaves of bread .
Thirty-five pounds of meat............
Three-quarters of a pound of suet ......
Three pounds of flour................ } amongst them.
One pound of raisins ....
Four pounds and a half of cheese ......
Four pounds and a half of butter ......

And half a barrel of beer in a fortnight.

The following diet is established for the boys on feasts on holydays :

18th of March, the Founder's-Day .... { Sixty pounds of roast beef and dumplings rubbed in the dripping-pan, with vegetables.

Saint George's-Day .... { Sixty pounds of roast beef and fifty pounds of good plum pudding, with vegetables.

Easter Sunday.. { Roast beef and Yorkshire pudding, with vegetables.

Last Sunday in April .... { Sixty pounds of roast beef and fifty pounds of good plum pudding, with vegetables.

Whit Sunday .. { Sixty pounds of shoulders of veal and gooseberry pies, with vegetables.

The Sovereign's Birth-Day ... { Sixty pounds of shoulders of veal and gooseberry pies, with vegetables.

Annual Visitation { Sixty pounds of shoulders of veal, with fruit pies and vegetables.

Last Sunday in October	Sixty pounds of roast pork and apple pies, with vegetables.
Lord - Mayor's - Day	Sixty pounds of roast pork and apple pies, with vegetables.
Christmas-Day .	Roast beef and good plum pudding, with vegetables.*

And on these feast-days the boys have two pence each allowed them, which is increased to sixpence to every boy who is examined on the Annual Visitation and who gains a prize.

* On the feast-days the beef is to be the sirloin or ribs as far as the seventh.

IMMEDIATE GOVERNMENT OF THE HOSPITAL.

The immediate government and superintendence of the establishment is vested in five members of the court of assistants of the Drapers' Company, to be annually chosen by the court on the election-day in August, to be called the SCHOOL COMMITTEE; and any three of them are to be a quorum, and the power deputed to the committee is so full and ample as to render any application to the court on any ordinary subject connected with the hospital unnecessary, but with the view of reserving a controlling power in the court, no repairs or alterations, involving an expense above £ 50, shall be carried into effect without the sanction of the court.

The school committee are to give orders for the purchase and supply of provisions, either by contract or otherwise from time to time, as they shall see fit, pursuant to the rule of diet established, with such variations as occasional circumstances may render advisable.

The school committee for the time being, or any three of them, at least four times in the year, on such day as they shall settle amongst themselves, are to visit the hospital, and there shall examine the boys and almsmen, and give such directions for the management of the hospital as they shall see fit, provided the same shall not be in violation of the rules contained herein. Minutes of the proceedings and orders made on such occasions shall be taken by the head master, or in his absence by the under master, and such minutes shall afterwards be drawn out at length by the head master, or in his absence by the under master, and a copy thereof from time to time, shall be transmitted to the clerk of the Company, to the end that such minutes may be preserved in duplicate, and be always resorted to as well at the hospital as at the Hall.

In case of any sudden emergency, the masters of the hospital are forthwith to give notice thereof to the clerk of the Company, to the end that he may take such steps as may be necessary therein.

The accounts of the household expenditure are to be kept quarterly, and show the provision, consumption, and price of each article distinctly within each quarter.

The general committee of the court of assistants are to visit the hospital, to hear the children publicly examined and catechised, on the last Thursday in July, to carry out the directions contained in the Founder's will.

The boys are to be examined on the last Sunday in April, in St. Helen's Church; and on the last Sunday in October, in St. Michael's Church, in Cornhill, or in such other church as the master and wardens of the Drapers' Company shall appoint, in accordance with the directions contained in the Founder's will.

The remnants of furniture which from time to time may be worn out, and all the woollen and linen rags, and all the remnants of every description arising from the boys' clothes, and every sort of kitchen stuff (if any) and all sorts of offal, however trifling, which shall not be used at the hospital, are to be sold on account of the trust.

RULES AND ORDERS

FOR THE

GENERAL CONDUCT OF THE INSTITUTION.

———◆———

I.   That the Head Master have the management of, and be responsible for, the general conduct of the whole establishment, and see that the other officers and servants perform the duties of their several stations : and that the under master be in all things subordinate to the head master.

II.   That in the absence or sickness of the head master the under master perform all his duties as Master ; and in the absence or sickness of the under master the head master perform all his duties.

III.   That the masters read prayers in the chapel morning and evening, alternately or otherwise as they may themselves arrange ; and take care that the alms-men and children devoutly attend the said service, unless hindered by sickness or other reasonable cause, to be admitted by one of the masters, to whom application must be made for exemption from attendance.

319

IV. That full divine service be regularly performed in the chapel once every Sunday throughout the year, and also on Christmas-Day and Good-Friday, at such hour as shall, from time to time, be fixed by the head master; and that during the time of the service the hospital gates be closed and locked.

V. That the daily chapel service commence at seven A. M., and half-past four P. M., from Lady-Day to Michaelmas; and at half-past seven A. M., and four P. M., from Michaelmas to Lady-Day.

VI. That each master keep a register, and set down therein such faults and offences as are worthy of notice, which shall from time to time be committed in breach of any of the Rules to be observed by the alms-men; and deliver in the same to the visiting committee at their first meeting in every month: to the end that they may be informed of the same.

VII. That the masters never leave the hospital at the same time; to the intent that one master may at all times, as well out of school hours as in school hours, and in holiday time, be upon the spot for the government of the alms-men and boys: excepting only on such extraordinary occasions as shall be specially sanctioned by the visiting committee; and then the matron shall be apprised of it that she may have more especial care of the boys.

VIII. That the alms-men, unless hindered by sickness or other reasonable cause, do devoutly attend the public worship of God in the chapel, morning and evening regularly, in their gowns; and take their seats there in order as they come.

IX. That one of the alms-men, or other person appointed by the master and wardens, officiate as clerk in the chapel whenever divine service is performed; and that the bell be tolled for the space of five minutes on week days, and a quarter of an hour on Sundays, before the prayers commence.

X. That after the bell hath been tolled for the stated time, the chapel clerk note down the names of such alms-men as may be absent, and make a weekly report thereof to the head master.

XI. That in case the master and wardens shall have permitted the wives of any of the alms-men to reside with their husbands, such wives do constantly attend divine service every Sunday morning and afternoon; unless hindered by sickness or other just cause to be allowed by one of the masters.

XII. That one of the alms-men, or other person appointed by the visiting committee, do sweep and keep the chapel and school in clean and decent order, and bring up coals, and light the fires in the school and chapel when necessary: and also sweep and keep clean the portico, stone steps, and pavement before the chapel, school, and masters' houses.

XIII. That the two alms-men appointed to reside in the lodges, do each keep the key of his respective gate, and lock up the same so soon as the clock shall have struck the hour of nine in the winter, and ten in the summer; and that in case any alms-man shall be found to have been absent without leave after the gates have been closed more than four times within the space of one year, he shall not be received again into the said alms-houses, or be entitled to the pension or allowance of an alms-man; unless afterwards restored thereto by an order of the court of wardens, on good assurance of amendment for the future.

XIV. That the alms-man who shall have been appointed to keep the east gate do every morning, before ten o'clock, sweep and clean the whole of the gravel roads, and roll them when necessary; that he sweep also the foot-path in front of the hospital without the walls, next to the highway; and that every night from Michaelmas to Lady-day, at half past eight P. M., and from Lady-day to Michaelmas, at half past nine P. M., he toll the bell fifty strokes by way of warning of the time of locking up.

XV. That either of the masters, when he shall see just cause, may give licence to any one or more of the alms-men, not exceeding two in number at one time, to be absent from his habitation and prayers for the space of one day and night, so that he do not licence any one person to be absent more than four times in one year : and that the persons obtaining such licence from time to time, give notice thereof to the other master, to the end that he may note the same.

XVI. That any two or more of the wardens, or the visiting committee, from time to time, as they shall see cause, may give licence under their hands to any of the alms-men to be absent from their habitations for any space of time, not exceeding twenty-one days. And in case the court of assistants or the master and wardens for the time being shall think fit, for the better support and encouragement of any of the said alms-men, to employ any of them in the Company's service at the Hall ; that the said wardens, or any two of them, may licence such of them as shall be employed to be absent from time to time, in the day-time only, as the duty of such service may require, giving notice thereof to the masters.

XVII. That the said alms-men and their wives (if permitted to reside with them) behave with submission and respect to the masters, and live in brotherly love and friendship towards one another.

XVIII. That no alms-man nor his wife use any railing, bitter, or uncharitable speeches to any of the other alms-men or their wives; and that no alms-man presume to strike any brother or brother's wife, under the penalty of a private reprimand for

D

the first offence, a public reprimand for the second, and for the third offence expulsion from the hospital for ever.

XIX. That if any alms-man or his wife presume to take the name of God in vain, or be drunk, such offender receive for the first offence a private, and for the second a public, reprimand. If after the second time he or she offend in like manner, that the party so offending be forthwith reported to the court.

XX. That if any of the said alms-men haunt or frequent any public house, and resort thereto after notice given him by either of the masters to refrain therefrom; the person so resorting thereto, after such notice given as aforesaid, receive for the first offence a private, and for the second a public, reprimand. If after the second time the offence be repeated, that the party so offending be forthwith reported to the court.

XXI. That if any of the inmates of the hospital commit adultery or fornication, or be guilty of theft, or such like enormous crime, he or they so offending be for ever expelled.

XXII. That if the wife of any of the said alms-men, who shall have been permitted to reside with her husband, prove with child, she shall not be permitted to lye-in in any of the said alms-houses;

but shall be removed by her husband (so soon as it shall have been discovered that she is with child) until she be delivered, under the penalty of his being for ever expelled in case of breach or disobedience of this order.

XXIII. That neither of the said alms-men presume to take an apprentice, or do any other act by which any charge may possibly accrue to the parish where the said alms-houses are situate, under pain of expulsion.

XXIV. That neither of the said alms-men presume to marry during his continuance in the said alms-houses, without leave of the wardens for the time being, under pain of expulsion.

XXV. That if any alms-man, or his wife, presume to beg during the time that he or she may be harboured in the said alms-houses, the offender suffer expulsion for the same.

XXVI. That no alms-man, or his wife, sell any chandlery ware, liquors, or fruits within the grounds of the hospital, or keep any bulk or stall there, or any public shop for exposing any thing for sale, or put up any sign or show-board within the premises, under the penalty of forfeiting three months' pension for the first, and expulsion for the second, offence.

XXVII. That no linen be laid upon, or dried in the ground before the alms-houses.

XXVIII. That no alms-man, nor his wife, keep any swine or rabbits or poultry within the ground, under the penalty of five shillings for every such offence.

XXIX. That none of them keep any dog within the said alms-houses or ground, under the penalty aforesaid.

XXX. That none of them take in any inmate, servant, or other person, to inhabit the said alms-houses, other than such as shall be allowed by the visiting committee for the time being, in case of sickness, or inability, under the pain of expulsion.

XXXI. That every alms-man daily, before the hour of ten in the morning, sweep and make clean the pavement before his dwelling; and that no ashes, soil, dust, nor any other thing, be cast out or laid in any part of the ground belonging to the said alms-houses, other than in the places appointed for that purpose.

XXXII. That none of the said alms-men presume to take down, break, or deface any of the brickwork, tiling, wainscot, or other thing belonging to the hospital under pretence of altering or amending the same, or otherwise, under the **penalty** of forty shillings, over and above the expense of restoring the same to the condition it was in before such alteration was made.

XXXIII. That the alms-men from time to time repair the glass windows of their respective houses at their own charge, to the end they may be careful to prevent the same from being broken.

XXXIV. That upon the death, expulsion, or other removal of any alms-man, all the grates, cupboards, dressers, shelves, locks, bolts, and similar improvements which he may have put up in his house, be left therein for the benefit of the said house.

XXXV. That for the better observation of the foregoing ordinances, and that no person concerned may plead ignorance thereof, it is ordered that the same be printed and framed and constantly hung up in the chapel, and that they be read by one of the masters twice in each year, viz., on the first Monday in March and the first Monday in September, in the said chapel, immediately after divine service.

END.

E

A HISTORY OF BANCROFT'S SCHOOL

Index

328

329

330

333